I0605834

CLIMATE ART

Powering Island Communities in the 21st Century

SigaWai Canopy Park

Jie Zhao, Liang Ma, Yan (Jennifer) Zeng, I-Shan Tam

See page 64

CLIMATE
ART
Powering Island
Communities
in the 21st Century
Land Art
Generator Initiative
Fiji
HIRMER

CONTENTS

Valelaca Rokataki: Prismatic Parasol

Michael Kokora, Marcus Carter, Miranda Lee, Jon Marcos (OBJECT TERRITORIES); James Richardson, Chase Rogers (One Hermitage); Nadir Abdessemed, Moritz Muetschele, Valentin Granger, Francisco Gallardo, Mohadese Banaeialishah (Transsolar Klima Engineering); Tony Tsui (noodo lab); Demian Szklar (Oaki Studio)

See page 176

Marou: The Power of Community

Grigorii Matiunin, Vladislav Larunin

See page 150

7

FOREWORD

Ilisari Naqau Nasau

Acting Chief and Sau Turaga (Chief Maker)
of Marou Village of the Mataqali Koro (Koro Clan)

"If you should give of yourself for the hungry and satisfy the needs of the afflicted, then shall your light rise in the darkness and your night will become like noonday sun."
— Isaiah 58:10

I am Ilisari Naqau Nasau from the Village of Marou of the Mataqali Koro. I hold the role of Chief Maker (Sau Turaga) — the one who presents the bowl of kava to our Chief — and at this time, I am honored to serve as the Acting Chief of our village.

On behalf of myself, the elders, and the entire community of Marou, I wish to extend our deepest and most heartfelt thanks to all of the designers who participated in the LAGI 2025 Fiji competition. From our mouths, we give sincere gratitude for the ideas you have brought from around the world to our shores.

It is a great privilege for Marou to be chosen as the host site for this most ambitious and important pilot project. We feel truly blessed. The proposals you have shared — systems for energy and water that we could never have imagined — will not only benefit us today, but will also support our future, and the futures of our children and grandchildren.

Thanks to your gifted hands, this project is now part of the story of our village. While delivering what we have long needed — power and safe water — it also brings with it the hope of greater resilience for our island. For LAGI, and for each and every one of you who contributed your time and creativity, this project will be known far beyond Fiji — it will travel the world as a symbol of collaboration and care.

Blessings to you all. You are helping us in this moment and helping generations to come.

Vinaka vakalevu.

“For LAGI, and for each and every one of you who contributed your time and creativity, this project will be known far beyond Fiji—it will travel the world as a symbol of collaboration and care. Blessings to you all.”

—Ilisari Naqau Nasau
Acting Chief and Sau Turaga (Chief Maker) of Marou Village of the Mataqali Koro (Koro Clan)

PREFACE

Elizabeth Monoian and Robert Ferry

Co-Directors, Land Art Generator Initiative (LAGI)

Sometimes a name finds its true meaning only through the course of its journey.

When we first abbreviated the Land Art Generator Initiative to LAGI in 2008, the choice was pragmatic—an easier way to refer to a rather long name that described our vision to merge art in the landscape with renewable energy infrastructure. We never imagined that, years later, the acronym would carry unexpected layers of meaning in a distant part of the world.

In the Fijian language, lagi (pronounced /lɒŋhɪ/ with an 'n' sound before the 'g') refers to the sky, to the heavens above. It speaks to a realm of ancestral presence and divine energy. It is from the lagi that rain falls and from which sunlight shines. To design for energy and water in Marou, then, is not only a technical task — it is a gesture of reverence toward lagi itself.

This serendipitous alignment of name and place has become more than a coincidence. It has become a point of connection between intention and place, vision and language. LAGI 2025 Fiji is not simply a design competition — it is an invitation to listen closely to land and sky, to people and place, to the rhythms of ocean, weather, and time. It is a call to imagine how renewable energy and water harvesting systems can serve as opportunities for creativity inspired by local knowledge and ecology.

The pages that follow are filled with transformative ideas — near futures imagined by interdisciplinary teams from around the world in response to the call of a single village. Each project embodies a different facet of what lagi might mean.

We hope that what you find here will inspire and challenge your sense of what is possible when regenerative infrastructures are co-created by the people they serve.

“In the Fijian language, lagi (pronounced /lɒŋhɪ/ with an ‘n’ sound before the ‘g’) refers to the sky, to the heavens above. It speaks to a realm of ancestral presence and divine energy. It is from the lagi that rain falls and from which sunlight shines.”

—Elizabeth Monoian and Robert Ferry
Co-Directors, Land Art Generator Initiative (LAGI)

Climate Islands

Elizabeth Monoian and Robert Ferry

Co-Directors, Land Art Generator Initiative (LAGI)

Harnessing the Sun's Energy

Sa siga na vanua. The land is full of sunshine.

Everything begins with the energy of the sun. All that gives us life, our consciousness, all our wealth flows from it.

Every day — just as it has for billions of years — the sun floods the Earth with energy. Each square meter receives about a kilowatt of solar power, peaking at full strength around 20% of the time. Over the course of a year, that adds up to 1,752 kilowatt-hours on average falling on every patch of land — a staggering abundance that life has evolved to capture, store, and transform in countless ways.

Billions of years ago, the energy of stars, like our sun, formed the minerals we mine today from the earth. It powered the cyanobacteria that gave oxygen to our atmosphere. Later, as the sun shone upon our planet hundreds of millions of years ago, its warmth germinated seeds that grew into ferns that absorbed carbon dioxide. The sun collaborated with chlorophylls to convert that carbon dioxide and rainwater into sugars and fibers that decayed underground to become the oil and gas deposits we unwittingly burn today.

The energy contained in the photons of the sun are the Planck units of measurement for the entire global economy. They are the ultimate backstop that gives value to every other thing.

The sun's energy is the collateral that backs up all investments and reinsures all reinsurance policies. Every unit of energy that we mine, convert, transmit, or combust to make our steel, our fertilizer, our electricity, our transit, our homes, and our smartphones all began as energy from the sun. It grows the leaves that allow us to breathe. It grows the food that sustains our human energy. We are the sun, not merely stardust.

It is a miracle. One kilowatt of energy beams down on every square meter — the only significant input to an otherwise mostly closed system that Buckminster Fuller famously called "Spaceship Earth."

Natural systems harvest the sun's energy with the intention and reverence it deserves. A healthy forest wastes almost none of it. From the emergent canopy in the sky to the microbes in the soils, the energy in that one kilowatt per square meter gets used to build proteins, vitamins, and sugars, to transmit information, and to move matter. Tiny factories combine sunlight's catalyst with oxygen, CO_2, nitrogen, hydrogen, and methane into various complex molecular arrangements. Millions of specialized species of life forms coevolve in symbiotic relationships that work collectively to increase the efficient use of energy. Over ages they resolve into resilient system balance.

Humans are one of those species. When we exist in balance with the abundant natural resources that surround us, we act as mutually symbiotic animals. Our need for food, water, shelter, and energy — when taken with intention, honor, and an appreciation for our place in the larger ecosystem — can be beneficial to all the species with whom we share the land and oceans. By taking from nature only what we need, while leaving in place what nature needs to regenerate, we can ensure that there will always be more for the taking. In *Braiding Sweetgrass*, Robin Wall Kimmerer calls this way of living in mutual thriving with nature the "honorable harvest."[1]

Even today, the residents of Naviti Island and Marou Village in Fiji's remote Yasawa Islands mostly live in a way that maintains balance with the populations of fish, clams, coconut trees, and other natural resources. The Indigenous (iTaukei) communities farm the land and tend to livestock in ways that do not deplete the nutrients of the soil or despoil the landscape. The only impacts that can be seen are those that are imported — the litter that washes up on the beaches, the fumes from plastic trash incineration and diesel fuel generators.

Access to the knowledge for how to live in mutual symbiosis with our local ecosystems is critically important as we shift to net-zero economies. According to the Intergovernmental Panel on Climate Change (IPCC), "Indigenous, local, and traditional knowledge systems and practices, including Indigenous peoples' holistic view of community and environment, are a major resource for adapting to climate change, but these have not been used consistently in existing adaptation efforts. Integrating such forms of knowledge with existing practices increases the effectiveness of adaptation."[2]

What does it look like to consider energy and water infrastructure from the framework of the "honorable harvest"? If we were to begin from scratch with the goal to design and build a human support system on Spaceship Earth that sustainably harvests the energy of the sun, we would first need to limit ourselves to 1 kW per square meter or 1,752 kWh per m^2 per year. This is the fundamental unit of sustainability. It is what we know with certainty will be renewed.

1 Robin Wall Kimmerer, *Braiding Sweetgrass: Indigenous Wisdom, Scientific Knowledge, and the Teachings of Plants* (Minneapolis: Milkweed Editions, 2013).

2 Intergovernmental Panel on Climate Change (IPCC), *Climate Change 2014: Impacts, Adaptation, and Vulnerability. Part A: Global and Sectoral Aspects. Contribution of Working Group II to the Fifth Assessment Report of the Intergovernmental Panel on Climate Change*, ed. Christopher B. Field et al. (Cambridge: Cambridge University Press, 2014), 758.

3 Sandia National Laboratories, *Solar FAQs*, February 2022, https://www.sandia.gov/app/uploads/sites/153/2022/02/Solar-FAQs.pdf.

4 Emanuele Bevacqua, Carl-Friedrich Schleussner, and Jakob Zscheischler, "A year above 1.5 °C signals that Earth is most probably within the 20-year period that will reach the Paris Agreement limit," *Nature Climate Change* 15 (February 2025): 262–65.

5 Karn Vohra et al., "Global mortality from outdoor fine particle pollution generated by fossil fuel combustion: Results from GEOS-Chem," *Environmental Research* 195 (April 2021): 110754, https://doi.org/10.1016/j.envres.2021.110754.

6 Charles A. S. Hall, Jessica G. Lambert, and Stephen Balogh, "EROI of different fuels and the implications for society," *Energy Policy* 64 (January 2014): 141–52; Vinay S. Tripathi and Adam R. Brandt, "Estimating decades-long trends in petroleum field energy return on investment (EROI) with an engineering-based model," *PLOS ONE* 12, no. 2 (February 2017): e0171083; Emmanuel Aramendia, Paul E. Brockway, Peter G. Taylor, et al., "Estimation of useful-stage energy returns on investment for fossil fuels and implications for renewable energy systems," *Nature Energy* 9 (May 2024): 803–816.

7 Jan Rosenow, "Have we been duped by the primary energy fallacy?" *Medium*, November 21, 2024, https://medium.com/@jan.rosenow/have-we-been-duped-by-the-primary-energy-fallacy-167f53c58961.

The first piece of good news is that the sun provides many orders of magnitude more energy than we need to run our global economy. More energy strikes the Earth's surface in one and a half hours than the global economy consumes in a year.[3]

The second piece of good news is that we now have all the technology we need to efficiently convert the sun's energy into useful electricity and transmit or store that energy to use for any purpose we could possibly want or need. We even have the technology to convert sunlight directly into hydrocarbons by combining it with water and air in much the same way that a leaf converts sunlight into carbohydrates.

The composition of our thin and delicate atmosphere is remarkable. Along with every other living thing on this planet, we have evolved to be finely attuned to it. The planet breathes through cycles of carbon as it makes its way around the sun. Its circulation systems are balanced and resilient to the shocks that come from random events like solar flares or volcanic eruptions.

Plants help the climate stay in tune by absorbing carbon dioxide from the air and storing some of it in roots and soils. Over millions of years, through different geological eras, the remains of ancient plants and microorganisms were buried, compressed, and transformed into fossil fuels—hydrocarbons stored deep beneath the Earth's surface.

The Case for a Clean Energy Future

The ancient sunlight we've burned over the past 150 years fueled a leap in technology and global prosperity. Fossil energy powered the breakthroughs that led to today's clean systems, from solar PV to advanced batteries. In that sense, we owe a paradoxical debt to the carbon age. But the next chapter it has enabled cannot come soon enough — because there are many reasons we should be transitioning away from a fossil fuel economy.

Firstly, there is the Earth's delicate climate balance. Burning fossil fuels adds greenhouse gases to our thin atmosphere. Regrettably, 2025 marks the year when scientists and policymakers have acknowledged that global average temperature has irrevocably passed the 1.5 °C threshold of warming above pre-industrial climate levels.[4] This is a fateful milestone because for every tenth of a degree above 1.5 °C, we risk disturbing serious Earth system feedback mechanisms — like ocean currents — that are irreversible and could trigger a mass extinction event. Surpassing 1.5 °C may seem abstract, but it is literally a matter of life and death for island nations such as Fiji whose land is already being lost to rising oceans.

Beyond the climate impacts, fossil fuel use is a public health crisis. It contributes to air pollution that is responsible for 1 in 5 deaths worldwide.[5] When we stop burning fossil fuels, we will literally save millions of human lives, which is enough of a reason on its own regardless of climate considerations. Remote communities that rely on old and inefficient diesel generators or burning wood and charcoal will be some of the greatest beneficiaries of the energy transition.

Burning fossil fuels is also not sustainable in the strictest meaning of the word. It takes energy to make energy. This is known as "energy return on investment" or EROI—a measure of how much usable energy we get out compared to how much energy we have to put in to extract and process it. The amount of energy required to produce a barrel of oil goes up every year because the easy-to-access and high-quality petroleum reserves have already been used up. We're now scratching the bottom of the barrel, literally fracturing rocks to suck up tar and drilling impossibly deep and risky wells in more ecologically sensitive environments. When we use more energy to get at oil reserves and require more refinement to make useful fuels from the oil we can access, the EROI goes down.[6] We might not run out entirely anytime soon, but our entire system is getting less efficient. We are always going to need some quantity of hydrocarbons to make pharmaceuticals and other products in the future, so if we're getting close to the end (and we likely are), then let's keep what we have remaining for those uses instead of burning it.

Burning fossil fuels is inefficient. Combustion engines waste tremendous amounts of energy as heat that dissipates into the surrounding environment. More than 60% of every ton of coal or barrel of oil will be converted into waste heat (rejected heat) instead of going to anything useful like electricity or mechanical energy. Thinking we need to replace all the energy in all those barrels of oil is called the "primary energy fallacy." In fact, a world powered by renewable energy would require only about 60% as much primary energy as a fossil-fuel-based one, due to the far greater efficiency of renewables in converting energy into useful work.[7]

If we get the policy right and ensure just social distribution of shared resources, a clean energy future could unleash a world of energy affordability and super-abundance.

One of the features of renewable energy technologies is that they are variable. While this feature has been used to question the viability of a 100% clean energy grid, the fact is that we already have perfected the solutions we need to transform variable energy into dispatchable energy, matching generation perfectly to loads. Battery energy storage systems (BESS) are already replacing gas-fired power plants on grids like California's, where installed capacity has surged from nearly zero in 2015 to over 16 gigawatts by 2025.[8] That's more than thirteen times the output capacity of an AP1000® nuclear reactor.

Another way to make sure we have enough energy to last us through periods of weak wind and cloudy weather is to deploy more renewable energy capacity than we would if the sun was always shining and the wind was always blowing. What that means is there will be times when our clean energy systems are making way more energy than we can use or even store. At these times of energy abundance, we will have the opportunity to use nearly free energy for purposes that we cannot even imagine today. Rather than the energy transition being about sacrifice or going backwards, it is exactly the opposite. A renewable energy economy will open doors to innovation and shared prosperity unknown in all human history.

On large grids, these mid-day periods of energy abundance could be used to power data centers to solve complex problems, desalinate water, pull CO_2 from the air, make green hydrogen using energy-intensive electrolysis, or even combine green H_2 and captured CO_2 to make sustainable jet fuel.

In communities like Marou Village, when the sun is high in the sky and after the battery banks have been topped off to get through the night, a slightly oversized solar mini-grid can power atmospheric water generation, make ice, or purify harvested rainwater.

A clean energy future will be more equitable and democratic. Today, the means of energy generation are tightly controlled by centralized institutions that have monopoly power over what might be the most important aspect of daily life. These institutions establish a cost they charge each consumer for every kilowatt-hour. But the energy of the sun falls the same on every square meter of land, and it is not possible for any single institution to control it. As access to energy becomes increasingly decentralized — enabling individuals to generate and use their own power — the implications for the distribution of wealth and resources could support greater equity in opportunity.

We could value the sun's energy more. When we build machines that harvest it for our use, we would be wise to do it with intention and reverence.

Fiji as a Model for the World

For nations like Fiji — where nearly half of export earnings go to purchasing imported fuel oils — turning to solar power makes perfect sense.[9] Remote island nations such as Fiji are in a unique position to demonstrate best practices for 100% renewable energy and sustainable systems. As islands with no connection to large continental power grids, they must locally generate all the energy required to light homes, cook food, power appliances, manufacture goods, transport people and materials, and provide clean drinking water. Sustainable models already exist in small island communities, from Eigg in Scotland to Samsø in Denmark, where integrated systems of renewables have enabled energy independence.

In this way, island communities like those on Fiji's Naviti island offer the potential of a demonstration in the Pacific context for the rest of the world to follow, whereby interconnected mini-grids and regional systems for human thriving are designed to be incredibly self-reliant, resilient, zero-carbon, and circular in their material stocks and flows.

Fiji has a stated policy of deriving 100% of national electricity production from renewable energy sources by 2030 and achieving net-zero annual greenhouse-gas emissions by 2050.[10]

Of the approximately 1,200 GWh of utility electricity Fiji generates each year, a surprisingly small percentage (only 30 GWh or about 2.5%) is generated from solar and wind — abundant natural resources that are currently underutilized. Hydroelectricity makes up more than half of the electricity mix, which helps Fiji maintain a relatively low carbon intensity for electricity despite the significant use of imported carbon fuels, which contribute around 40% to the electricity mix.[11]

8 California Independent System Operator, *2024 Special Report on Battery Storage: May 29, 2025* (Folsom, CA: CAISO, 2025), 2, https://www.caiso.com/documents/2024-special-report-on-battery-storage-may-29-2025.pdf.

9 Ravita D. Prasad and Atul Raturi, "Low carbon alternatives and their implications for Fiji's electricity sector," *Utilities Policy* 56 (February 2019): 1–19, https://doi.org/10.1016/j.jup.2018.10.007.

10 Republic of Fiji, *National Climate Change Policy 2018–2030* (Suva: Secretariat of the Pacific Community, 2018), objective 4.1; also see Fiji National Energy Policy 2023–2030 for updated reaffirmation.

11 International Trade Administration, "Fiji - Renewable Energy," *Fiji Country Commercial Guide*, U.S. Department of Commerce, last modified July 14, 2023, https://www.trade.gov/country-commercial-guides/fiji-renewable-energy.

12 Ravita D. Prasad and Atul Raturi, "Prospects of Sustainable Biomass-Based Power Generation in a Small Island Country," *Journal of Cleaner Production* 318 (October 2021): 128519, https://doi.org/10.1016/j.jclepro.2021.128519.

13 Molly Quell, "Closely-watched international climate case in The Hague wraps up its first week of testimony," *AP News*, December 6, 2024, https://apnews.com/article/climate-international-court-justice-a7449cb84e5bc555ddee909a1967719e.

14 Zeke Hausfather, "How unusual is current post-El Niño warmth?" *The Climate Brink* (blog), November 25, 2024, https://www.theclimatebrink.com/p/how-unusual-is-current-post-el-nino; Copernicus Climate Change Service, "2nd warmest April globally remains 1.5°C above the pre-industrial level," *Copernicus.eu*, May 9, 2024, https://climate.copernicus.eu/2nd-warmest-april-globally-remains-15degc-above-pre-industrial-level.

Biofuels make up the balance of electricity generation at 14%. While biofuel as a replacement for diesel is considered lower carbon and renewable, biofuels in Fiji are obtained through a mix of sugarcane ethanol and coconut oil, and there is potential to add pine forestry residues.[12] These require a far greater land use intensity than solar or wind. Biofuel production results in large monocultural landscapes that destroy natural habitats and compete with limited space for food agriculture.

These numbers apply mainly to the three larger islands of Fiji (Viti Levu, Vanua Levu, and Ovalau). Over 100 remote inhabited islands, like Naviti Island, rely almost entirely on imported fuel for electricity generation. Electricity accounts for less than 1/5 of Fiji's primary energy consumption. Transportation and industry are almost entirely dependent on imported fossil fuels and this is where the vast majority of energy is consumed. Electrification of these sectors will be critical for nationwide decarbonization and will greatly benefit the economy of Fiji.

As appliances, industry, and transportation begin to electrify in Fiji, the demand for renewable power and storage solutions is expected to increase significantly. Electric engine marine transport, for example, can offer a more sustainable solution for traveling between islands, but the carbon intensity of electric motors will always be a reflection of the carbon intensity of the land-based electricity grid that powers their on-board batteries.

Annual solar insolation in Fiji is very good, measuring as high as 2,500 kWh/m^2/year (exceeding that of the American Southwest). And yet solar power generation in Fiji presents some interesting challenges. Considerations must be made for the conservation of tropical forests, protection of water systems, maintenance of agricultural lands, and the preservation of the natural beauty of Fiji. An invaluable resource in its own right, the beauty of the landscapes and seascapes of Fiji must be considered practically in terms of the sustainability of the local economy, which relies on the tourism industry for 25% of its GDP.

For a nation where land is a precious resource, practical design solutions for renewable energy generation that shares land with other uses, such as parks, cultural destinations, farms, and habitats, can help to increase the potential for a 100% renewable island economy. These new energy system designs can also consider how their aesthetic manifestation can support and enhance the beautiful landscapes that bring one million tourists each year from around the world.

For rural villages like Marou, solutions for sustainable infrastructure can also be considered in the context of their ability to contribute more than just kilowatt-hours to the community. LAGI 2025 Fiji is an experiment in how to bring multiple systems and learning from nature together to arrive at beautiful solutions that merge aesthetically with the landscape, provide spaces for community, and attract more visitors to stimulate the local economy.

Climate Justice

On December 4, 2024, Fiji's Permanent Representative to the United Nations, Ambassador Luke Daunivalu, spoke passionately to the International Court of Justice in The Hague about the plight of his nation on a rapidly warming planet. "This is a crisis of survival. It is also a crisis of equity. Fiji contributes 0.004 percent of global emissions, yet our people bear the brunt of climate impacts with marginalized groups — women, children and the poor — being disproportionately affected."[13]

For the past century, we have witnessed a repeating pattern. Global average temperatures have risen to new highs during each El Niño event and then dipped back down slightly during the La Niña years that followed. As we write this essay, global average temperatures have remained solidly above the critical 1.5 °C warming threshold for two years while the Earth's climate is in the process of diverging from its familiar patterns.

As climate scientist Zeke Hausfather notes in *The Climate Brink*, "Global temperatures rose earlier and have potentially remained elevated longer than in any prior El Niño event since at least 1940."[14] While it is not yet clear why, it could be that the ability of the Earth's oceans to absorb excess heat is beginning to ebb, with dire consequences for the rate of future warming.

15 Simon Evans, "Analysis: Which countries are historically responsible for climate change?" *Carbon Brief*, October 5, 2021, https://www.carbonbrief.org/analysis-which-countries-are-historically-responsible-for-climate-change.

16 Patrick Jowett, "Ecoprogetti releases fully automated solar panel recycling line," *PV Magazine*, May 20, 2025, https://www.pv-magazine.com/2025/05/20/ecoprogetti-releases-fully-automated-solar-panel-recycling-line.

For years, the rallying cry of those fighting for stronger and more rapid action on climate change was to "keep 1.5 alive." It was the famous target set forth in the Paris Agreement for staying below a certain amount of warming above pre-industrial levels deemed to limit the most harmful impacts to human societies.

While 1.5 will not have been officially overshot as a climate threshold until decadal average measurements can be made, this is little comfort to small island nations who are already seeing storms, rising sea levels, and degradation of their land and reefs. For coastal villages, passing 1.5 °C poses an existential challenge. This is despite the fact that the residents of these villages have not contributed to global warming, nor have they benefited from the growth of global wealth that resulted from dumping of 2.5 trillion tonnes of CO_2 ($GtCO_2$) into Earth's thin atmosphere since 1850.[15]

Launching LAGI 2025 Fiji

On our first visit to Marou Village on the invitation of the Acting Chief (Sau Turaga) Ilisari Naqau Nasau, we were greeted at the beach with guitar strumming and song as we walked from the boat to shore (during low tide one must anchor nearly a half kilometer away and wade through the curious tidal pools to reach the shore). As we stepped foot into the village, we offered the traditional "dua n'dua" greeting of visitors and were gifted beautiful white hibiscus salusalu (flower necklaces) as we reciprocated the gift by offering yaqona (dried kava root).

Prior to our arrival, the entire village had gathered to discuss hosting LAGI 2025 Fiji. When we arrived, residents were open to learning more. The welcoming sevusevu—a ceremonial gift exchange—set a generous and respectful tone. As the tu yaqona prepared the kava in the tanoa (the carved wooden ceremonial mixing bowl), we joined the circle, each taking turns to receive the bilo (coconut shell cup), clap our cupped hands, and call out "Bula!" (life!) before drinking. With the bilo moving from hand to hand and songs shared among us, the atmosphere shifted from formality to familiarity. We then began to introduce ourselves and speak about the ideas behind the project.

After presenting and answering questions with our host mataqali (the small clan), we then presented to the larger yavusa (the entire village community). Our visit happened to coincide with a workshop that was facilitated by Energy Action Partners and Arizona State University on behalf of the Fiji Department of Energy to simulate and measure the electricity demand curve of the village's 67 households. During the community event, we explained what a partnership with LAGI 2025 Fiji might be like, the schedule, how we would work together to craft a creative brief, and how being the LAGI 2025 Fiji design site partner could help determine the design of the solar mini-grid that would be installed in close coordination with the Fiji Rural Electrification Fund and the Fiji Department of Energy. Over the course of that first week, we came to have an appreciation for what the LAGI 2025 Fiji design guidelines might ask for.

Two months later, we returned with a first draft and went through it line-by-line with the Marou community. We refined the site boundary and came to better understand constraints. As we drank kava around the tanoa, we discussed the residents' desire to attract more tourists and their interest in offering homestays for visitors — of which there are none yet in Marou. We also discussed designing for ease of operation and the residents' commitment to ensuring the new solar mini-grid remains functional over the long term.

One of the challenges that face solar mini-grids in remote communities is continued maintenance. If a component breaks down and there is no one who can repair it, the entire investment can become worthless. A system of lesser-quality solar modules that never meets its nameplate capacity or is abandoned for parts failures before it can pay back its embodied carbon is worse for the climate than if it had never been installed. Abandoned solar equipment that sits idle gives the entire idea of the clean energy transition a bad reputation.

Our goal from the start was to co-create resilient local infrastructure with the residents of Marou in a holistic way to reflect the culture of the community. If the infrastructure could exist as a cherished and frequented place, rather than a monoculture of solar modules set behind a fence, if it could expand the shared uses of the land, if it could complement the beauty of the tropical island setting, perhaps our design approach would support more sustainable operations over its entire life cycle, which will hopefully last for generations. In contrast to an obscure, utilitarian machine of aluminum and glass, this infrastructure would be warm, welcoming, and familiar. Rather than have technological systems installed by a team who is not present afterwards, what if the project was installed in collaboration with the community, so that there was an exchange of knowledge in the process? Could the village be better equipped to handle frequent maintenance? Could the risk of obsolescence be mitigated?

Climate Challenges Facing Marou

During our initial conversations in Marou, we learned about the challenges faced by communities like it — those confronting some of the most severe impacts of global warming.

There has always been a season of rain (November through March) and a season of sun (May through September), but as a warmer atmosphere holds more energy and moisture, these seasons are becoming more extreme. During the wet season, it is more likely that the village will find itself flooded, knee deep in muddy water as a meter of rain falls in one month, washing away topsoil, eroding the landscape, and carving ever-widening gullies through the village streets. During the dry season there can be months of no rain at all. On a small agrarian island with no standing freshwater lakes and with a few ground wells and cisterns that are quickly depleted, these conditions can become life threatening — farming is challenging, the school must close, and water must be imported from the mainland if it can be afforded.

Far from the electricity grid of the mainland, there is no reliable access to power. Some more fortunate households have a solar panel or two and a battery. There are rooftop solar panels on Yasawa High School, and a diesel generator is shared at selected times and for important uses, being careful to conserve costly fuel. As temperatures become hotter, access to electricity for refrigeration becomes more important to keep fish catch fresh so it can be sold to market, or to preserve the bodies of deceased loved ones prior to burial in traditional coastal grave sites that themselves are being reclaimed by the rising seas.

As sea levels rise, the village faces a triple threat. Storm surges and king tides pull land into the ocean. Summer floods further erode the land and cause subsidence. Seawater permeating the water table threatens to turn once reliable ground wells brackish and non-potable.

This is to say nothing of the increasing severity of cyclones driven by the energy in warmer South Pacific waters. Even when storms leave buildings mostly intact, gutters that used to feed rainwater from rooftops into above-grade cisterns are often blown away and take years to repair with limited resources, adding further to water scarcity. Everywhere in Marou it seems that challenges build upon challenges.

And yet Marou Village is also a community of resilience and abundance. Vegetation grows rapidly in the tropical climate. The soils are nutrient rich with lava rock and require little if any fertilizer to grow crops during seasons when rainfall is sufficient yet not overwhelming.

Co-Designing Solutions for Efficiency

As we work together to build the energy infrastructure of the 21st and 22nd centuries, we should ask ourselves: What is the most enduring way to plan and build these systems? In other words, what is the most efficient use of energy and resources over the entire life cycle of the system? What energy systems will best meet the needs of the present while preserving natural resources and biodiversity so future generations of humans and non-humans may also flourish on this beautiful miracle of a planet?

One way to think about efficiency is to focus only on saving upfront on the production costs of the system — limiting the time and material that goes into making it. But if we go too far cutting costs in that direction, we may see infrastructures fail before their ideal design life-expectancy, because too many corners were cut at the start. It's not efficient to rebuild every few years.

Another way to think about efficiency is by considering how much raw material we need to use versus how much can be either recycled or harvested sustainably from rapidly renewable materials. Recycling more and using natural local materials means less impact on the environment and less energy expended.

For LAGI 2025 Fiji, many of the designers seized upon the idea of using local materials that regenerate quickly, such as bamboo and coconut palm leaves, as the primary structural and cladding materials of their proposed energy and water systems for Marou.

One of the unheralded benefits we are starting to see with solar energy is that it can be almost infinitely recyclable. In 2025, the Italian company Ecoprogetti launched "an automated photovoltaic recycling line that separates and recovers up to 100% of the aluminum, copper, glass, plastic, and silicon in solar panels."[16] We're starting to glimpse a future where solar-powered facilities reclaim old solar panels and make new ones — where

17 Hannah Ritchie, "The low-carbon energy transition will need less mining than fossil fuels," *Sustainability by Numbers*, November 6, 2023, https://www.sustainabilitybynumbers.com/p/energy-transition-materials; International Energy Agency, *Net Zero by 2050: A Roadmap for the Global Energy Sector*, revised version (Paris: IEA, 2021), https://www.iea.org/reports/net-zero-by-2050.

once we have built up the clean energy infrastructure to power the world for the first time, we may not need to mine that much in raw materials to perpetuate that infrastructure indefinitely. Compare that to our current global economy where we must continuously extract deeper and more remote deposits of coal, oil, and gas just to keep the generator turbines spinning and the motors running.

Data scientist Hanna Ritchie has done the math on the raw materials required to complete the global energy transition using the International Energy Agency's estimate of 43 million metric tons of raw materials to meet its Net Zero Scenario by 2040. She reminds us that while that is indeed a large number, it pales in comparison to the 15 billion metric tons of fossil fuels that we dig out of the earth every year just to burn them.[17]

And while it will take burning fossil fuels to build out our new energy system, that is only a temporary condition. In a world where solar panels, wind turbines, and batteries are made using renewable energy, they will have zero embodied carbon and therefore all the energy they produce will have zero carbon intensity.

Another way to think about efficiency is how much we can save on operational and maintenance costs over the life cycle of a system, making sure it is designed well and built to last without much repair needed.

One of the ways to save over the life cycle on operational and maintenance costs is to limit the number of moving parts. The hours of repair required to keep a coal or nuclear power plant running are orders of magnitude greater than the hours required to keep a solar-power system running. Cleaning solar panels can certainly improve performance, but the rain does a pretty good job in most climates.

Another way to save on operating expenses is to reduce the cost and volatility of the feedstock of the energy. Where does the primary source of energy come from? Is it barrels of fuel oil? Is it train cars full of coal? Is it fossil methane gas? Is it processed uranium? Is it clear-cut forests? How much does it cost to continue to extract and deliver these feedstocks? How reliable or volatile are the supply and the market price of that energy feedstock over the entire life cycle of the system?

Or does the source of energy come from rays of sunlight or the power in the waves and wind that flow as free and endless gifts of nature?

When we focus on the simple metrics that govern finance instruments for energy development projects — the capital costs versus the sale of kilowatt-hours into wholesale markets — and neglect the more complex ecosystem metrics that often work on timelines longer than 20 years, we are inadvertently doing harm to ourselves now or in the future. When we build energy landscapes as monocultures of modules, without consideration for what co-habitable and mutually symbiotic shared uses could be, we are missing opportunities to protect biodiversity and limiting the potential co-benefits to communities. When we adhere to a utilitarian aesthetic without engaging in considerations for local culture, we are failing to win over a generation of potential supporters of the energy transition.

Rather, we should think about the idea of "cost" more broadly to include social and environmental costs as well. Just because such costs don't show on the ledger does not mean they are not real. This is why a system that externalizes the cost of its pollution by hiding it in an ever-warming atmosphere or subjecting poorer communities to its poisonous byproducts is not one that is most enduring. Shifting the burden of cleaning up our mess onto future generations and the most vulnerable communities is surely not the way to be remembered as good ancestors.

At the end of the day, this is what it is all about: How do we make the wisest choices with our one precious life on this one beautiful planet to ensure that thousands of future generations also get to have the experience we have had?

In Marou, the community is embarking on a creative answer to this question, working together with the designers who answered the call of the LAGI 2025 Fiji design brief and who dedicated their time and creativity to imagining and detailing solutions.

By generously inviting LAGI to host the 2025 Fiji design competition in their village, and by committing to steward the regenerative creation that will be built, the residents of Marou are demonstrating what it means to design and build systems for human flourishing that are grounded in community and in balance with nature.

A Field Guide to Regenerative Water Technologies by the Land Art Generator was developed as a companion to LAGI's *Field Guide to Renewable Energy Technologies* and as supplemental material for LAGI 2025 Fiji. The PDF is available as a free download on the LAGI website.

DESIGN GUIDELINES

A Qualified Entry Must Meet the Following Criteria

Use solar photovoltaic modules as part of the media for a work of art in the landscape: a creative and aesthetic installation for Marou Village that is conceptually engaging to visitors and inspires people about the beauty of renewable energy;

Have an installed solar photovoltaic (PV) nameplate capacity of no less than 75 kW that fits within the energy design site boundary area;

Provide some amount of water harvesting and storage to help see the Village of Marou through the dry season each year. This could be as simple as collecting the rain that falls on the solar modules, but more ambitious ideas are also welcome;

Be pragmatic, constructible, maintainable, and resilient to the forces of nature (Marou Village experiences Category 5 cyclones);

Consider modularity so that the pilot project in Marou Village might be expanded in the future as the village grows and demand for energy and water increases;

Consider replicability and scalability so that the design can be implemented within other island communities;

Be designed to cost not much more than $15 USD per installed watt for the 75 kW solar photovoltaic array. For reference, a purely utilitarian installation in Marou might cost as much as $10 USD per watt (higher than global averages mainly due to the complexity of logistics). The cost of water harvesting or other proposed systems may be in addition to the cost of the PV array;

Not incorporate imported living materials or materials that could possibly contain foreign seeds, plants, insects, or living creatures of any kind (the use of living materials native to Naviti Island is okay);

Be safe for people by housing power electronics, energy storage systems, or other potentially harmful features away from easy access, especially by curious children and animals;

Not generate greenhouse gas emissions or other forms of environmental pollution;

Provide a brief statement that explains how your team intends to approach the prototyping and pilot implementation processes and how you intend to collaborate with the local community in those efforts;

Provide a brief statement that explains how your design will be operated and maintained during its life and how the local community will contribute to operations and maintenance;

Provide a brief environmental assessment as a part of the written description in order to identify the effects of the project on natural ecosystems and to outline a strategy to mitigate any foreseeable issues;

Not use AI-generated images or text for final submission (the use of generative AI is acceptable as a design tool during your concept development process);

Use English language for all text and metric scale for all drawings.

Entries May Also (not required)

In addition to the 75 kW solar PV and water harvesting, entries may also incorporate other renewable energy technologies (e.g., hydro, wind, tidal)—either inside or outside the energy design site area. Generating additional electricity when the sun is not shining might help reduce the sizing requirements of energy storage and help eliminate or minimize generator use. Keep cyclones in mind when proposing any wind power installations.

Energy Considerations

Energy is the primary system for which LAGI 2025 Fiji is seeking design solutions. In order to qualify, your entry must provide a 75 kW or greater solar photovoltaic mini-grid for the Village of Marou within the energy design site.

The solar photovoltaic technologies you incorporate can be as simple as you like but they do not need to be purely utilitarian. Custom shaped modules, flexible modules, and modules with custom face glass that is tinted or textured are acceptable, as is any BIPV product or solar roofing tile available on the market. In order to be installed, the technology must be able to comply with testing standards (IEC 61730-1 and IEC 61730-2, or EN 61730-1 and EN 61730-2, or UL Standard 1703). To this end, your design should use photovoltaic cell technologies and encapsulant technologies that are available in the market and that have at least a 25-year lifespan. This excludes emerging technologies such as OPV, DSSC, or Perovskites.

Consider thoughtful energy storage solutions so that the residents of Marou can access electricity for lighting and other uses at night, before sunrise, and on overcast days. Lithium iron phosphate (LFP) batteries are a safe and low-cost option, but we encourage you to think creatively. When it comes time to pilot your winning project, you can always fall back on LFP if necessary.

In addition to the 75 kW solar photovoltaic capacity, you may decide to include other forms of renewable energy technology. These systems can help to provide electricity when the sun is not shining and may be proposed anywhere within the Marou Village or Yasawa School watersheds. Please consider long-term maintenance and the impact of saltwater on moving parts when proposing other energy technologies.

LAGI 2025 Fiji is working with Arizona State University (ASU) and in collaboration with Fiji Rural Electrification Fund (FREF). These institutions have previously identified Marou Village as a viable candidate for electrification with a mini-grid system and have a plan in place for local distribution. Thus, it is not a requirement to design the layout of electricity distribution within the village. This work will be done in collaboration with local authorities during the detailed design process for the winning proposal(s).

Water Considerations

Rainwater harvesting and storage must be considered as a secondary component of your LAGI 2025 Fiji design proposal. Even a modest amount of rainwater harvesting is welcomed by the community (for example, storing the rainwater that is shed by the solar modules themselves). We also encourage creative thinking that can lead to more substantive solutions. You may integrate your water solution into your design as an integral component of your solar energy system, as a separate element entirely, or both.

Freshwater is a seasonal challenge for Marou Village. During the rainy season (November through April) there is usually plenty of freshwater available. During this time the village does their best to store water in large above-ground storage tanks (mostly polyethylene). Still, this supply is often depleted by the middle of the dry season. Water is consumed by the 67 households in Marou Village and by the nearby primary and secondary schools. Existing storage capacity is around 600,000 liters (in the village) and 300,000 liters (at the school), distributed in 5,000 – 10,000-liter tanks attached to the roofs of homes, churches, and community buildings.

You may propose solutions for water treatment, water recycling, water distribution, or other ancillary water systems, but these are not required. Consider creative water purification solutions such as distillation or nature-based systems. When it comes time to pilot your winning project, you can always fall back on a reverse osmosis system if necessary.

Rainwater harvesting is likely the most energy efficient way to provide freshwater, but ocean water desalination systems and atmospheric water generation may also be proposed while considering their energy demand and maintenance requirements.

You can see on the maps and photos provided in the LAGI 2025 Fiji supplemental materials where water channels flow from the mountains to the sea and the areas where stormwater is eroding the land within and around the village. You may consider how interventions within these areas can help improve resilience against seasonal flooding while assisting with freshwater harvesting and storage, but such adaptation systems are not required.

JURORS

The LAGI 2025 Fiji jury comprised an expert panel from the Pacific Islands, Fiji, and Marou Village, along with global leaders, whose disciplines span policy, art, culture, climate science, distributed energy systems, adaptation, storytelling, architecture, landscape architecture, and planning.

Ilisari Naqau Nasau
Acting Chief and Sau Turaga (Chief Maker) of Marou Village of the Mataqali Koro (Koro Clan)

Oliver Broughton
Energy Portfolio Management, Renewables and Efficiency, Elemental Group

Deb Guenther
Landscape Architect and Partner, Mithun, FASLA, LEED AP, SITES AP

Elena van Hove
Director of Global Energy Access, Laboratory for Energy and Power Solutions, Julie Ann Wrigley Global Futures Laboratory, Arizona State University

Fenton Lutunatabua
350 Pacific Regional Director; Storyteller and Climate Change Activist

Dr. Ramendra Prasad
Associate Professor, Department of Science, School of Science and Technology, The University of Fiji, Lautoka, Fiji; Centre for Climate Change, Energy, Environment and Sustainable Development, The University of Fiji, Lautoka, Fiji

Jale Samuwai
Manager, Global South CFAN Program, RMI

Paula Schaafhausen
Artist

Setoki Tuiteci
Architect and Director, Ethos Edge Design Studio; General Secretary of the Fiji Association of Architects

Residents of Marou
Ilisari Naqau Nasau (Acting Chief), Paula Nakarawa, Vesivesi Bose, Seru Lasa, Naibuka Kamayavu, Onisimo Yabakidrau, Solomoni Naqoli, Apasai Kaitoga, Samuela Nabolaniwaqa, Meciu Vuli, Viliame Tuwawa, Siliveno Tuitavua, Inia Lesu, Meli Tauvoli, Joseva Nasau, Vika Seru, Siteri Sawea, Melita Buna, Malelita Nainiata, Miriama Tuwawa Bainivalu, Rota Salio, Lanieta Mavama, Vika Tuirotuma, Timaima Cagilau Ralulu, Akanise Tipo, Lewatu Rejieli, Sera Tamudere, Aralai Vuranovo, Asilika Momoyalewa, Vasiti Talatoka, Ruci Drau, Remivani Toga, Watisoni Daku, Ilisari Vuda, and others

DESIGN SITE

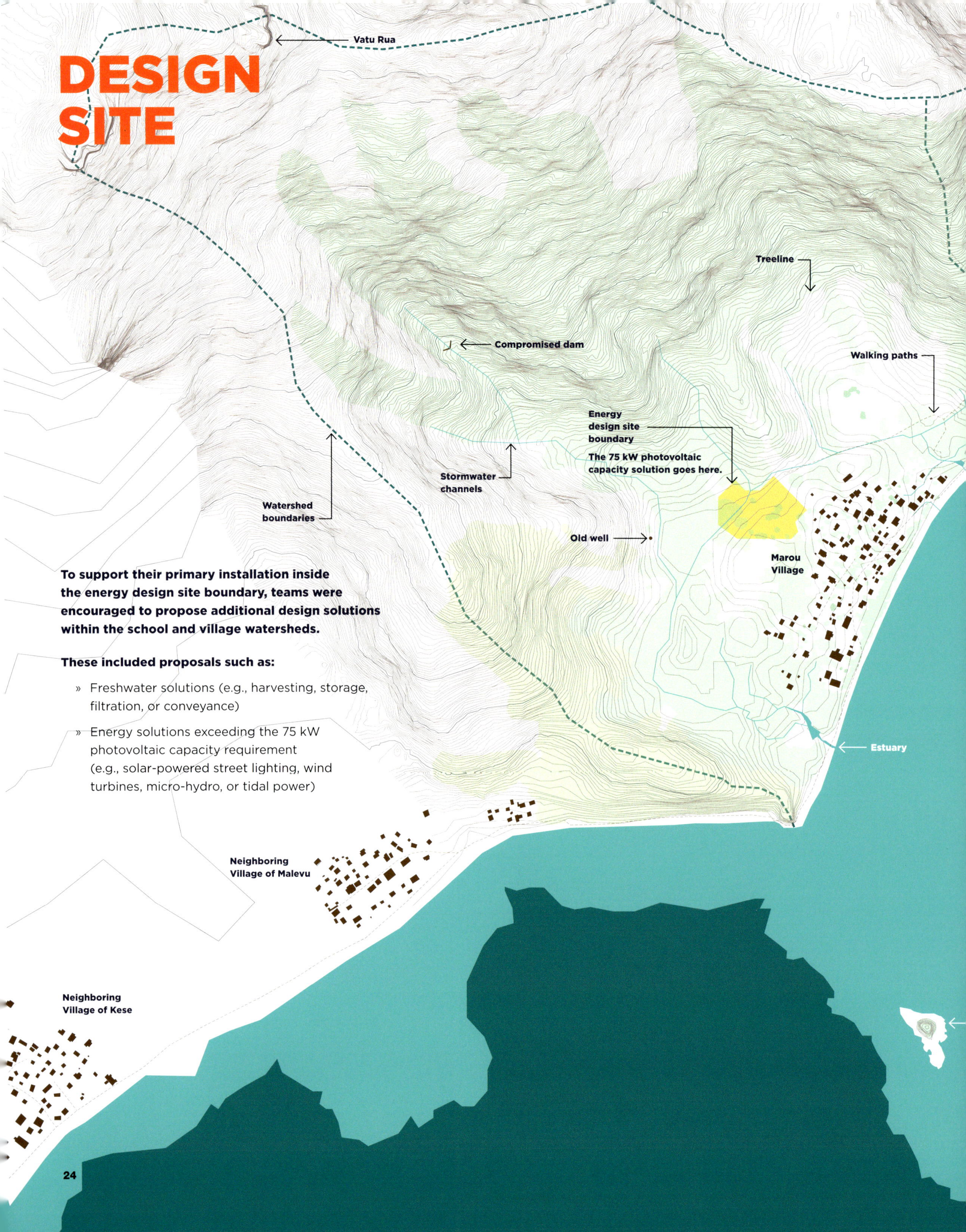

To support their primary installation inside the energy design site boundary, teams were encouraged to propose additional design solutions within the school and village watersheds.

These included proposals such as:

» Freshwater solutions (e.g., harvesting, storage, filtration, or conveyance)

» Energy solutions exceeding the 75 kW photovoltaic capacity requirement (e.g., solar-powered street lighting, wind turbines, micro-hydro, or tidal power)

20 meter contours
1 meter contours
Yasawa School
Low tide line
Existing rubble mound jetty
Vakatawa Island "The Watchman"
This box represents the area shown on this page.
Naviti Island Context Map

Energy as Freedom: Building with Purpose, Designing for Pride

Elena van Hove

Director of Global Energy Access, Laboratory for Energy and Power Solutions, Julie Ann Wrigley Global Futures Laboratory, Arizona State University

1 Amartya Sen, *Development as Freedom* (New York: Alfred A. Knopf, 1999).

Power That Belongs: An Invitation to Marou

Some of my most memorable moments in Fiji have taken place after sunset — sitting with community members under the stars, sharing kava, surrounded by the low hum of conversation and the soft glow of solar lanterns. These lights offered more than visibility. They created the conditions for safety, connection, and continuity — extending the day just a little longer. In those quiet evenings, the link between energy and quality of life was unmistakable.

My path into this work has been shaped by a belief in development not as a fixed outcome, but as the expansion of choice. Economist Amartya Sen describes development as "the expansion of the real freedoms that people enjoy."[1] That framing has guided my approach: development as a means of creating the conditions for people to pursue the lives they value. In that context, energy is not simply a utility — it is an enabler. It supports health, education, safety, and opportunity. It provides the basic infrastructure upon which other freedoms can be built.

For many years, I saw energy access through a strictly technical lens. My focus was on delivering reliable power systems, ensuring coverage, and optimizing costs. But over time, I've come to recognize the role of design and aesthetics — not as luxuries, but as elements that influence how infrastructure is received, maintained, and valued. Beauty can evoke pride and belonging. Well-designed systems invite stewardship. Communities are more likely to care for infrastructure that reflects their identity and aspirations.

This understanding is central to the spirit of LAGI 2025 Fiji. The competition asks us to move beyond utilitarian solutions and toward a more integrated approach, where energy systems are functional, culturally relevant, and visually resonant. It challenges us to consider infrastructure not as something imposed, but as something co-created with the people it is meant to serve.

Marou Village represents this opportunity clearly. Located between mountain and sea, the community is already actively shaping its own development pathway. The goal is not to insert a system, but to support a locally-driven vision. LAGI's role was to facilitate an international design competition that inspired new ways of thinking about infrastructure — bringing creativity and global design talent into conversation with local needs and values. Implementation will be carried forward by the Fiji Rural Electrification Fund (FREF) and its partners, including Arizona State University, ensuring that the resulting system reflects both technical rigor and cultural relevance.

Energy, at its core, is about more than electricity. It's about enabling lives to unfold with dignity, choice, and possibility. That is the invitation of Marou — and of this work.

Designing Belonging: Systems, Symbols, and Co-Creation

In development work, there is often a tendency to look for singular solutions — a breakthrough technology, a one-size-fits-all policy, or a system that promises both scale and speed. But real-world infrastructure exists within complex, human systems. Success depends not just on the device or the design, but on how well that system fits its broader context: policy, financing, operations, environment, and culture.

LAGI's design philosophy speaks directly to this complexity. It challenges the idea that infrastructure must be purely functional, instead inviting designers to consider how energy systems can reflect cultural identity and social meaning. While technology may power devices, it is relevance, adaptability, and community investment that determine whether a system endures and is valued.

I came to appreciate this more deeply during one of my early projects: the deployment of a solar-powered clinic container in northern Uganda, adjacent to a health center that served approximately 20,000 refugees from South Sudan. I joined near the end of the implementation phase, just as the system came online. When the lights were turned on for the first time, the local clinicians — who had been providing care for nearly 200 patients a day in small buildings and tents — were jubilant. I remember their laughter, their wide grins. "It's like New York City," one said, pointing at the bright, clean interior. It may have looked ordinary to me — fluorescent lights and basic exam equipment — but to them, it signaled a shift: a safer, more capable, more dignified place to work.

The project powered the maternity ward, allowing the clinic to provide safe deliveries at night. It electrified staff housing, making remote assignments more comfortable and appealing.

Even something as simple as reliably charging a phone or cooking indoors contributed to a better quality of life. That experience expanded my understanding of how infrastructure can affect not just service delivery, but morale, retention, and a sense of possibility.

It also underscored the importance of participatory design. Certain features, such as the ventilation in the patient room or the location of the lab near the entrance, were later adjusted by clinicians to better align with their workflows. The original team had worked hard under time and resource constraints and had conducted a site visit to inform the design. But the limited opportunity for engagement meant some elements didn't fully match local use patterns. It was a reminder that even well-planned systems benefit from deeper collaboration.

That same principle has shaped my work in Fiji. Through the Fiji Rural Electrification Fund (FREF) and the Community Energy Toolkit (COMET) workshop process, we've worked closely with village leaders, government stakeholders, and technical teams to develop a mini-grid model that fits local realities. Many policymakers had seen how fully community-managed systems often failed — stranded assets from well-meaning projects that lacked technical support. At the same time, a private-sector-only model wasn't viable in remote Indigenous communities. These are tight-knit places with strong social cohesion and deep relationships to land. Infrequent visits from outside operators don't build trust or enable reliable service. In many cases, the logistics of access alone make technical troubleshooting costly and inefficient.

To address these challenges, we explored a co-ownership model structured around joint ventures between communities and private sector partners. Cooperatives represent the community in the joint venture, while also offering other relevant village services, such as micro-financing or agricultural processing. This approach allows for local representation, economic resilience, and sustained technical oversight. It wasn't a pre-designed model imposed from the outside—it evolved through dialogue, shaped by the lived realities of the villages themselves.

This is what genuine co-design looks like. It is not about symbolic inclusion, but shared responsibility, where technical, cultural, and economic considerations are integrated into a system from the outset. It requires listening, iteration, and a willingness to let assumptions shift.

Elena van Hove, Taniela Tabuya, and Viliame Finau carry solar power equipment to shore as part of the Accelerating Solar Mini-grid Deployment in Fiji project in December 2023.
Photograph by Joji Wata.

It also reinforces something more human: infrastructure shapes how people feel about their place in the world. A system that is thoughtfully designed — not only to function but to reflect the community it serves — can generate a sense of belonging and pride. It invites people to see the infrastructure as their own.

Across cultures, symbols matter. The carved tanoa in Fijian kava ceremonies, the Meiji Jingu Shrine in Tokyo, and South Africa's Freedom Park each embody memory, heritage, and collective meaning. They mark identity. They invite reflection. While not essential in the narrowest technical sense, these elements foster emotional connection. Energy infrastructure can do the same.

Designing for energy access in Marou isn't just about delivering power. It's about creating infrastructure that works, fits, and endures — solutions that reflect the values and spirit of the people who will live with these systems every day.

Scaling Care: Designing in Paradise, Planning for the Planet

Marou is undeniably beautiful. Its landscape, where steep green hills meet clear ocean water, is both striking and deeply lived in. The community is active, connected, and already shaping its own development path. But building infrastructure here is far from simple. Reaching the village requires careful coordination across ferry schedules, truck access, and weather conditions. Materials must be corrosion-resistant and cyclone-resilient. Labor, logistics, and maintenance plans must all be adapted to the pace and rhythm of island life. These factors don't make the work impossible, but they do require design that listens to the land.

Constraints like these are often seen as limitations, but I've come to view them as design inputs. They are reminders to simplify, to respect context, and to build with longevity in mind. In places like Marou, the challenge is not just technical — it's philosophical: how do we create infrastructure that is both resilient and relevant? How do we support systems that communities will want to keep, care for, and carry forward?

This is where LAGI plays a unique role. The initiative doesn't promise universal templates or instant solutions. It doesn't assume replicability. Instead, it offers a provocation, inviting designers to explore what infrastructure could look like if it were shaped not only by engineering constraints but by identity, culture, and imagination. In Marou, the LAGI competition serves as a "lighthouse project," not because every community needs a sculptural solar canopy or artful water catchment, but because it challenges us to think differently about what's possible.

At the same time, we must recognize the urgency and scale of the global energy access gap. More than 700 million people around the world still live without electricity. In that context, it is neither realistic nor appropriate to assume every project will incorporate high-design aesthetics or symbolic architecture. Not every system needs to be a landmark. But every community deserves infrastructure that is reliable, respectful, and designed with care.

That is the balance we're trying to strike through the Fiji Rural Electrification Fund (FREF), which is now preparing to implement the first 20 mini-grids across the country. With Arizona State University as one of the technical partners, the program is developing a scalable, public-private partnership model that blends community co-ownership with professional operation and maintenance. This hybrid approach allows for long-term sustainability without compromising community agency. It's not a perfect model, but it's one that's evolving through dialogue and grounded in lessons learned from both global experience and local reality.

Ultimately, I believe scale and care are not mutually exclusive. We can design systems that are both cost-effective and culturally grounded, both replicable and respectful. But doing so requires collaboration — across sectors, across geographies, and across ways of knowing.

What Marou offers the world is not a finished product, but a glimpse of what energy infrastructure can be when it is imagined expansively and built collectively. In this work, technology matters. Policy matters. But what matters just as much is the willingness to ask different questions — to center not only efficiency but also meaning.

The future of energy cannot be designed in isolation. It must be built with communities, shaped by place, and informed by the belief that power is not just about electricity — it's about the freedom to thrive.

“The competition asks us to move beyond utilitarian solutions and toward a more integrated approach—where energy systems are functional, culturally relevant, and visually resonant. It challenges us to consider infrastructure not as something imposed, but as something co-created with the people it is meant to serve.”

—Elena van Hove

Director, Global Energy Access, Laboratory for Energy and Power Solutions, Julie Ann Wrigley Global Futures Laboratory, Arizona State University

Water as Resilience

Lisa M. Farmen

Founder and Principal Engineer, Aquastry LLC

The man in the photograph recorded the ground elevation in the San Joaquin Valley of California and noted the changes over time on a telephone pole.
Public domain image courtesy of the USGS Denver Library Photographic Collection.

Growing up on the rainy side of Oregon's Cascade Range, water was a given. In the Willamette Valley and along the coast, it arrived each year in generous measure, marking the true start of summer only when it finally receded in July. It never occurred to me that water could become a source of crisis. I never imagined I'd live to see the day when water scarcity would define the global conversation about climate, equity, and survival.

That realization came slowly, and then all at once. In the early 1980s, I launched my career in Silicon Valley, running a state-certified water lab and working closely with the semiconductor industry. Over the decades, I saw firsthand how one of the world's most advanced industrial sectors depended on one of its most vulnerable resources. When Texas Instruments acquired our fabrication plant in Santa Cruz, we faced a tough mandate: double production while using 30% less water. At the time, this seemed impossible. The ultrapure water systems standard in 1995 recovered only 70% of water, with the rest discarded as waste.

But by commissioning one of the first High Efficiency Reverse Osmosis (HERO) systems, and designing a full water recycling loop, we achieved what had once seemed implausible. The new system recovered 98% of water and reused the rest for boiler and HVAC makeup. In the end, we more than doubled production while reducing total water use. The experience proved that even high-consumption industries can operate on a fraction of the water they once used.

But efficiency alone won't solve the larger crisis. Globally, the picture is far more sobering.

If all the water on Earth were represented by a 5-gallon container, the amount available as fresh, drinkable water would fill just a single teaspoon. That tiny fraction must sustain more than eight billion people and trillions of other living creatures. Most of Earth's water is locked in oceans, icecaps, and glaciers — out of reach without costly infrastructure. Much of the Earth's freshwater is suspended as vapor in our atmosphere and this percentage increases as temperature rises. It is possible to have a relatively high humidity and no rain. The atmosphere must contain particulates to nucleate condensation. Even heavy rainfall is often lost unless captured by systems like wetlands or reservoirs. Meanwhile, global water consumption has historically doubled every 20 years, outpacing population growth by a factor of two.[1] Driven by rising agricultural demand and industrial use, water needs could grow another 30% by 2050, even as freshwater sources shrink.

Water is a finite resource under infinite demand. More than 80% of global disease is water related.[2] A quarter of the world's population across 25 countries already lives under extreme water stress, using at least 80% of their available supply. More than half the world faces high water stress, withdrawing at least 40% of their renewable freshwater.[3] The narrower the margin between supply and demand, the more vulnerable a region becomes. Even under the most optimistic climate scenarios, another billion people are projected to face extreme water stress by mid-century.

Much of the water that sustains life and food production comes from underground. Groundwater, stored in the pores between soil and rock, is being extracted far faster than it can naturally recharge. As these aquifers deplete, their structure collapses, permanently reducing their capacity and causing the land above to sink. In California's Central Valley, land has subsided by up to 28 feet since the 1920s. One man famously marked the change by nailing boards to a telephone pole (image this page).

NASA's GRACE (Gravity Recovery and Climate Experiment) satellites monitored this loss between 2002 and 2017, and their successor, GRACE-FO, continues to measure global changes in aquifers, evapotranspiration, and regional water storage. Their findings are sobering: a third of the world's major aquifers are now in significant distress.[4]

As groundwater disappears, the risks extend beyond farmland. Coastal regions are particularly vulnerable to saltwater intrusion, which contaminates freshwater supplies.[5] Sea level rise, fueled by climate change, makes this threat more urgent. Roughly 90% of the excess heat from global warming is absorbed by the oceans, causing them to thermally expand.[6] This thermal expansion accounts for up to half of observed sea level rise, most of it concentrated in the upper 700 meters of the ocean.[7]

There are two types of sea level rise. Relative sea level rise (also known as isostatic rise) is experienced locally and includes not only rising seas but also sinking land. Both can be devastating. By 2100, as much as 52% of the global population and nearly half of the world's land area could be at risk of flooding and storm surge.

1 Deborah Zabarenko, "Water use rising faster than world population," *Reuters*, October 25, 2011, https://www.reuters.com/article/business/environment/water-use-rising-faster-than-world-population-idUSTRE79O3XY/.

2 World Health Organization, "Drinking-water: Key facts," *WHO Fact Sheets*, last modified September 13, 2023, https://www.who.int/news-room/fact-sheets/detail/drinking-water.

3 World Resources Institute, *Aqueduct Water Risk Atlas*, https://www.wri.org/aqueduct.

4 NASA Jet Propulsion Laboratory, "Water Storage," *GRACE-FO Science*, https://gracefo.jpl.nasa.gov/science/water-storage.

5 U.S. Environmental Protection Agency, "Climate Adaptation and Saltwater Intrusion," https://www.epa.gov/arc-x/climate-adaptation-and-saltwater-intrusion.

6 NOAA Climate.gov, "Climate Change: Ocean Heat Content," https://www.climate.gov/news-features/understanding-climate/climate-change-ocean-heat-content.

7 NASA Sea Level Change, "Thermal Expansion," https://sealevel.nasa.gov/understanding-sea-level/global-sea-level/thermal-expansion.

Global mean sea level rise (also known as eustatic rise) is the global average sea level compared to a fixed point, such as the center of the Earth. This is the kind of sea level rise most related to climate change and is driven by melting ice and thermal expansion. Most of the excess heat from global warming is absorbed by the seas, causing them to thermally expand. Sea level rise now threatens to displace entire communities. For coastal villages like Marou in Fiji's Yasawa archipelago, this danger is immediate — not only from flooding, but from the contamination of freshwater sources by encroaching salt.

But Marou is also a place of possibility. A five-year rainfall analysis shows an annual average of 1,960 mm. This is not a dry place — it's a place where rainfall is heavy for half the year and must be better captured and preserved for the other half of the year when rainfall is extremely scarce. Roof-based rainwater collection systems are one part of the solution. Atmospheric water capture (AWC) technologies, especially viable in humid coastal climates, can add resilience. Reverse osmosis (RO) desalination may also play a role, though it is energy intensive, requires consistent maintenance, and produces high-salinity waste.

Perhaps most promising are nature-based solutions. Constructed wetlands can manage stormwater, reduce erosion, trap sediment, and help recharge aquifers. They also help maintain the freshwater-seawater pressure balance that prevents saltwater intrusion. A single millimeter of rainfall over a hectare equals 10,000 liters of water. Every drop counts. A wetland system designed to align with the local rainfall patterns of Marou could harvest extraordinary volumes of freshwater. Based on a five-year rainfall average in the Yasawas, the broader watershed could yield nearly 278 million liters per year, while the LAGI 2025 Fiji design area alone could contribute more than 33.5 million liters annually.

Aquifer recharge through wetlands also protects water from evaporation and helps prevent insect-borne diseases — an important public health benefit in tropical regions. With appropriate filtration and treatment, this stored water can meet human needs reliably and safely. It also helps ensure that aquifers, once restored, can remain viable for future generations.

Globally, we are waking up to the idea that there may be no such thing as a truly "clean" source of natural water anymore. Even bottled mineral water brands now rely on filtration and UV disinfection. In this new reality, water must be actively managed, protected, and regenerated. We must shift from a model of extraction to one of stewardship.

By pairing renewable energy with regenerative water design, LAGI 2025 Fiji challenges us to rethink infrastructure as an ecosystem — functional, beautiful, and alive with meaning. I'm glad to see that LAGI is extending their vision of designing energy infrastructure with communities to include water — asking not just how we power the future, but how we can sustain life.

The global climate system is delicate, complex, and increasingly unstable. It is the communities that have contributed least to this crisis — like Marou — that face the most immediate threats.

This is what makes the work in Fiji so urgent. If we can figure out how to design climate-resilient energy and water systems for a remote island community, we can figure it out anywhere. The design solutions generated through this competition will be locally rooted, but their implications are universal.

The effects of global warming are serious and life threatening. Still, we must meet them not with despair, but with imagination, accountability, and resolve. We must act as though the future is not something we inherit, but something we co-create, drop by drop.

Bridging Energy Access Through Community-Centered Development in Fiji's Small Island Context

Dr. Ramendra Prasad

Associate Professor, Department of Science, School of Science and Technology, The University of Fiji, Lautoka, Fiji; Centre for Climate Change, Energy, Environment and Sustainable Development, The University of Fiji, Lautoka, Fiji

Renewable energy (RE) plays a pivotal role in the global transition toward sustainable and environmentally responsible energy systems. Solar, wind, and hydropower offer clean alternatives that reduce dependence on finite fossil fuel resources, and they significantly lower carbon emissions compared to conventional energy sources.[1] Ongoing technological advancements have improved the accessibility and cost-effectiveness of renewable energy, supporting its growing adoption worldwide.

Despite these encouraging developments, the integration of renewable energy into both centralized electricity grids and decentralized mini-grids still faces several challenges. One of the most significant barriers is the intermittency and variability of variable renewable energy (VRE) sources, such as solar and wind. Fluctuating weather patterns, inconsistent sunlight, changing wind conditions, and erratic cloud cover can all impact the ability of these systems to reliably meet real-time energy demand.

Globally, the past decade has seen a concerning rise in fossil fuel use — up 13.1% between 2012 and 2022, according to the *Global Status Report 2024*.[2] The South Pacific reflects this dependence, with fossil fuels still dominating electricity generation across the region. While RE capacity has doubled during the same period, it remains a small share of the total energy mix. Within Oceania, Australia has made the most significant progress, increasing its installed renewable capacity by about 150%. New Zealand's growth has been much more modest at around 10%. In Fiji, uptake has grown by approximately 15%.[3]

An even further breakdown of the different RE sources in the Oceania region showed, from 2020 onwards, the total installed capacity of solar has overtaken hydro as the major RE source. However, the situation in Fiji has been different as hydroelectricity has always had a larger share in energy generation over the decade (2012–2021) compared to other Oceania countries.

Fiji's energy transition is shaped by its geography. As an archipelago of over 300 islands with a population of around 885,000, nearly half of whom live in rural areas, infrastructure deployment is complex.[4] The islands lie between the equator and the Tropic of Capricorn, with consistent solar radiation and average temperatures ranging from 18 °C at night to 32 °C during the day. Annual rainfall ranges from 2,000 to 3,000 mm on the main islands and up to 6,000 mm in the mountains, providing strong hydropower resources. Wind speeds vary seasonally but not by much, averaging between 18.8 km/h in the dry season to 21 km/h in the wet season.[5]

Today, between 50% and 60% of Fiji's grid-connected electricity comes from renewable sources. Hydroelectric power still dominates, but recent years have seen growing contributions from bioenergy and a small but growing portfolio of solar installations. Most solar projects to date have been small-scale rooftop systems installed by institutions for their own use, with excess electricity exported to the grid.

Some recent examples include:

- 1.1 MWp rooftop solar system at Coca-Cola Amatil in Suva
- 412 kWp installation at the Radisson Blu Resort in Nadi
- 250 kWp combination rooftop and ground-mounted system at Fiji National University (Nadi campus)
- 45 kWp ground-mounted array at the University of the South Pacific (Suva)
- 1.44 kWp rooftop unit at the University of Fiji (Lautoka)

Looking ahead, Energy Fiji Limited (EFL) is actively expanding its solar infrastructure. A 1 MWp solar facility has been commissioned in Taveuni, and a 5 MWp solar farm is being developed in Qeleloa, near Nadi.[6]

1 Wadim Strielkowski, Elena Tarkhanova, Natalia Baburina, and Justas Streimikis, "Corporate Social Responsibility and the Renewable Energy Development in the Baltic States," *Sustainability* 13, no. 17 (2021): 9860, https://doi.org/10.3390/su13179860.

2 REN21, *Renewables 2024 Global Status Report* (Paris: REN21 Secretariat, 2024), https://www.ren21.net/reports/global-status-report/.

3 International Renewable Energy Agency (IRENA).

4 Fiji Bureau of Statistics (FBoS), *Fiji Bureau of Statistics Releases 2017 Census Results*, October 1, 2018, https://www.fiji.gov.fj/Media-Centre/News/Fiji-Bureau-of-Statistics-Releases-2017-Census-Res.

5 Tourism Fiji, *Weather & Climate*, 2020, https://www.tourismfiji.com/fiji-weather.html.

6 Energy Fiji Limited (EFL), *Annual Report 2020* (Fiji: EFL, 2020).

For rural electrification initiatives, the Fiji Department of Energy (DoE), with funding from the government, has been deploying solar home systems (SHS). The DoE oversees the implementation of these projects and manages major maintenance. The initial SHS installations, known as Type I, consisted of two 50 Wp solar panels, one 100 Ah battery, a 10A charge controller, and DC lights. After 2014, a larger version, the Type II SHS, was introduced. These included two 135 Wp solar panels, one 200 Ah battery, a 20A charge controller, DC LED lights, and a 300W inverter capable of supporting increased household demand, including AC loads. With rising energy needs, larger systems and mini-grids have become necessary. Notably, solar mini-grids have been installed on the islands of Kadavu (249 kW), Lakeba (153 kW), and Rotuma (153 kW). To address mini-grid financing challenges, the government of Fiji established the Fiji Rural Electrification Fund (FREF) to secure funding and implement rural electrification projects.

In 2018, FREF installed a solar mini-grid system on Vio Island in the Yasawa Archipelago as a pilot project with seed funding from the Leonardo DiCaprio Foundation. Since then, FREF has secured additional grants, including from the governments of New Zealand and Australia. A feasibility study, conducted by Arizona State University (ASU), has recently been completed for 75 potential solar mini-grid sites. Marou Village is one of the sites that was chosen, and the LAGI 2025 Fiji project has benefited through its alignment with the FREF program.

The adoption and deployment of renewable energy in small islands like Fiji face additional challenges. High capital costs, compounded by limited income-generating opportunities in remote and maritime communities, constrain economic development and perpetuate a cycle of cash scarcity. Accessibility is also a concern, as ships may visit some islands only once a week or even once a month, and local infrastructure remains underdeveloped. Developers must often incur additional costs to transport specialized civil works equipment to these sites.

Furthermore, the limited availability of land, especially under communal ownership, can intensify project challenges. For these reasons, effective community engagement is critical to the success of rural electrification projects, particularly those focused on expanding energy access in remote and underserved areas.

In Fiji, there is a diversity of settlement types, ranging from traditional iTaukei villages to Indo-Fijian farming communities and maritime settlements. In the former, hierarchical structures, chiefly authority, and communal land ownership are prevalent. At the same time, all remote and maritime communities face significant access and logistical challenges. Indo-Fijian settlements are typically agriculturally oriented and based on individual land tenancy. Peri-urban areas, which combine both rural and urban characteristics, present yet another distinct context.

These variations necessitate tailored strategies that take into account cultural norms, governance systems, and socio-economic conditions. Such contexts shape not only how communities respond to energy interventions but also what forms of engagement are culturally and practically appropriate. A blend of traditional and modern methods is essential to build trust and gather meaningful input. The Talanoa method — a culturally embedded form of open dialogue — has proven to be a valuable and widely accepted tool for fostering inclusive participation. Successful engagement is grounded in mutual understanding, respect for traditional protocols, and a shared commitment to co-development.

The success of energy projects in Fiji depends on respecting and understanding local traditions, including:

- Governance and ownership: The iTaukei governance system is hierarchical, shaped by village bylaws and communal decision-making.
- Land tenure: Customary land ownership can complicate the siting and operation of energy infrastructure.
- Community buy-in: Projects that lack social licensing or community endorsement often fail, even if technically sound.

All rural electrification initiatives should begin with systematic community engagement and the establishment of local buy-in. The LAGI project is demonstrating this approach through community involvement from the project's inception through design selection. Going forward, the team will continue the co-creation process with the residents of Marou village through prototyping and pilot project implementation to help ensure that energy and water systems are authentically woven into the fabric of the community. The interconnectedness of community engagement, policy frameworks, and infrastructure development is critical to the long-term sustainability of energy projects.

Implementing targeted policy interventions is essential to break the cycle of poverty and support income-generating opportunities that will ensure the long-term sustainability of climate technologies in Fiji's smaller maritime islands. The productive use of energy (PUE) goes beyond basic electrification for lighting and includes co-benefits, such as enhanced economic activity, retention of value chains within the community, greater load diversity, and more stable energy demand. These factors are critical for the financial viability of mini-grids and for improving livelihoods through business development and job creation. PUE encourages a shift from passive consumption to active entrepreneurial engagement.

To ensure resilience against extreme weather events, all on-site construction should comply with Category 5 cyclonic windspeed civil engineering standards. Imported solar photovoltaic (SPV) modules and inverters must be of high quality to withstand Fiji's challenging environmental conditions. At a minimum, PV modules should meet international standards—IEC 61215, IEC 61730, and IEC 61701—and include a 25-year power output warranty. To ensure performance and reliability, modules should be sourced from Tier 1 manufacturers. It is recommended that all SPV components, including batteries and inverters, be approved by the Clean Energy Council. Mounting structures, cables, DC connectors, switchgear, system control components, and transformers should all meet international standards to ensure long-term durability. All aspects of construction must comply with the Sustainable Energy Industry Association of the Pacific Islands (SEIAPI) standards.

Overall, small island communities face unique challenges in achieving energy access, including limited economies of scale, scarce income-generating opportunities, and high logistical costs. In these contexts, communal land ownership and the implementation of community mini-grids require that engagement with communities is not treated as an add-on, but rather as the foundation of successful rural energy transitions in Fiji. Respect for cultural structures, participatory planning, and alignment with national policy objectives are all essential. Projects, like LAGI 2025 Fiji, that prioritize community-led development, encourage productive energy use, and foster enabling environments for entrepreneurship will be more sustainable, equitable, and resilient over the long term.

“The Talanoa method — a culturally embedded form of open dialogue — has proven to be a valuable and widely accepted tool for fostering inclusive participation. Successful engagement is grounded in mutual understanding, respect for traditional protocols, and a shared commitment to co-development.”

—Dr. Ramendra Prasad

Associate Professor, Department of Science, School of Science and Technology, The University of Fiji, Lautoka, Fiji; Centre for Climate Change, Energy, Environment and Sustainable Development, The University of Fiji, Lautoka, Fiji

During an initial visit to Marou Village in June 2024, the LAGI team walked the potential design site areas, documenting them with ground and aerial photographs. Pictured: Robert Ferry and Ilisari Naqau Nasau.

After incorporating insights from the initial visit, Elizabeth and Robe returned in September 2024 to revise the design guidelines draft and redefine site boundaries in collaboration with Marou residents.

Robert Ferry sits with Ilisari Naqau Nasau, Acting Chief of Marou Village, as they review design solutions submitted to the LAGI 2025 Fiji competition in May 2025.

Representatives of Mataqali Koro participating in the selection process for the LAGI 2025 Fiji design competition. Bula vinaka!

Tanoa: The Bowl of Life

Puya Khalili, Aziz Khalili, Iman Khalili

See page 174

SOLUTIONS

WINNING SOLUTIONS

The O

Ligavatuvuce: Hands that Offer and Uplift

FEATURED SOLUTIONS

Drau

Between the Sky & Earth

Coconet

SigaWai Canopy Park

Vunilagi

Vatu Rua Kaukauwa: Two Resilient Rocks

Energy Forest

Unleashing the Vanua: Living Systems for Community Resilience

TALI-TALI-LAND

Solar Waves

The Arc of Nature

Just a Roof

The Cloud

Solar Pavilion for the Community

Solar Forest

Land Actuator

Na Lomalagi, na Qele, kei na Tamata: The Sky, the Earth, and the People

Vaka ni Lomani: Vessel of Compassion

Bula Sun

Solar Leaf

Sky Letters: Letters to the Invisible

Land Sails

Marou Vula

Drua

Independence

Vanilla Energy

Mangrove Bridge

The Drua Fleet of Energy

Vanua Sun-Well: Building Community with Water & Energy

Marou: The Power of Community

Meke na Mana: The Power Dance

Navigating Light, Holding Rain

The Flowers of New Life

Palm Heart

Sun + Rain Network

Arrays of Vanua

The Flow of Life: Currents of Continuum

Vale ni Siga

The Kaleidoscope of Marou

Plug-in Solar Sheds

Solar Vessels

A Place Becoming

Energy Bloom

Stretch Point

Tanoa: The Bowl of Life

Valelaca Rokataki: Prismatic Parasol

Under One Roof

Marou Totem Landscape

TAGI LAGI: Plugins for Clean Energy

Threadscape

Vale ni Wai Siga: Aqua Nest Solar Habitat

Eco-EnergyScape

Marou Gathers: A Constellation of Voices, Energy, and Worlds

TRIvibe

Loto Kava Ring

Koro Coral

Ever Present Naviti

Synergistic Garden

The Fifth Element

Sun and Mist Harvest

UmbraWell

Savu

Mataliki

Hibiscus

Herpolitha Weberi

Tree of Life

Solar Shelter

Braided Nature: The Power of Welcoming

Salusalu Marou Solar Park

The Breath of Marou

Veilomani Energy Pavilion

Voivoi Future

The Living Thread

Waqa ni Rarama: Canoe of Light

Vakabula

Grid of Light and Land: A Living Framework for Village Resilience

Solar Village

Aqualillies

LAN'GI

de la terre

RAY

“By pairing renewable energy with regenerative water design, LAGI 2025 Fiji challenges us to rethink infrastructure as an ecosystem—functional, beautiful, and alive with meaning.”

—Lisa M. Farmen
Founder and Principal Engineer, Aquastry LLC

The O

DESIGNER: Alberto Roncelli

TECHNOLOGIES: solar photovoltaic, battery energy storage, rainwater harvesting, multi-stage water filtration (flush diverter, screen filter, sediment filter, carbon filter, UV), underground cisterns

ANNUAL PRODUCTION: 150 MWh of electricity, 1.2 million liters of filtered water

DESIGN TEAM LOCATION: Denmark

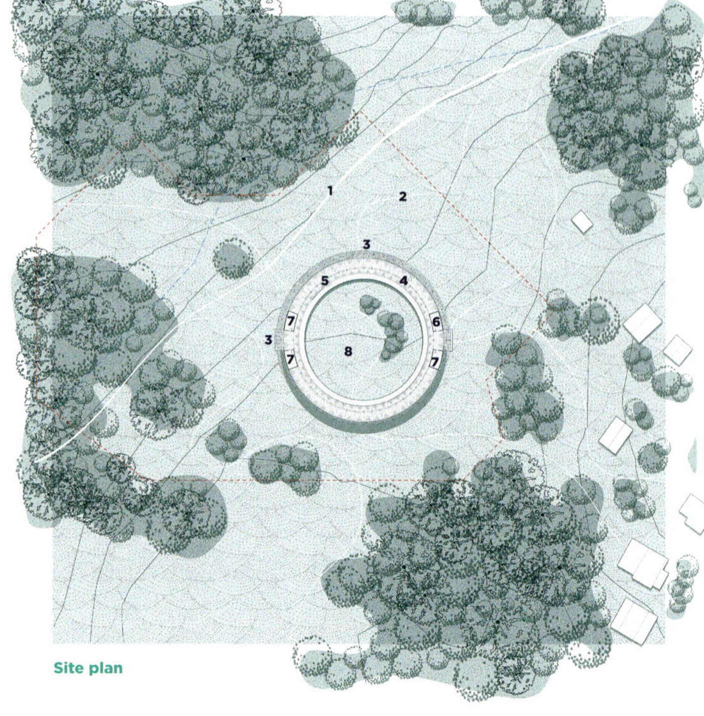

Site plan

1. Extension of the main walking path
2. Secondary paths to *The O*
3. Main access points to the structure
4. Covered space under the canopy
5. Floor with masi-inspired pattern decoration
6. Battery storage and inverters housed within a 15 m² insulated room
7. Enclosed rooms for flexible use and storage
8. Underground modular water tanks

Shaped as a perfect circle, *The O* is a symbol of harmony between architecture, energy, and landscape. Its 40-meter-wide solar canopy floats above the ground like a quiet halo, providing renewable power, harvesting rainwater, and creating a generous, shaded gathering space for the Marou community.

Constructed primarily from timber, the installation merges ecological sensitivity with technological precision. The canopy, composed of 336 monocrystalline solar panels, generates 150 MWh of clean electricity each year — enough to supply household energy for the village. Beneath it lies a 600-square-meter ring of open space, adaptable for cultural events, learning, and everyday use.

Rainwater is gathered from the 768-square-meter roof, filtered through a multi-stage system, and stored in ten modular underground tanks, with a combined capacity of 100,000 liters. Over the course of a year, more than 1.2 million liters of rainwater can be harvested, supporting either potable or domestic use, depending on the filtration approach determined by the community.

Designed for resilience and simplicity, *The O* uses modular systems that are durable, intuitive to operate, and easy to maintain. A central technical room houses the battery bank, inverters, and controls, with clear, illustrated manuals. A team of trained local stewards will oversee basic maintenance tasks, supported by occasional visits from technical partners if needed.

The O is a living platform that supports cultural expression, seasonal events, and evolving community needs. It invites participation not only in its function but in its meaning, transforming the act of gathering energy and water into a collective, regenerative practice.

Sitting lightly on the land, *The O* stands as a tangible embodiment of Fiji's *Vision 2050* — uniting clean energy, low-carbon construction, and community empowerment in a single, poetic form.

RIGHT: The curving form of *The O* rises dynamically on the south side of the installation, as the landscape flows nearly uninterrupted below. The walkway is elevated above the high floodwater line to ensure long-term resilience.

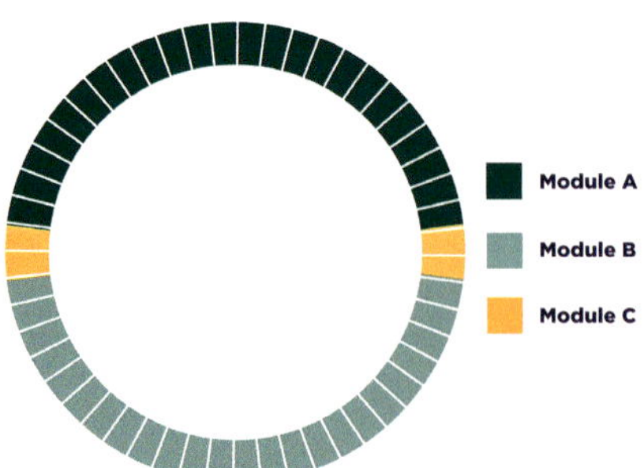

The structure is designed from simple, modular, and small elements that can be easily manufactured, transported, and assembled.

Two primary modules define the overall geometry, with a third module connecting them. There are 24 modules of type A, 24 of type B, and 4 of type C.

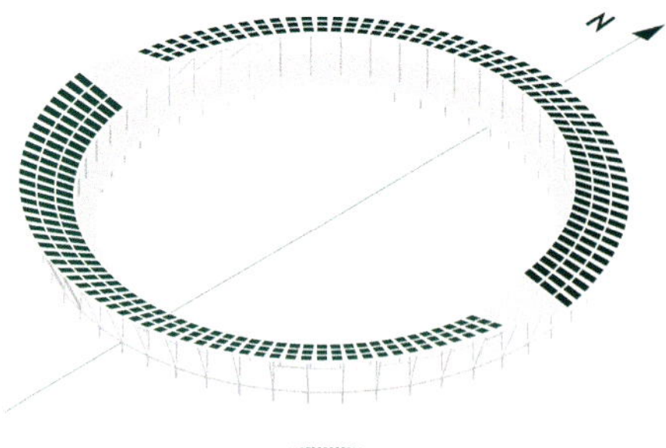

Energy production
The solar panels are installed along the canopy in three rows, tilted at 19° to maximize solar exposure year-round. They are grouped into 18 strings to optimize energy output and minimize electrical losses. Fifteen batteries, each with a 50 kWh capacity, are housed in a ventilated and secure electrical room.

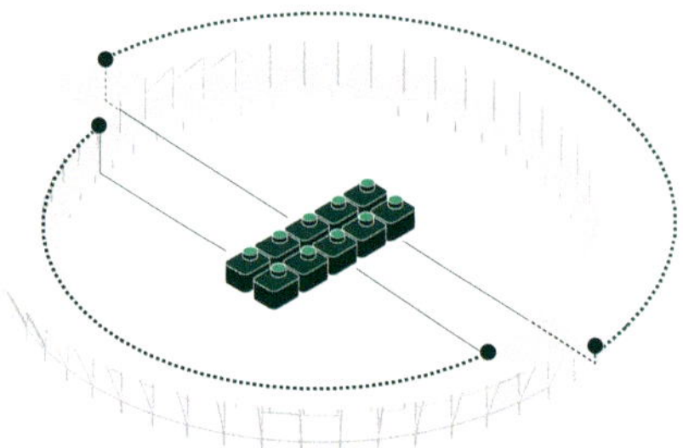

Water harvesting
The entire 768 m² roof functions as a rainwater collection surface. Water is captured by two gutters and stored in underground cisterns after passing through membranes and filters for purification. The system can be expanded by adding additional storage tanks, either above or below grade.

A new social heart of the village
The area beneath the roof and within the central circle serves as a multifunctional community space. Workshops with the community during later design stages will help identify materials and additional design elements. The structure can be adapted over time and modified for specific events or seasons.

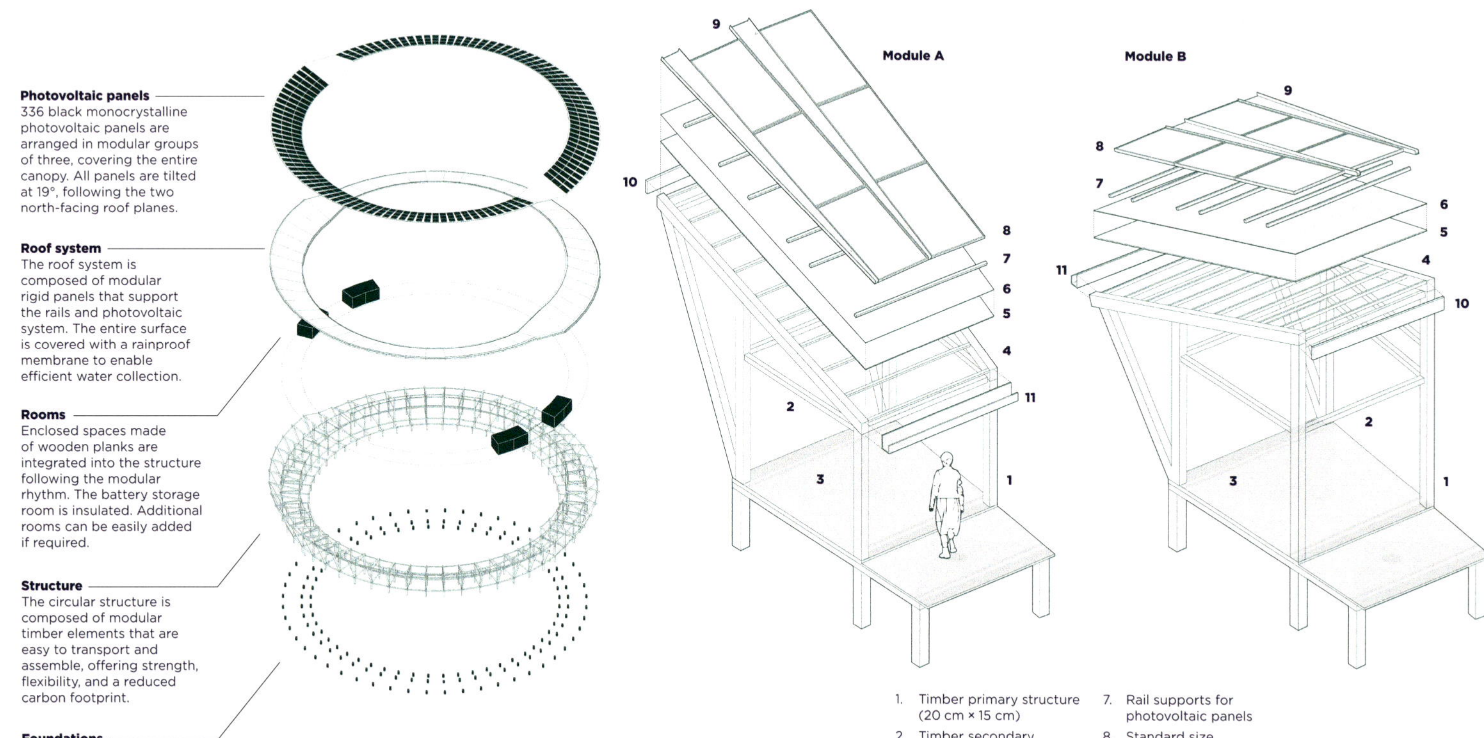

Photovoltaic panels
336 black monocrystalline photovoltaic panels are arranged in modular groups of three, covering the entire canopy. All panels are tilted at 19°, following the two north-facing roof planes.

Roof system
The roof system is composed of modular rigid panels that support the rails and photovoltaic system. The entire surface is covered with a rainproof membrane to enable efficient water collection.

Rooms
Enclosed spaces made of wooden planks are integrated into the structure following the modular rhythm. The battery storage room is insulated. Additional rooms can be easily added if required.

Structure
The circular structure is composed of modular timber elements that are easy to transport and assemble, offering strength, flexibility, and a reduced carbon footprint.

Foundations
Screw pile foundations are used to minimize ground disturbance and allow vegetation to grow beneath.

1. Timber primary structure (20 cm × 15 cm)
2. Timber secondary structure (10 cm × 10 cm)
3. Timber flooring (with masi geometries developed with the community)
4. Timber roof supports
5. Rigid panel
6. Rainproof membrane
7. Rail supports for photovoltaic panels
8. Standard size monocrystalline photovoltaic
9. Metal profile between photovoltaic panels
10. Protective and aesthetic profile
11. Gutter for efficient rain collection

The sweeping central space formed by the installation offers a destination where visitors can learn about art, ecology, and sustainable energy and water systems. It is also a place for Marou residents to gather, perform, or sit alone in the quiet of the landscape.

Seen from the north, the solar modules define the roof of the installation.

Ligavatuvuce
Hands that Offer and Uplift

The view from just above the village reveals the full profile of the left hand.

DESIGNER: Young Kang

TECHNOLOGIES: solar photovoltaic, battery energy storage, rainwater harvesting, biofiltration, underground cisterns

ANNUAL PRODUCTION: 120 MWh of electricity, 4.5 million liters of filtered water

DESIGN TEAM LOCATION: United Arab Emirates

A visitor approaches the hands from the north, pausing on the walkway to take a photograph.

Shaped by the traditional gesture of open palms offering yaqona (kava), *Ligavatuvuce*—a compound of three Fijian words that come together with the poetic meaning of "Hands that Offer and Uplift,"— rises from the land as a sculptural expression of resilience and generosity. Drawing from Fijian ritual and craftsmanship, the artwork reinterprets the bilo (the traditional kava drinking vessel made from the shell of a coconut) as an integrated system for solar energy and clean water, linking cultural symbolism with environmental stewardship.

Two hands emerge from a compacted earth platform, framed with cross-laminated timber and finished in a layered blend of traditional thatching: Soga palm leaves, reeds, and coconut fronds. Between them rests a large timber bowl structure supported by 15 timber frames and structural battens. Its soffit is thatched in the same local materials, and its concave form tilts north, both to cradle sunlight and to guide rainfall into an open well below.

Mounted across the upper surface of the bowl are 181 high-efficiency photovoltaic panels, generating enough electricity to power Marou Village and oriented to provide a regular supply of electricity throughout the day. The rainwater collection system spans over 2,800 square meters of surface area, harvesting 4.5 million liters annually. Rainwater is first settled to remove coarse sediment, then purified through a multistage filtration system using gravel, sand, and activated carbon before being stored in an underground cistern.

A gabion wall anchors the site and shapes rainwater runoff paths, while a main access trail leads visitors to the shaded interior, which functions as a space for ceremony, storytelling, and rest. The structure's minimal footprint preserves agricultural land, while its symbolic form strengthens cultural identity.

Ligavatuvuce offers the generous gift of clean water, renewable energy, and social cohesion — held aloft by the hands of the land and its people.

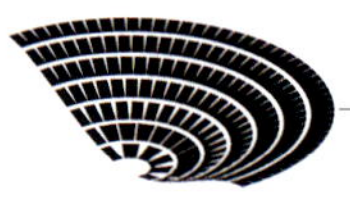

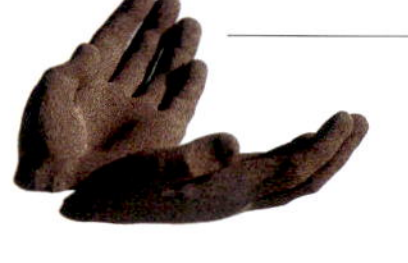

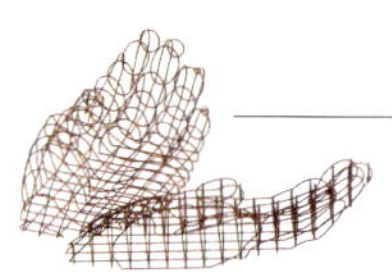

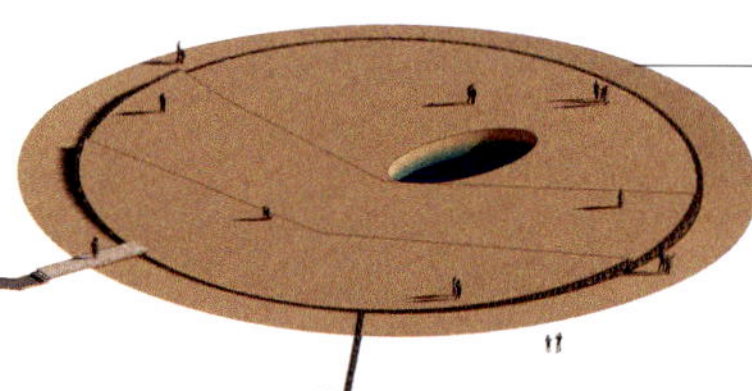

Solar panels clad the interior of the bowl—a conceptual representation of water that also directs rainwater toward the well.

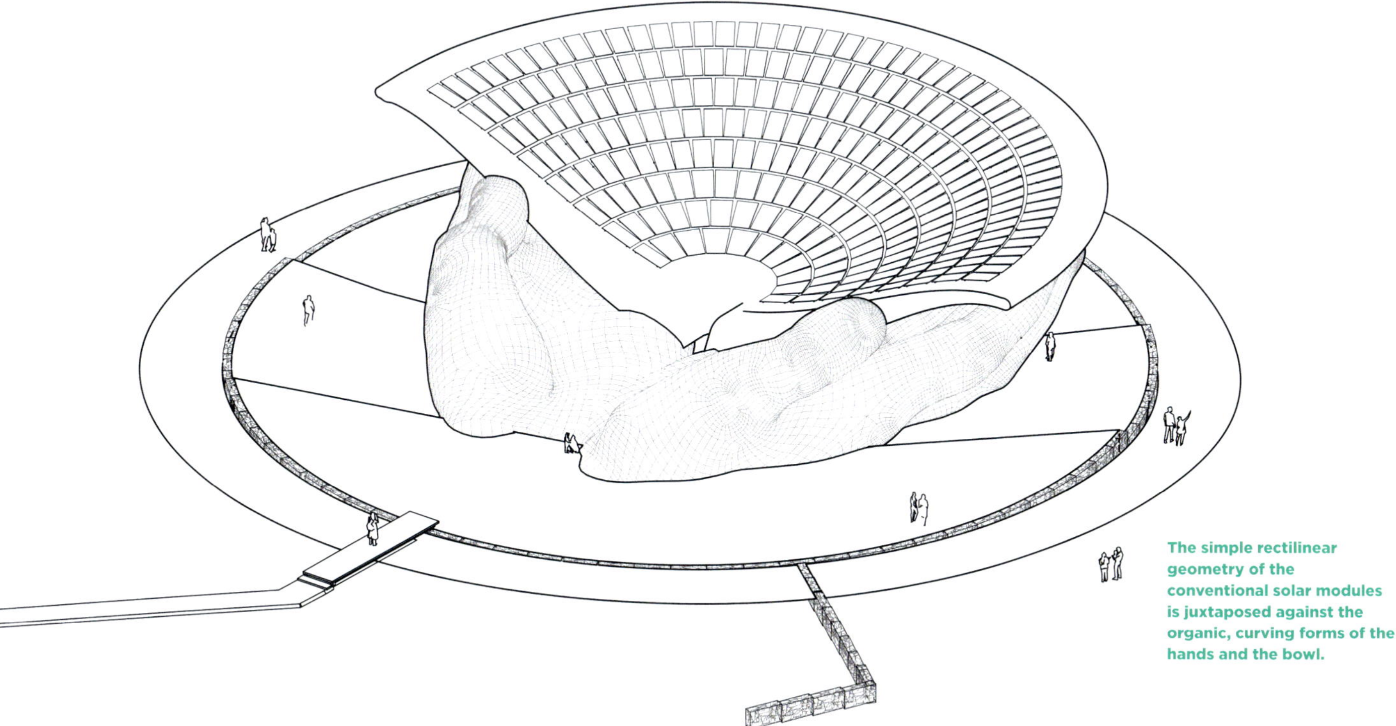

The simple rectilinear geometry of the conventional solar modules is juxtaposed against the organic, curving forms of the hands and the bowl.

The history and significance of thatching in Fijian culture

Thatching remains central to Fijian architecture, embodying the relationship between environment, craftsmanship, and community. It serves as the primary roofing material for bure (houses and communal structures), using soga palm, reeds, and coconut fronds to respond to Fiji's tropical climate while reflecting generations of Indigenous knowledge.

Building a bure is a communal endeavor that reinforces social cohesion. Skilled craftsmen, or mataisau, hold respected roles for their mastery of techniques passed down orally to ensure strength and longevity. Regional variations reflect local conditions, and well-crafted thatching endures for decades.

Beyond its practical function, thatching carries symbolic meaning. The roof can be viewed as sacred, its intricate weave representing the interconnection of land, people, and ancestors. Maintenance serves both practical needs and ritual obligations, reinforcing respect for nature and tradition.

Although modern materials are increasingly common, traditional thatching continues in resorts, cultural sites, and sustainable design projects. It stands as a living tradition—an enduring symbol of Fijian identity that bridges past and future.

Drau

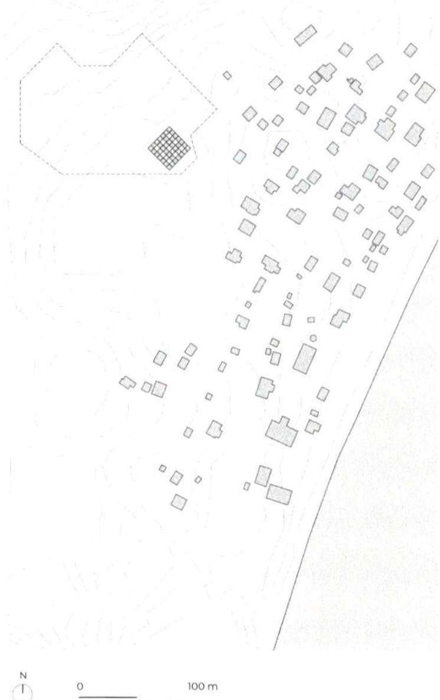

Site plan of a 40-module configuration of *Drau* installed near Marou Village

DESIGNERS: Mateusz Góra, Agata Gryszkiewicz (Tamaga Studio)

TECHNOLOGIES: solar photovoltaic, battery energy storage, rainwater harvesting, above-ground cisterns

ANNUAL PRODUCTION: 160 MWh of electricity, 1.245 million liters of filtered water (40-module configuration)

DESIGN TEAM LOCATION: Poland

Named after the Fijian word for "leaf," *Drau* is a modular solar pavilion that draws from the organic geometry of palm fronds and the symbolic patterns of Fijian masi weaving. Designed for tropical environments, the installation provides clean energy, drinking water, and shaded public space, transforming off-grid infrastructure into an adaptable, community-centered landscape.

Each 3.5 m × 3.5 m unit supports a diamond-shaped roof that rests lightly on cylindrical hardwood columns reminiscent of the trunks of palms. Slatted timber beams fan overhead in elegant repetition, forming a canopy that is both shelter and sculpture. Below the canopy, woven mat-covered rain harvesting tanks with a storage capacity of 2,400 liters per module are tucked between structural columns. The roof is tilted and rotated to deflect wind, matching solar production to demand, and facilitating the collection of rainwater.

Modules can be arranged in clustered formations with solar panels facing north, east, and west. Producing consistent energy throughout the day in this way reduces the need for large battery energy storage. A 40-module configuration has a capacity of 104 kW and can store 38,400 liters of rainwater at a time.

Beneath the canopy, hardwood beams and round columns evoke a forest of palms. The modular spaces below serve diverse local uses: elevated wooden platforms for gathering or play, garden plots for native plants, or agrivoltaic zones supporting food production. Shared infrastructure between grouped modules reduces cost and complexity, while the decentralized system ensures that failure in one unit doesn't affect the rest.

Clustered modules share batteries, a small string inverter, and plumbing. If one unit fails, the others continue to operate independently. The structure is cyclone-resistant, built with local hardwoods and durable glass-glass solar panels, and may be adapted with steel columns or screw-pile foundations as needed.

Detailed design and installation includes local builders and craftspeople in both design and assembly, creating opportunities to build local knowledge. Maintenance is low-tech and community led.

From its structural logic to its symbolic form, *Drau* honors tradition while offering a versatile and replicable model for energy independence in remote island communities.

RIGHT: The rotated, sloping roofs of *Drau* create dappled shade for community agriculture and gathering spaces. Rainwater cisterns are decorated with traditional woven pandanus leaves.

Solar shelter
Six glass-glass monocrystalline panels are mounted on the elevated steel-sheet roof, providing protection from sun and rain. The 19° tilt ensures optimal energy collection.

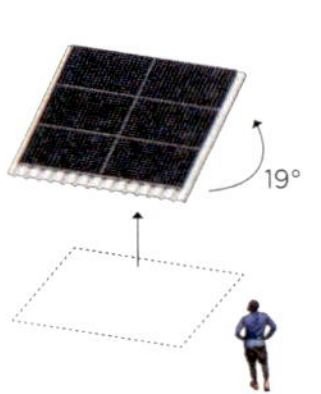

Wind deflection
The 45° roof rotation reduces wind pressure and uplifting.

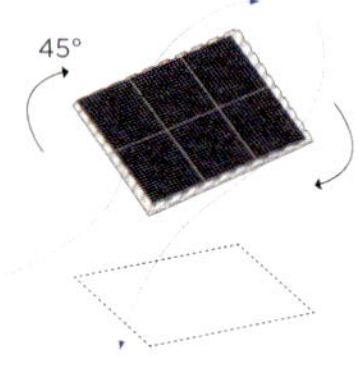

Leaves and trunks
The wooden roof structure references the patterns of palm leaves, while the circular wooden columns evoke the form of palm trunks.

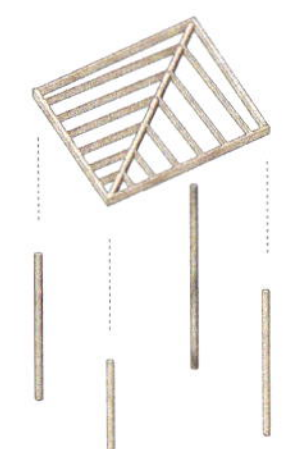

Social terrace
The wooden platform provides an adaptable public space for meetings, relaxation, play, and other activities, elevated to allow stormwater to flow beneath.

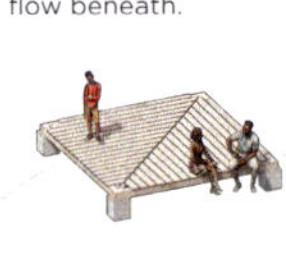

Rainwater harvest
Rainwater is efficiently collected and directed to filtered storage tanks. The tanks are covered with impregnated woven palm leaves, visually distinguishing each module.

Independent module
Each unit contains its own energy infrastructure with batteries, a small string inverter, and a water harvesting system. A social terrace sits beneath the protective roof.

Masi solar cluster
The main fan-like arrangement features three modules oriented north, east, and west, balancing energy generation throughout the day while aligning with morning and evening demand peaks.

Clusters can be expanded into larger units that share batteries, inverters, and rainwater collection systems, allowing for multiple scalable configurations.

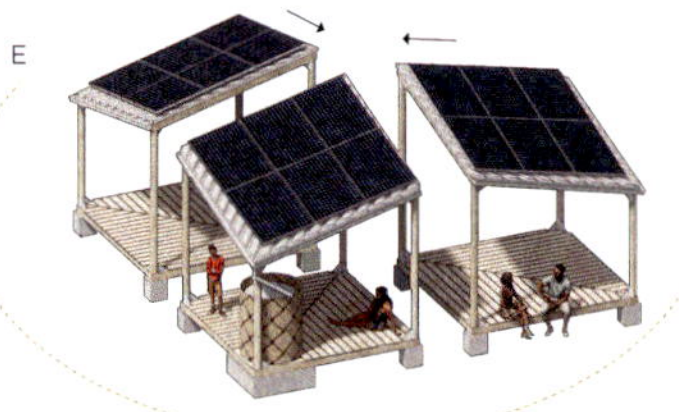

Configuration examples

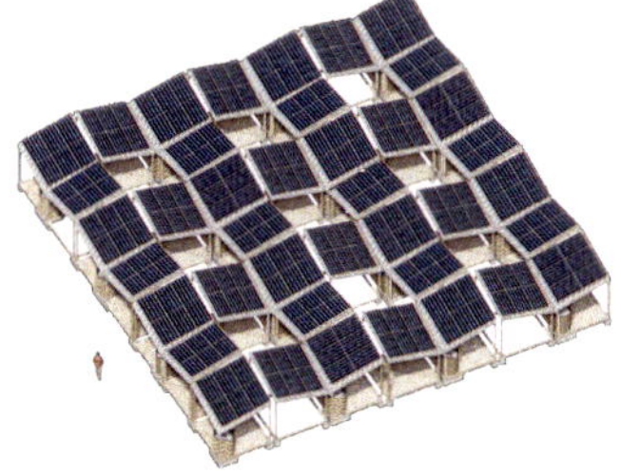

Example of extra large composition

Module variations

M1
Garden, playground, agriculture/agrivoltaic

M2
Rainwater tank, agriculture/agrivoltaic

M3
Social terrace seating, lounge, meeting place

M4
Rainwater tank, social terrace

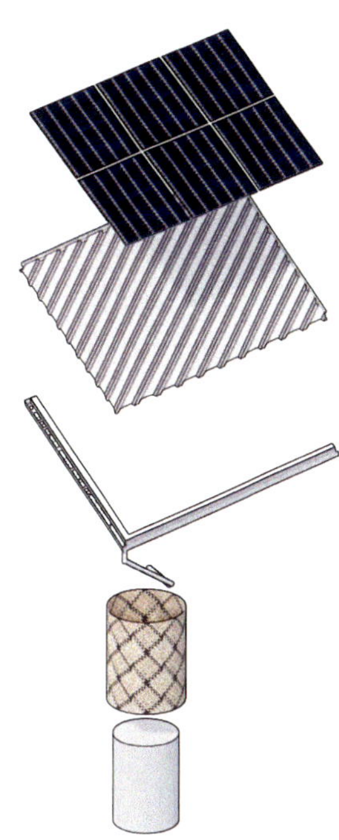

Solar modules
- Six 430-watt 1.1 m × 1.7 m monocrystalline glass-glass panels
- Cyclone resistant mounting system
- 45° rotation and offset from the roof edge to reduce wind pressure and uplifting

Roof diaphragm
- Recycled corrugated steel sheet metal
- 45° rotation to reduce wind pressure and uplifting
- Rainwater flows easily into a single corner gutter.

Water collection
- Steel gutter
- First flush diverter

Water harvesting cistern
- Decorative tank cover made from impregnated woven palm leaves
- 2,400-liter stainless steel rainwater tank with mechanical, ceramic, and carbon filtration systems
- Two outputs for utility and drinking water

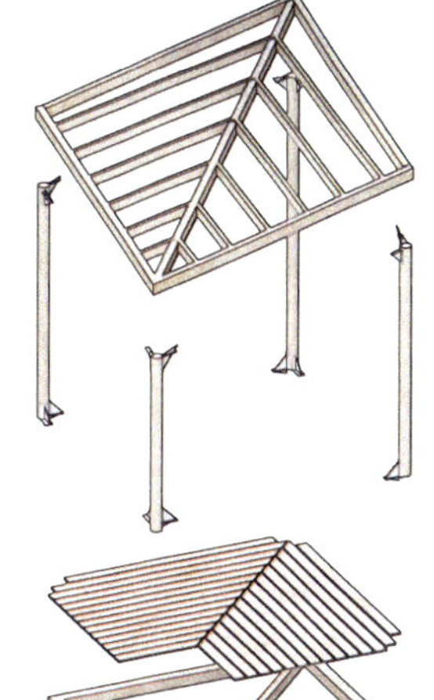

Structure
- Leaf-like beam structure made from local hardwood
- Cyclone metal strap stiffeners
- Four hardwood columns with circular cross-section to improve wind-flow
- Triangular corner steel brackets provide protection against lateral forces.

Energy system
- Small string inverter under the roof
- Two 7 kWh LFP batteries located beneath the deck in a protective housing

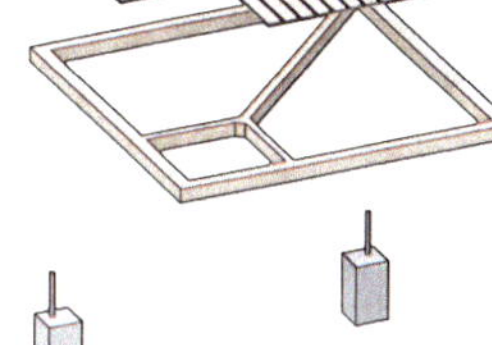

Decking
- Elevated deck made from local impregnated hardwood
- Deck beams below stiffen the entire wooden frame

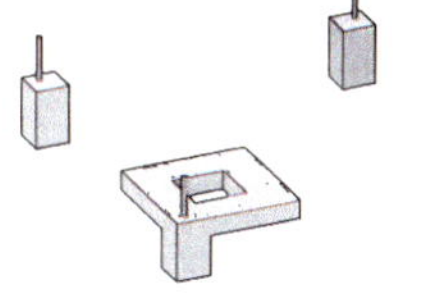

Foundation
- Concrete and rock foundations with steel column pins
- Slab foundation to support rainwater tank

LEFT: A view from the south reveals openings above the courtyard spaces.

Between the Sky & Earth

DESIGNERS: Yi Yang Chai, Ng Yi Ming (Off Grid Studio)

TECHNOLOGIES: bifacial solar photovoltaic with custom color encapsulant, battery energy storage, rainwater harvesting with constructed wetlands and sand filtration

ANNUAL PRODUCTION: 233 MWh of electricity, 720,000 liters of filtered water

DESIGN TEAM LOCATION: Malaysia

Site plan

RIGHT: The colors of the photovoltaic panels bring the artwork to life when seen from above. Visitors can navigate the gently sloping ramp to take in sweeping views across the landscape of Naviti Island.

Framed by the Fijian concepts of *lomalagi* (sky) and *vanua* (land), *Between the Sky & Earth* is an artwork designed to harmonize tradition and technology. Situated on elevated ground in Marou Village, the pavilion draws on local materials, cultural motifs, and ecological cycles to provide clean energy, filtered water, and shared community space.

The design is composed of two interlocking circular planes — one grounded, one elevated — symbolizing the connection between Earth and sky. Inspired by masi patterns and Fijian storytelling, the form incorporates bamboo structures, radiant gable roofs, and a central wetland basin. The pavilion serves as a venue for gatherings, farming, and celebration, while also functioning as off-grid energy and water infrastructure for the village.

At its heart, a 48-meter diameter canopy supports 360 bifacial colored photovoltaic panels mounted on steel frames. The panels generate 233 MWh per year, using both direct sunlight and reflected light from the wetland below. Between roof modules, rain is directed into the basin where a constructed wetland and sand filtration system purify up to 720,000 liters annually. Water is then gravity-fed to a lower village tank for household use.

Construction emphasizes local resilience: bamboo columns, recycled timber decking, and rammed earth walls are paired with modular, easily transportable components. Assembly is low-tech and community-led, with educational workshops throughout the design and build process.

Regular monitoring and daily observations are carried out by a trained village caretaker. Monthly maintenance includes visual inspection and gentle cleaning of PV panels to remove dust, organic debris, or salt spray. More comprehensive annual checks are paired with seasonal events or gatherings to build collective ownership and visibility of the system.

A living classroom, *Between the Sky & Earth* becomes a guardian of landscape and culture, and a model for island communities.

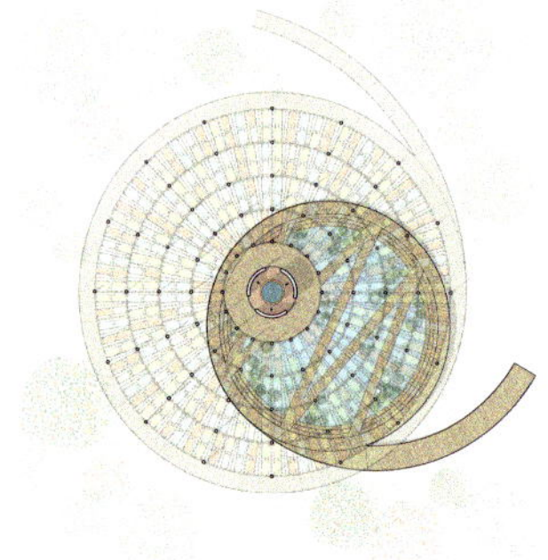

Visitors wave to each other from above and below.

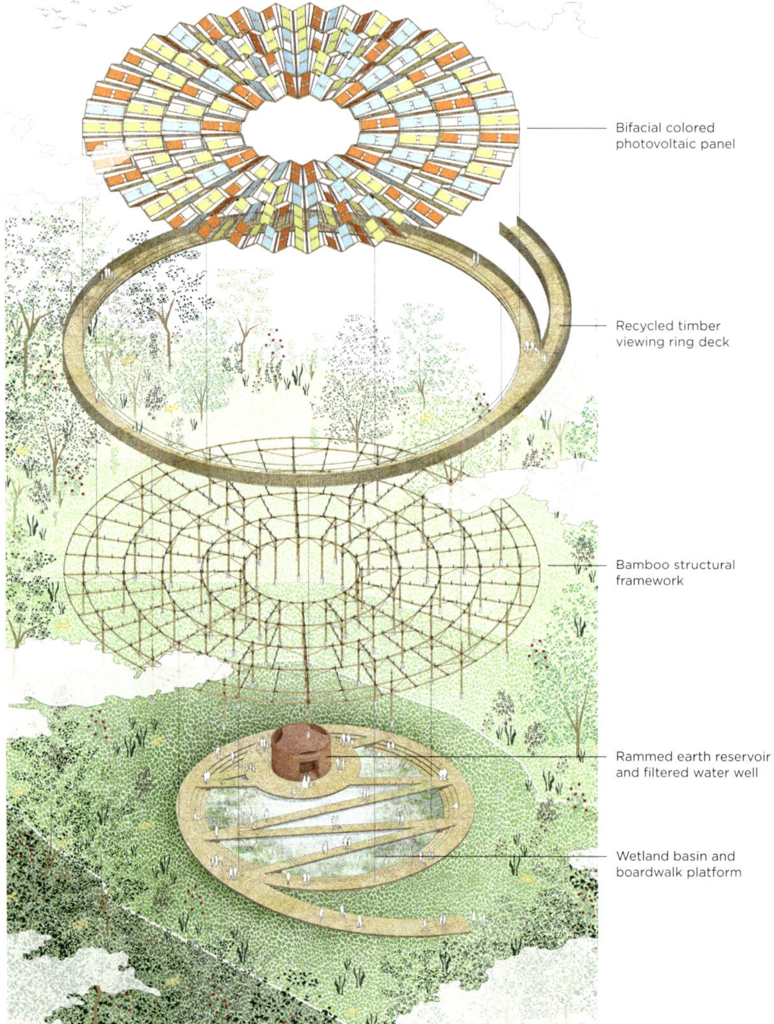

Exploded axonometric

Views from inside the artwork reveal the constructed wetland areas, with boardwalk platforms that lead to public access points for safe drinking water.

A section through the center of the artwork reveals the constructed wetland leading to the rammed earth water well.

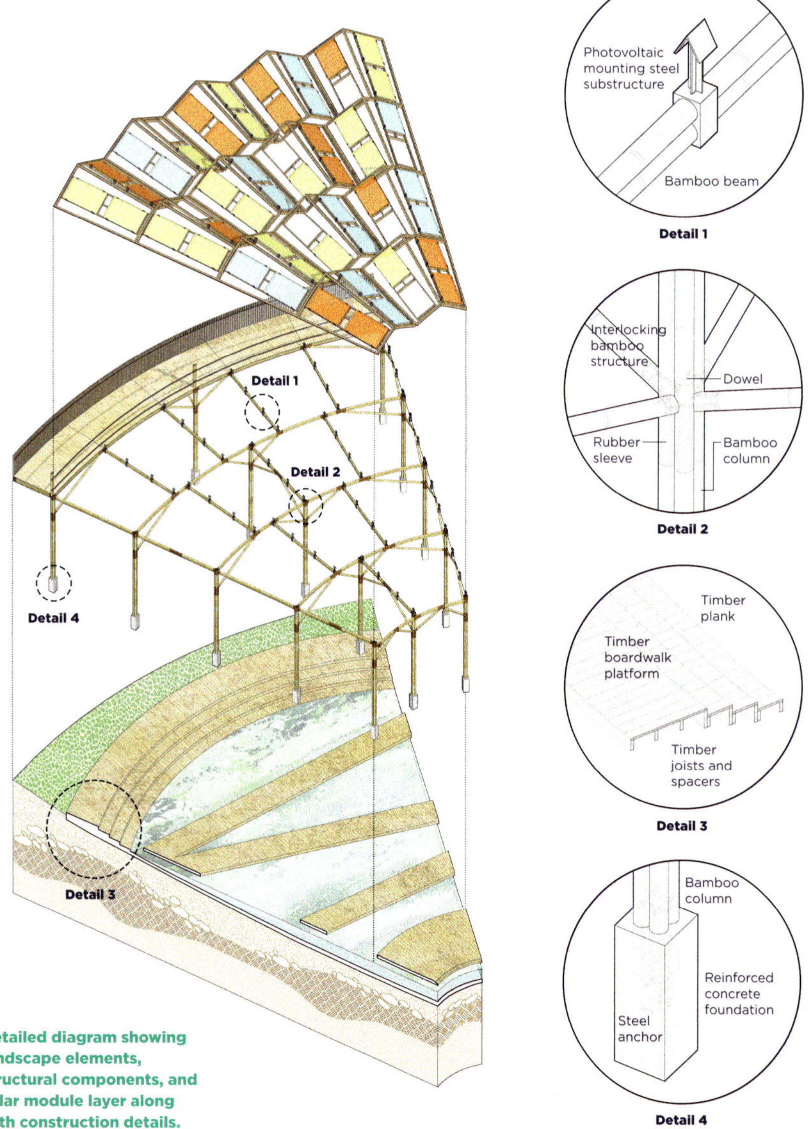

Detailed diagram showing landscape elements, structural components, and solar module layer along with construction details.

Detailed wall section

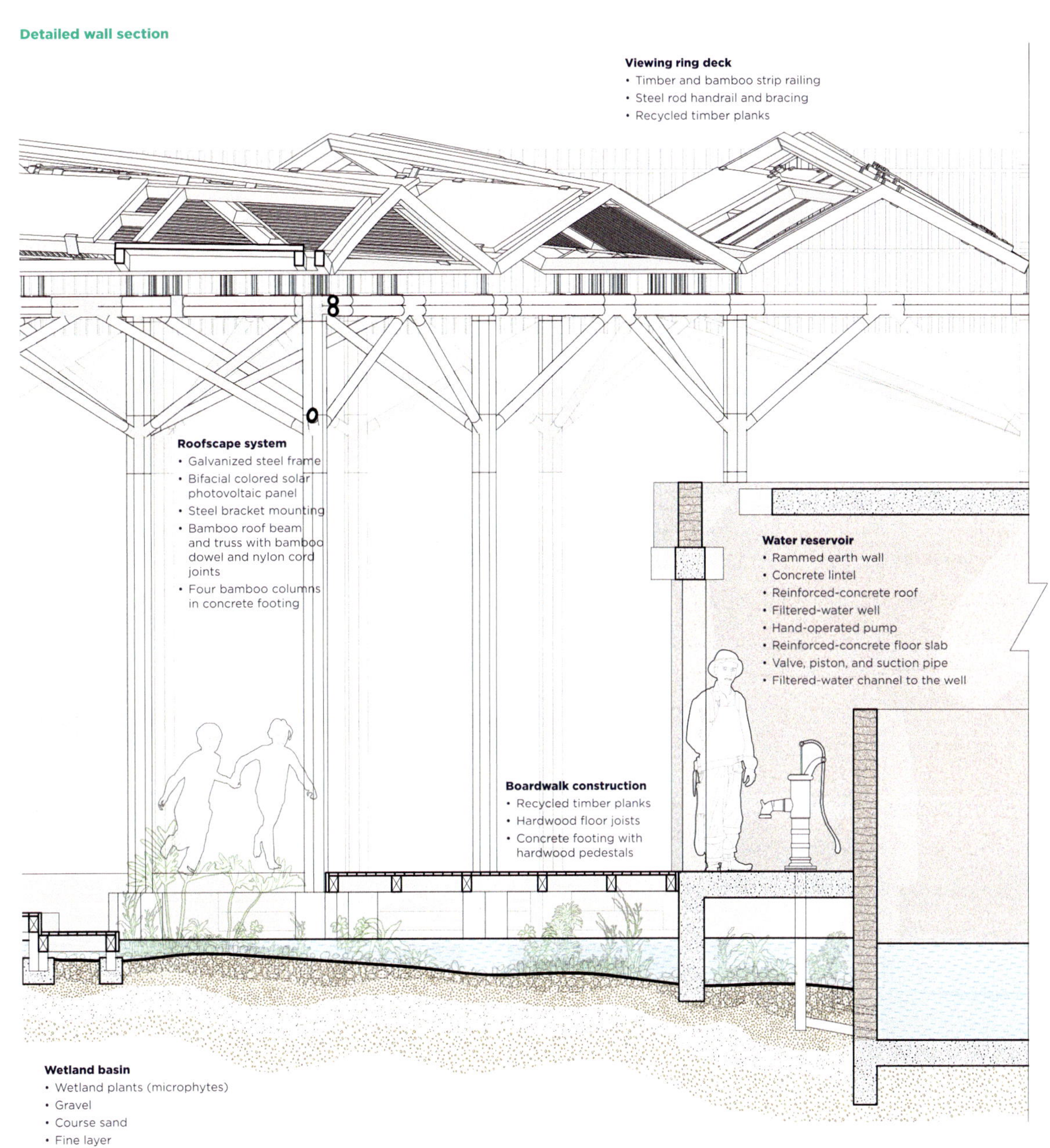

Coconet

DESIGNERS: Yicen Zhong, Zhai Jingxuan

TECHNOLOGIES: solar photovoltaic, battery energy storage, atmospheric water condensation, underground cisterns

ANNUAL PRODUCTION: 128 MWh of electricity, 600,000 liters of filtered water (40-unit configuration)

DESIGN TEAM LOCATION: China

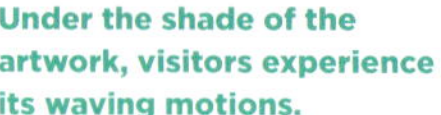
Under the shade of the artwork, visitors experience its waving motions.

Inspired by the coconut sapling, *Coconet* imitates the natural intelligence of tropical flora. Like the young palm reaching toward the sun while storing water in its roots, this modular installation gathers clean energy and drinking water from the sky and air, creating a kinetic landscape that supports both daily life and ecological beauty.

Each unit consists of a rotating, wind-responsive canopy outfitted with solar photovoltaic panels. Lightweight and finely balanced, the canopy spins with the breeze, activating a simple mechanical air pump below. As humid air is pushed underground into a cooler stainless steel chamber, water vapor condenses into clean water, which is stored for community use.

A single unit generates up to 3.2 kWh of electricity annually and produces an estimated 15,000 liters of water. Forty such devices are planned for installation, creating a landscape animated by movement and purpose.

The structure's upper assembly uses fiberglass keels and ETFE film for minimal weight, while its base and water collection system are constructed from stainless steel — a food-grade material that ensures clean water storage and efficient heat transfer. When deployed in rows, the devices create a dynamic visual field, their canopies spinning in synchronized response to wind currents.

Maintenance is designed for accessibility: photovoltaic panels can be cleaned with long-handled mops; the water collection chamber opens for periodic rinsing; and in cyclone conditions, the canopy can be easily detached and secured. Battery monitoring is supported by manufacturer-led community training and remote monitoring diagnostics.

Visually striking and functionally elegant, *Coconet* transforms renewable infrastructure into a mesmerizing gesture of energy, air, water, and wind.

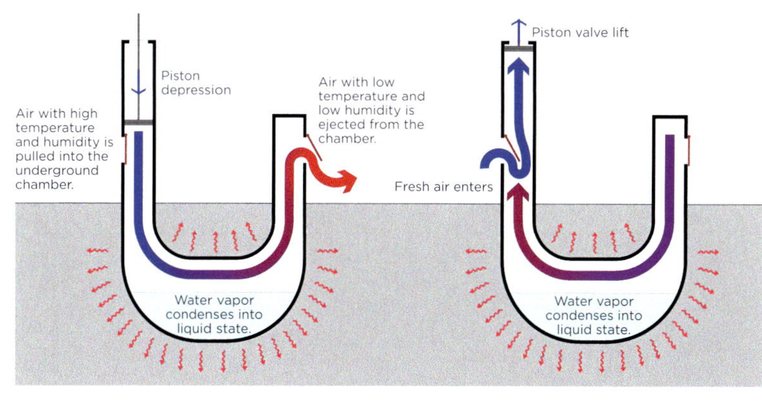
Piston depression
Air with high temperature and humidity is pulled into the underground chamber.
Air with low temperature and low humidity is ejected from the chamber.
Water vapor condenses into liquid state.
Piston valve lift
Fresh air enters
Water vapor condenses into liquid state.

SigaWai Canopy Park

DESIGNERS: Jie Zhao, Liang Ma, Yan (Jennifer) Zeng, I-Shan Tam (University of Pennsylvania)

TECHNOLOGIES: solar photovoltaic, hybrid battery and ice storage, rainwater harvesting, wetland filtration and storage

ANNUAL PRODUCTION: 135 MWh of electricity, 1 million liters of filtered water

DESIGN TEAM LOCATION: United States

RIGHT: Daily life unfolds beneath the shade of the canopies and along the edge of the wetland after rainfall.

Named from the Fijian words siga (sun) and wai (water), *SigaWai Canopy Park* embodies the union of light, water, and land in service of climate resilience. This community infrastructure project weaves renewable energy and ecological design into a modular, low-cost canopy system and sponge park—providing power, potable water, flood control, and public gathering space for Marou Village.

The system integrates 15 solar modules, each with a 5.7 kW capacity, for a total of 86 kW. Electricity is stored through a lithium iron phosphate battery array and an insulated ice battery system, which maintains refrigeration through nights and overcast days. Smart controls automate performance monitoring and energy distribution. The canopy, made of recycled sailcloth and bamboo, is collapsible for cyclone conditions and provides shade for social activities and cultural gatherings.

Rainwater flows from canopy surfaces into a sculpted wetland, passing through reed beds, gravel filters, and a biofiltration pond before undergoing a three-stage mechanical filtration system. Wetland elements absorb stormwater, reduce flooding, and promote biodiversity.

The design supports local jobs during installation and operation, offers shaded markets for crafts and commerce, and integrates traditional materials and motifs—hexagonal solar arrays with masi patterns, recycled sails evoking drua vessels, and a constructed wetland modeled after the form of Naviti Island.

Materials are chosen for durability and circularity, with recyclable metals, modular components, and biodegradable bamboo fencing. Wildlife-safe, solar-powered lighting protects nocturnal species and preserves the night sky.

SigaWai Canopy Park is a living demonstration of how infrastructure can nourish both community and ecosystems, restoring balance through design and creating space where energy, water, and tradition flow together.

SigaWai Canopy Park
in maintenance mode

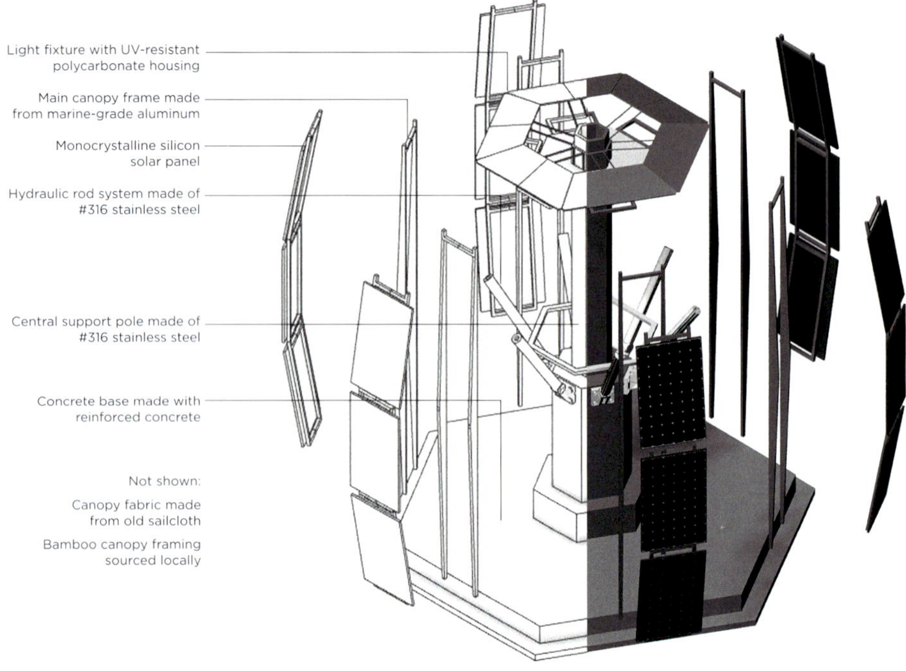

Exploded axonometric diagram

The solar units are designed to withstand passive flooding without compromising the electrical systems.

The modules are easily accessible during maintenance mode.

Shaded community gathering space

Storm mode

View of the installation in the late afternoon

Vunilagi

DESIGNERS: Stephen Burton, Nicholas Stevens, Felipe Crisostomo (POMO)

TECHNOLOGIES: solar photovoltaic, battery energy storage, rainwater harvesting, water filtration and storage

ANNUAL PRODUCTION: 140 MWh of electricity, 320,000 liters of filtered water

DESIGN TEAM LOCATION: Australia

RIGHT: The narrow and vertical entrance opens up on the other end of the curve into sweeping views of the landscape.

In Fijian, *vunilagi* is the place where earth, sea, and sky meet — the horizon that connects all things. In Marou Village, it becomes a place of protection and possibility: a cyclone-resilient bamboo structure that brings shelter, solar power, and freshwater to the heart of the community.

Shaped by deep community dialogue, *Vunilagi* is designed to serve as a refuge during storms and flooding, while also offering a shared space for everyday life — gatherings, workshops, knowledge exchange, and the welcoming of guests. The open-air, 500 m² structure breathes with the tropical climate, harnessing breezes beneath a roof that supports a 75 kW solar array and harvests rainwater.

Vunilagi supports community knowledge and provides new skills via practical and replicable construction methods. Bamboo — widely available across Fiji and endorsed for agribusiness by the Ministry of Forestry — is the core structural material. Its strength-to-weight ratio, ease of transport, and capacity for local fabrication make it ideal for remote construction without heavy machinery. Raised above flood lines and assembled with hand tools, rope, and very little concrete, the design minimizes external dependencies and maximizes local empowerment.

Energy from 200 solar modules feeds a 100 kWh battery energy storage system, delivering reliable off-grid power for the village. Rainwater flows from the angled roof into centralized tanks and is filtered through sand and charcoal for safe household use. Both systems are designed for ease of maintenance and future expansion.

The architecture is rich with symbolism: triangular entrances evoke volcanic origins, palm mat walls recall drua sails, and geometric repetitions echo traditional Fijian motifs. Modular frames express the interconnection of people and place, earth and sky.

Vunilagi provides a foundation for autonomy, climate resilience, and community-led design. It stands as a model for how coastal communities can protect their futures while honoring their pasts, turning shared aspirations into enduring infrastructure.

Workshops and classes take place beneath the breeze-filled shade of *Vunilagi*.

Roll down wall detail

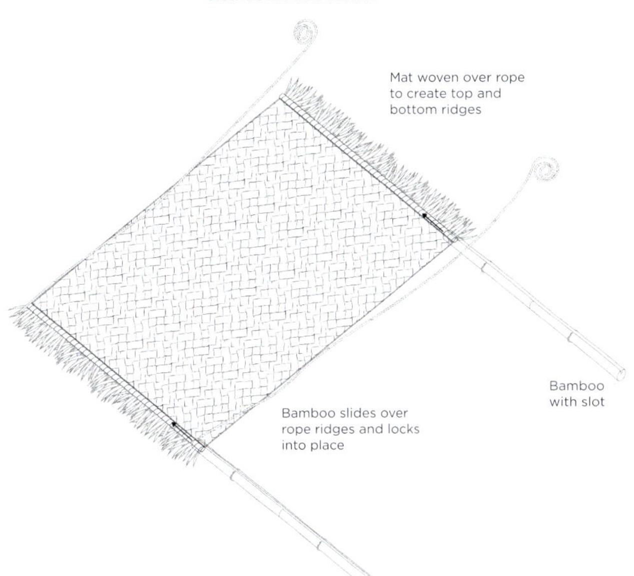

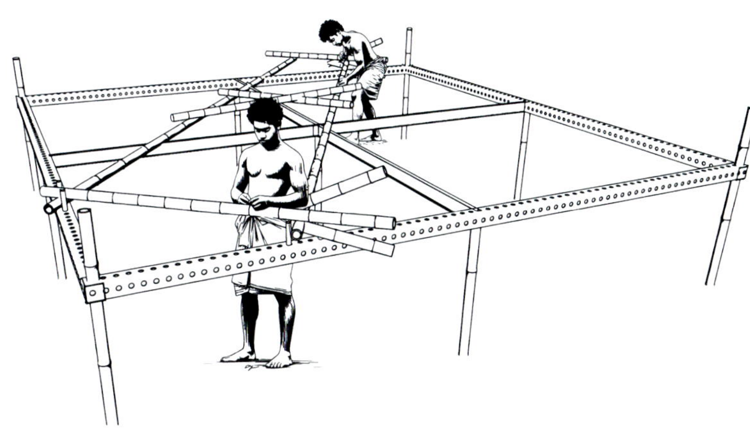

Vunilagi's curved form takes inspiration from the coconut palm leaf, embodying a vital source of life for the village in its very shape.

The Fijian drua boat uses a hand woven sail stretched between two points and hoisted by ropes. *Vunilagi* invokes this cultural heritage through its roof covering, and more notably through its walls, which are tensioned and modulated by rope.

The structure is composed of straight bamboo frames, each set at a different angle to create a curving form. This geometric repetition reflects cultural patterns found in Oceanic art, such as tapa cloth, and serves as the fundamental framework of *Vunilagi*.

Vunilagi modulates airflow to invite cooling breezes or seal itself against harsh weather, adapting fluidly to changing conditions.

The entrance evokes a volcano, rising in a dramatic triangular form. Lit with flexible red LEDs, the portal pays homage to the volcanic origins of the ancient Yasawa Islands.

Vatu Rua Kaukauwa
Two Resilient Rocks

DESIGNERS: Jonathan Hernández López, Felipe Vargas Romero (OWN NOW)

TECHNOLOGIES: solar photovoltaic, vertical axis wind turbines, modular battery energy storage, rainwater harvesting, advanced filtration, above-ground cisterns

ANNUAL PRODUCTION: 224 MWh of electricity, 564,000 liters of filtered water

DESIGN TEAM LOCATION: Germany, Australia

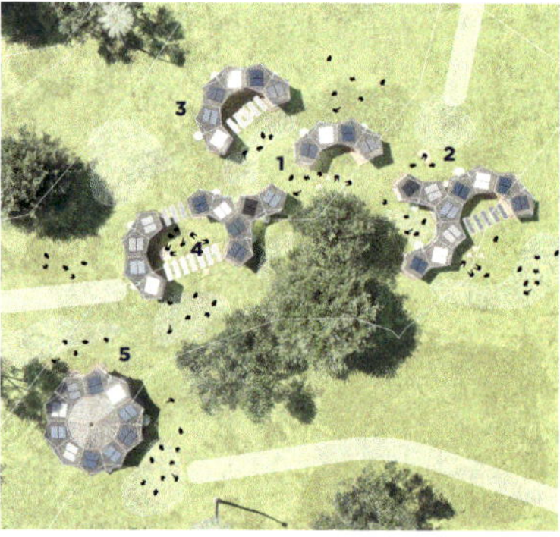

Site plan showing the five typology configurations

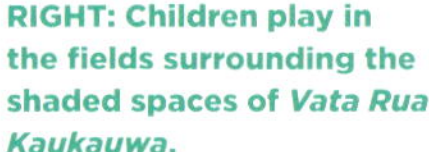
RIGHT: Children play in the fields surrounding the shaded spaces of *Vata Rua Kaukauwa*.

Named for the iconic twin peaks of Naviti Island, *Vatu Rua Kaukauwa*, meaning "two resilient rocks," stands as a living symbol of cultural endurance and ecological restoration. The design blends regenerative architecture, nature-based systems, and community co-creation to support energy independence, water resilience, biodiversity, and social cohesion in Marou Village.

At the core of the vision is a set of modular pentagonal bamboo structures arranged into adaptable typologies that respond to terrain, flooding, and community needs. Five typologies offer different configurations for housing, social gathering, food production, biodiversity support, and energy generation. Flexible and scalable, the modules can be deployed in phases to accommodate growth over time.

The 40-module design has the capacity to generate 224 MWh of electricity annually through a combination of rooftop photovoltaic panels, vertical axis wind turbines, and flexible solar membranes. Rainwater is harvested from 332 square meters of total catchment area and distributed to perimeter tanks with filtration provided by sand, charcoal, and optional reverse osmosis systems to ensure safe and reliable access to water throughout the year.

Beyond utility, *Vatu Rua Kaukauwa* restores ecological relationships. Structures are designed to host native flora and fauna — hibiscus, sedges, and habitat-integrated roofs support biodiversity and erosion control. Community gardens grow taro, yams, bananas, and cassava. The site layout incorporates flood-mitigating vegetation and creates gathering spaces that reinforce Fijian cultural practice.

Built primarily from fast-growing local bamboo, modules are cyclone-resistant, demountable, and easily maintained. Construction uses minimal concrete and prioritizes lightweight, modular components that can be assembled without heavy equipment. Local craftsmanship is celebrated through woven mat wall panels and traditional joinery techniques.

Vatu Rua Kaukauwa positions Marou Village as a beacon of circular design and community resilience — an ecological destination that nurtures both people and place.

Prototype exploded axonometric view

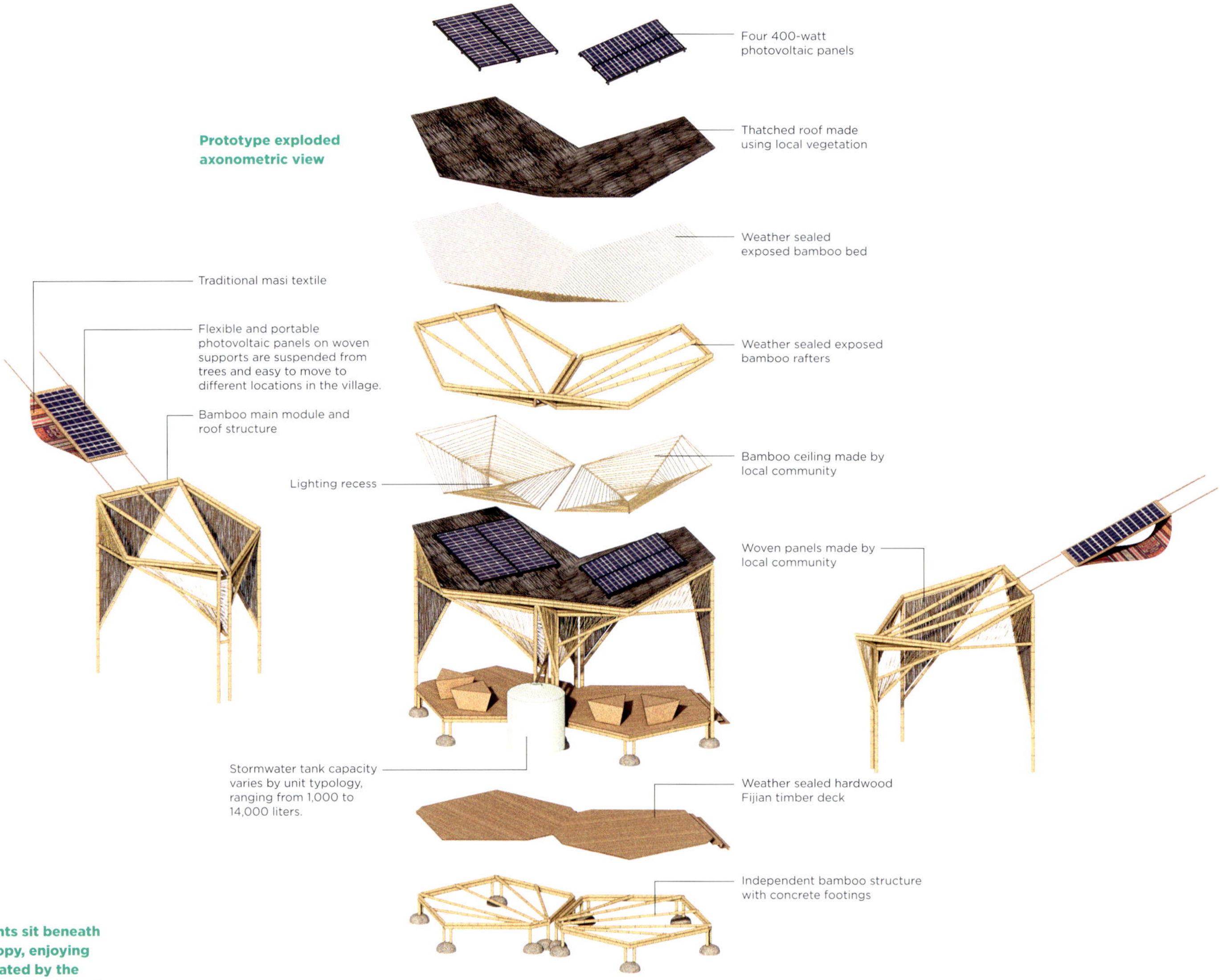

Four 400-watt photovoltaic panels

Thatched roof made using local vegetation

Weather sealed exposed bamboo bed

Traditional masi textile

Flexible and portable photovoltaic panels on woven supports are suspended from trees and easy to move to different locations in the village.

Weather sealed exposed bamboo rafters

Bamboo main module and roof structure

Lighting recess

Bamboo ceiling made by local community

Woven panels made by local community

Stormwater tank capacity varies by unit typology, ranging from 1,000 to 14,000 liters.

Weather sealed hardwood Fijian timber deck

Independent bamboo structure with concrete footings

Marou residents sit beneath the solar canopy, enjoying the space created by the textiles on the underside of the solar modules.

At night the solar and water energy system becomes a safe, lighted space.

The largest module creates a space for performances and celebrations.

Energy Forest

DESIGNERS: Peng Chien Chang, Ruo Jing Yuan, Cong Chen

TECHNOLOGIES: solar photovoltaic, battery energy storage, solar thermal water distillation, rainwater harvesting and storage

ANNUAL PRODUCTION: 147 MWh of electricity, 327,000 liters of distilled water, 542,000 liters of filtered water

DESIGN TEAM LOCATION: China

Evening activities take place under the glow of the *Energy Forest* modules.

Right: *Energy Forest* provides shade during the day while it generates clean electricity and distilled drinking water for the community.

Energy Forest reimagines essential infrastructure as a living canopy—an elevated grove of "Energy Trees" that generate electricity, produce clean water, and create spaces for shade, gathering, and resilience. Designed for modular deployment, the system grows organically with the needs of Marou Village, responding to climate extremes.

Each Energy Tree is made of three layers: photovoltaic panels above, a glass-enclosed solar still at the center, and a rainwater harvesting tank below. Together, these layers form a vertically integrated system that draws energy from the sun, collects and purifies water, and delivers both with minimal environmental impact. The structure also lifts essential utilities above flood lines, protecting resources during storms while freeing the space below for community use.

Beneath the Trees, an airy, dappled understory emerges—cool, protected, and open to possibility. Residents can gather here informally or formally, using the space for daily markets, storytelling, games, or celebration. At night, lights integrated into the canopies softly illuminate the site, extending its social utility into the evening and transforming the grove into a luminous commons.

Constructed from durable, corrosion-resistant materials and shaped by earthquake- and cyclone-conscious design, the Energy Trees are engineered for long-term service. Their dendriform supports create visual continuity with natural forms while reducing wind resistance. The structures are modular, easy to maintain, and designed for disassembly and reuse, ensuring low-impact and long-term flexibility.

Community members co-own and care for the system. Each household or group adopts a Tree, participating in its upkeep and designating its use. In this way, *Energy Forest* becomes a shared landscape of autonomy and innovation.

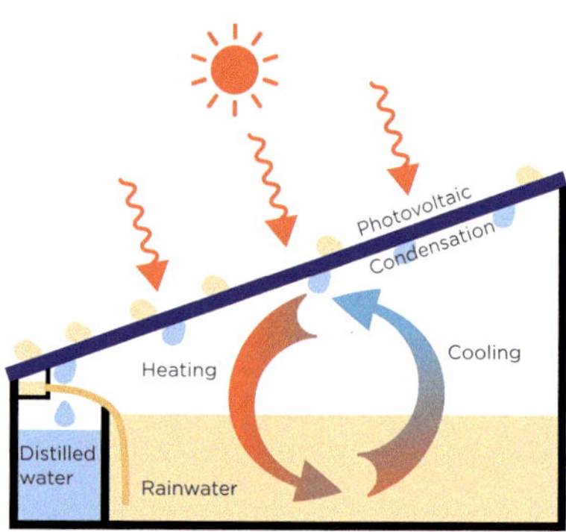

The residual heat generated by the solar panels is transferred to the rainwater collection tank below to assist the distillation process. While the water tank raises the temperature for distillation, it also helps cool the solar photovoltaic panels. In this way, the system's components work together to maximize efficiency.

A forest of energy and water modules rises in a clearing near Marou Village.

Energy Tree module diagram

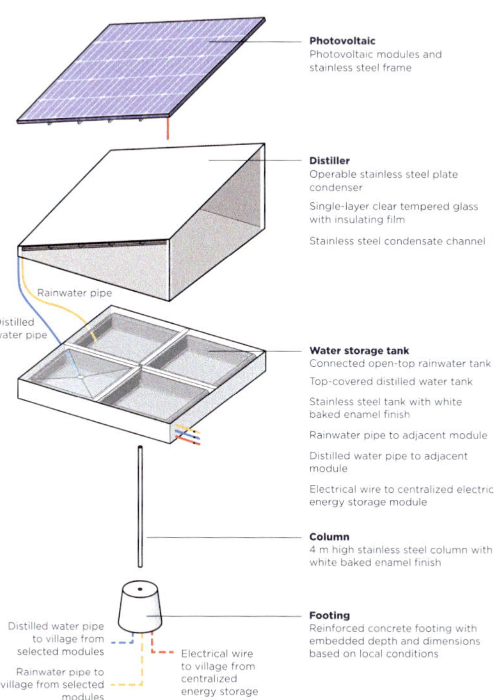

Unleashing the Vanua
Living Systems for Community Resilience

DESIGNERS: Jisoo Kim, Seung Hyo Chang, Jisoo Kim

TECHNOLOGIES: solar photovoltaic, battery energy storage, constructed wetlands, stormwater harvesting, modular UV purification system

ANNUAL PRODUCTION: 130 MWh of electricity, 1.2 million liters of filtered water

DESIGN TEAM LOCATION: United States

Fog lifts above the artwork.

TOP RIGHT: Solar modules are installed on top of the canopy.

RIGHT: Stormwater collects in the constructed wetland, mitigating flood risk while providing biofiltration for harvested water.

In Fijian culture, *vanua* means more than land — it signifies the unity of people, place, and spirit. *Unleashing the Vanua* reflects this Indigenous principle through a decentralized infrastructure system that integrates solar energy, clean water, ecological restoration, and shared community space. Rather than imposing new systems, the design grows from the rhythms and relationships already embedded in Marou Village.

At its heart is a network of bamboo-framed solar canopies that collect energy and harvest rainwater. These lightweight structures float above shaded courtyards, creating places for gathering, food cultivation, learning, and ceremony. Split bamboo gutters below the panels channel rain into visible, planted watercourses. These open channels double as constructed wetlands — slowing, filtering, and guiding water through the landscape before final purification via solar-powered UV systems.

Water becomes a connective tissue, linking homes, gardens, and communal spaces. Farming strips run alongside channels; taro and cassava take root at basin edges. As residents walk between dwellings, they trace the path of the water itself — witnessing, maintaining, and co-managing its flow as part of everyday life.

The structural language of the canopy echoes local vegetation. Bundled bamboo columns mimic native trunks, while rope-lashed joints combine strength with natural textures. The entire system is modular, repairable, and built with tools and materials already in use by the community. No part is hidden. Infrastructure is seen, felt, and inhabited.

This is a living framework — one that evolves with the village and adapts to climate pressures over time. As new nodes are added, wetlands expand, and energy networks grow. Meanwhile, soil stabilizes, habitats return, and young people inherit the skills and knowledge to maintain the system.

Unleashing the Vanua is a model for regenerative development where land, water, and community thrive together through a living design.

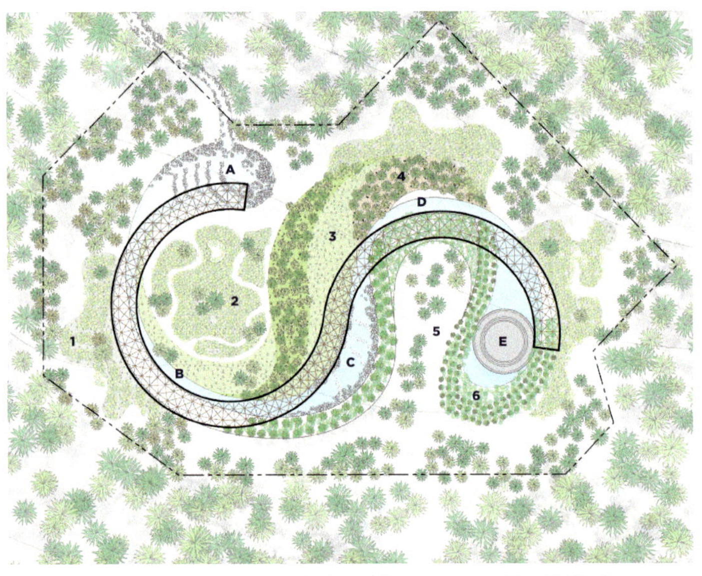

Outdoor public spaces
1. Community garden
2. Art lawn
3. Agro-ecological farming
4. Botanic garden
5. Entrance plaza
6. Medicinal garden

Water biofiltration system
A. Sediment basin
B. Settling channel
C. Constructed wetland
D. Water spine
E. Water tank

Unleashing the Vanua **offers a resiliency framework built on three integrated strategies: a water purification system that harnesses natural topography and ecological processes; bamboo structures constructed with local materials and labor to strengthen community capacity; and solar energy as a reliable, sustainable power source. Collectively, these elements support economic development and long-term sustainability in Marou.**

View of the Installation from Vatu Rua

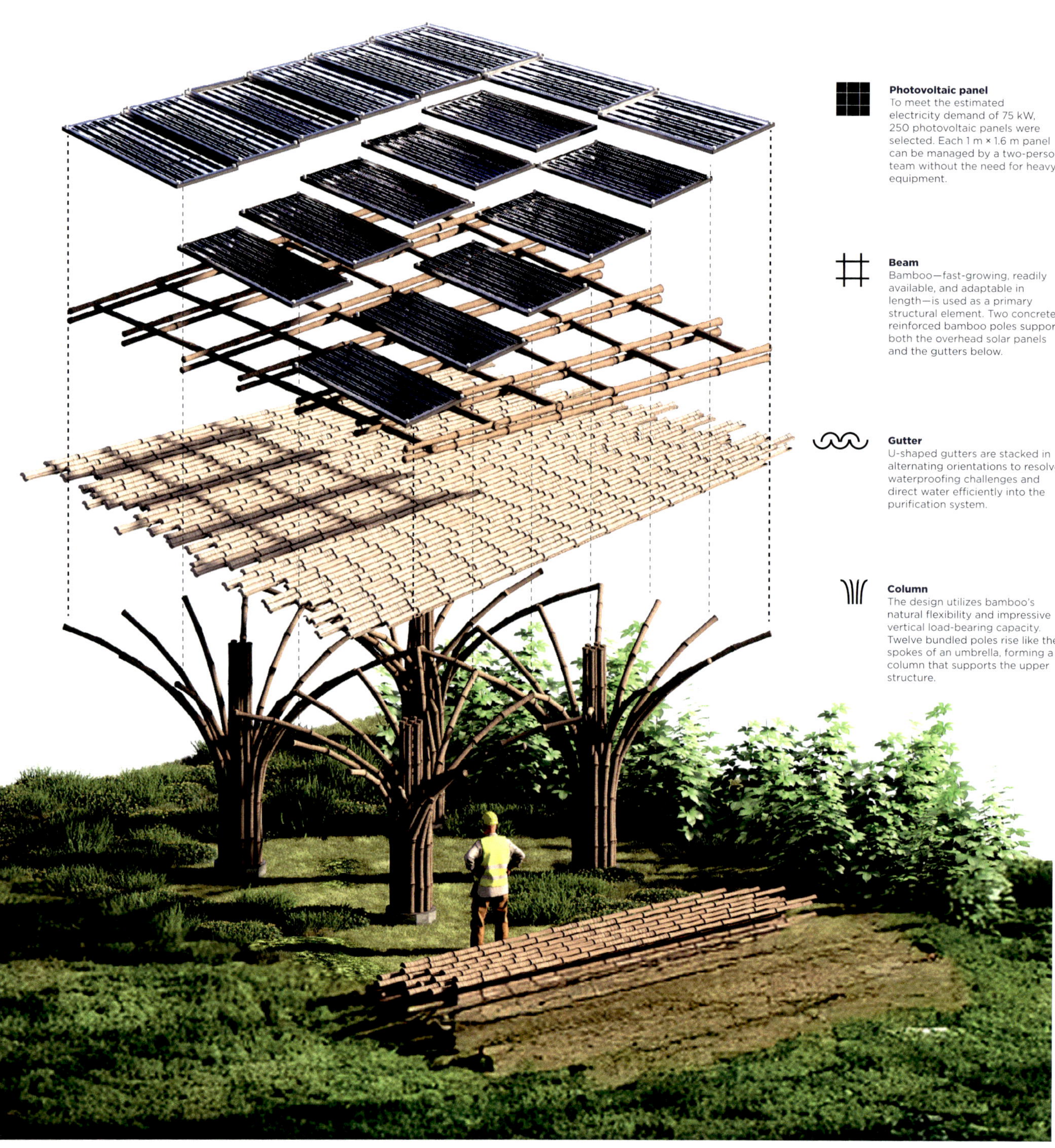
Photovoltaic panel
To meet the estimated electricity demand of 75 kW, 250 photovoltaic panels were selected. Each 1 m × 1.6 m panel can be managed by a two-person team without the need for heavy equipment.
Beam
Bamboo—fast-growing, readily available, and adaptable in length—is used as a primary structural element. Two concrete-reinforced bamboo poles support both the overhead solar panels and the gutters below.
Gutter
U-shaped gutters are stacked in alternating orientations to resolve waterproofing challenges and direct water efficiently into the purification system.
Column
The design utilizes bamboo's natural flexibility and impressive vertical load-bearing capacity. Twelve bundled poles rise like the spokes of an umbrella, forming a column that supports the upper structure.

Vegetation

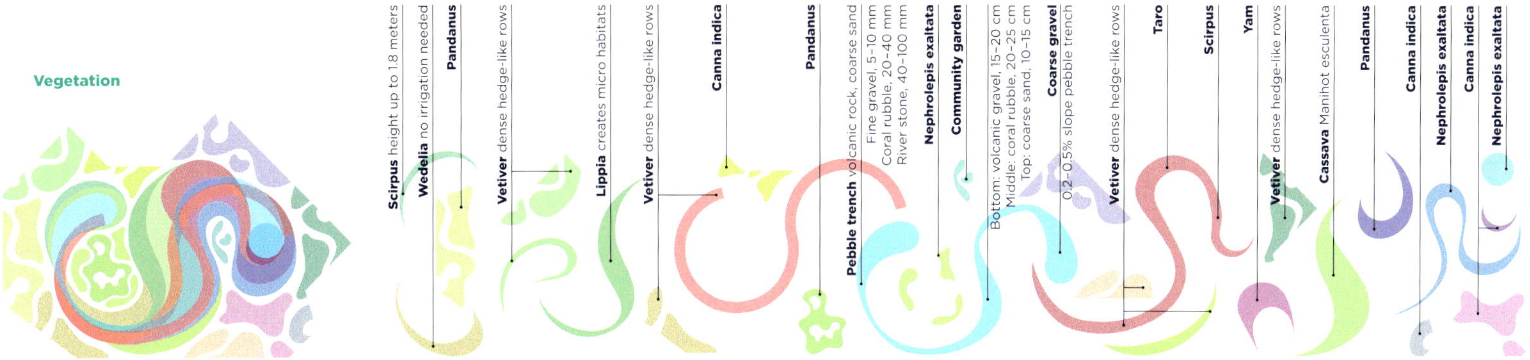

Scirpus height up to 1.8 meters
Wedelia no irrigation needed
Pandanus
Vetiver dense hedge-like rows
Lippia creates micro habitats
Vetiver dense hedge-like rows
Canna indica
Pandanus
Pebble trench volcanic rock, coarse sand
Fine gravel, 5–10 mm
Coral rubble, 20–40 mm
River stone, 40–100 mm
Nephrolepis exaltata
Community garden
Bottom: volcanic gravel, 15–20 cm
Middle: coral rubble, 20–25 cm
Top: coarse sand, 10–15 cm
Coarse gravel
0.2–0.5% slope pebble trench
Vetiver dense hedge-like rows
Taro
Scirpus
Yam
Vetiver dense hedge-like rows
Cassava Manihot esculenta
Pandanus
Canna indica
Nephrolepis exaltata
Canna indica
Nephrolepis exaltata

Water system

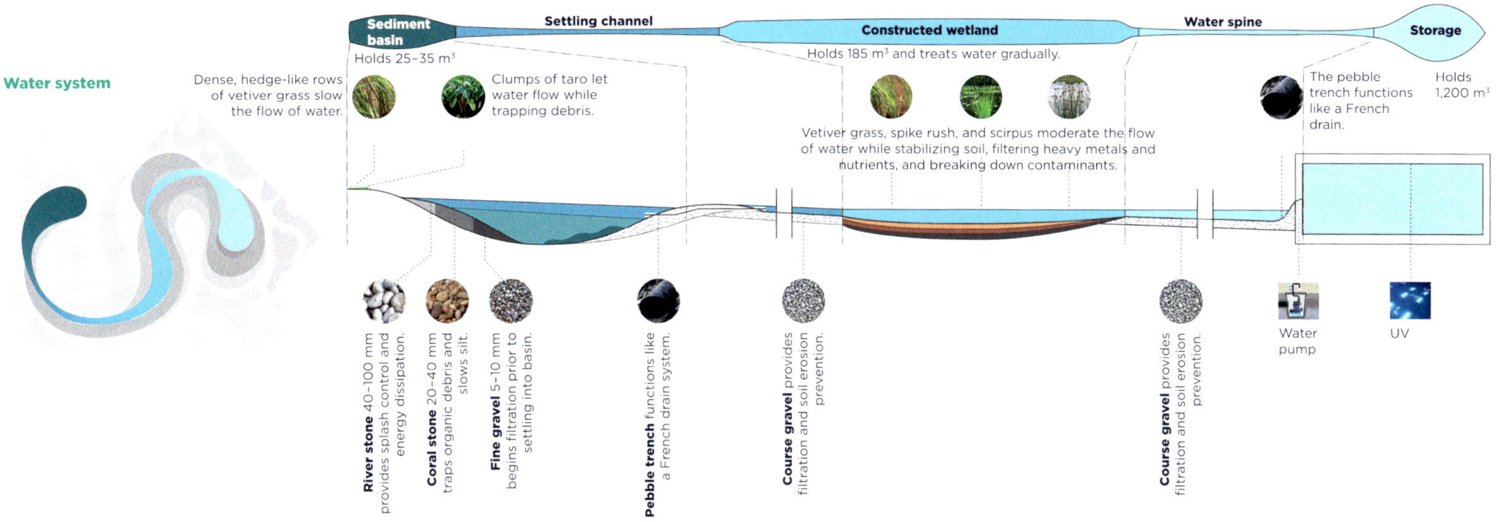

Sediment basin — Holds 25–35 m³
Settling channel
Constructed wetland — Holds 185 m³ and treats water gradually.
Water spine
Storage — Holds 1,200 m³

Dense, hedge-like rows of vetiver grass slow the flow of water.

Clumps of taro let water flow while trapping debris.

Vetiver grass, spike rush, and scirpus moderate the flow of water while stabilizing soil, filtering heavy metals and nutrients, and breaking down contaminants.

The pebble trench functions like a French drain.

River stone 40–100 mm provides splash control and energy dissipation.

Coral stone 20–40 mm traps organic debris and slows silt.

Fine gravel 5–10 mm begins filtration prior to settling into basin.

Pebble trench functions like a French drain system.

Course gravel provides filtration and soil erosion prevention.

Course gravel provides filtration and soil erosion prevention.

Water pump

UV

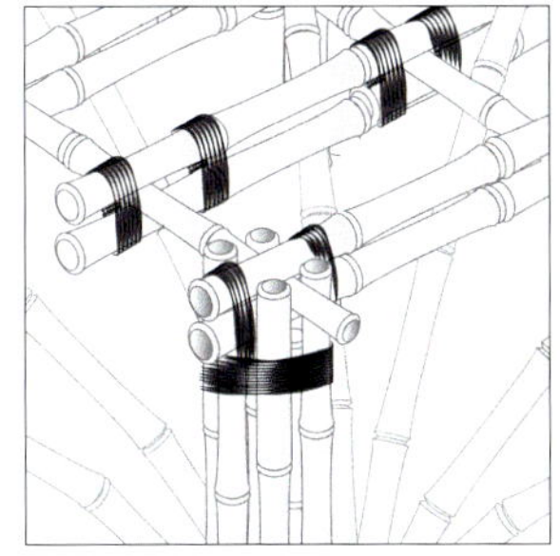

Detail 1
Tying the column to the beams

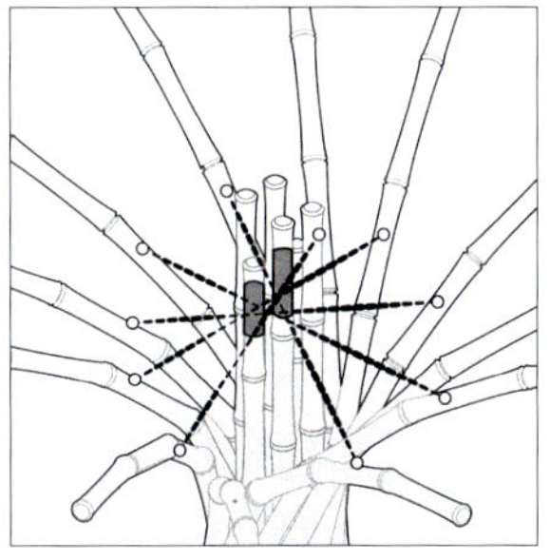

Detail 2
Steel tension ring

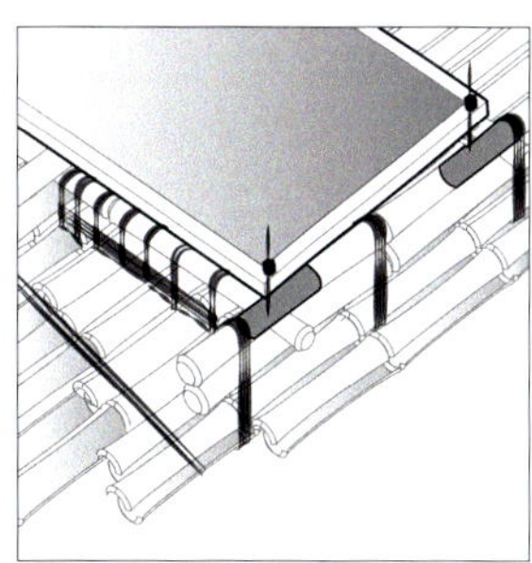

Detail 3
Photovoltaic panel pin joint and hanging gutter

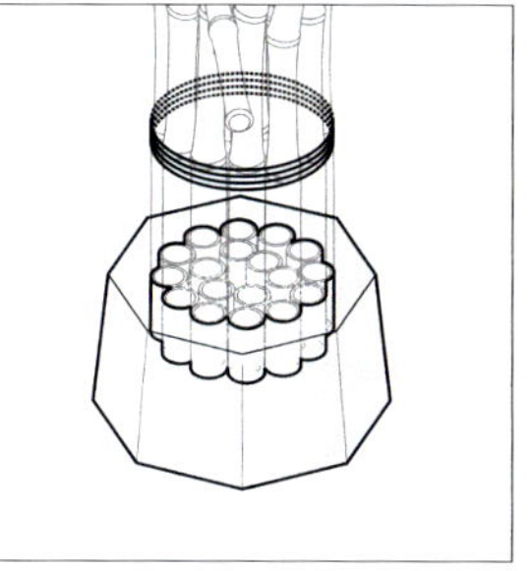

Detail 4
Bamboo lashing and precast concrete base

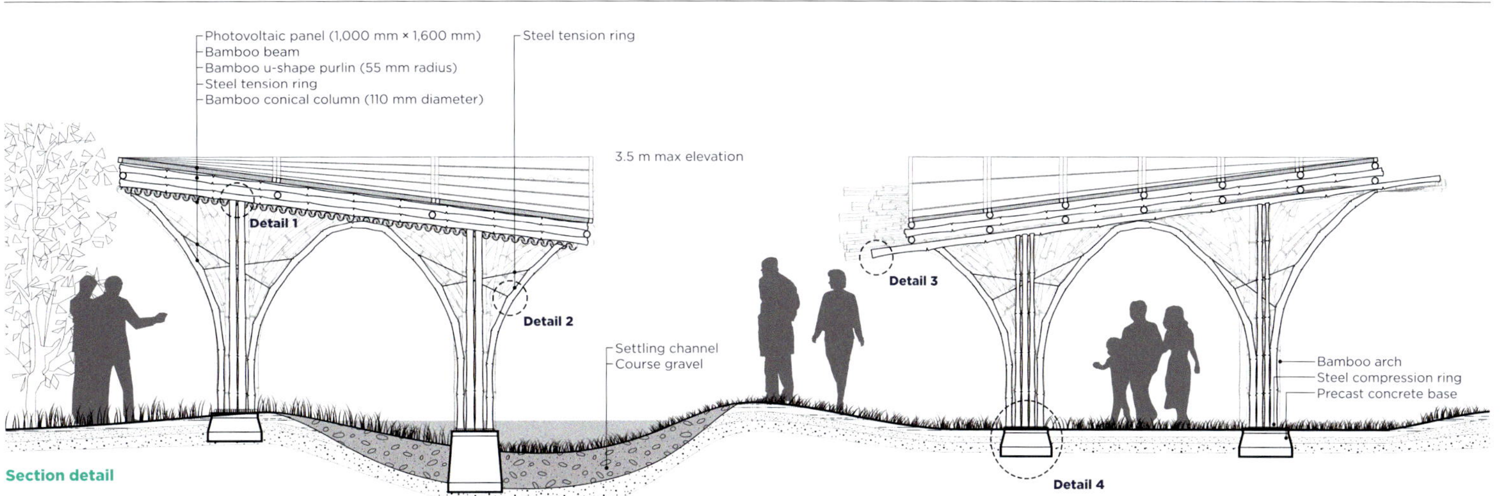

Section detail

TALI-TALI-LAND

Fabric panels are designed to be replaced and refreshed periodically by the local community. Patterns, colors, and techniques may evolve with time, reflecting the creative expression of individuals.

DESIGNERS: Lim Boon Hau, Pyaezone Aungsoe (Hau & Pyae)

TECHNOLOGIES: solar photovoltaic, battery energy storage, textile windbreak, rainwater harvesting, underground cisterns

ANNUAL PRODUCTION: 150 MWh of electricity, 1.25 million liters of filtered water

DESIGN TEAM LOCATION: Japan

RIGHT: Beautiful textures of local woven cloth create a unique landscape, concealing the structure and the solar photovoltaic rain harvesting canopies.

TALI-TALI-LAND, literally meaning "Weave-Weave-Land," transforms infrastructure into cultural expression. In Marou Village, this modular system of solar canopies and rainwater harvesting becomes a woven landscape: a place where tradition meets technology, and each resident has a hand in shaping the environment they rely on.

At its core is a steel structural module, designed for standardized fabrication, easy assembly, and resilience to storms. The roof collects solar power and rainwater. But its outermost layer—what makes it sing—is the cloth: masi, tapa, and woven mats designed and crafted by community members. These textiles act as windbreaks, insulation, visual identity, and cultural story. No two are the same. Each module is a unique expression, yet together they form a unified system.

Assembled in clusters, the structures offer shade, utility, and connection. They host playgrounds, open-air workshops, storytelling spaces, food gardens, and creative studios. This is not a fenced-off solar farm. It is infrastructure people live within, not just next to. Rainwater flows invisibly into underground tanks, filtered and stored for communal use. Electricity is stored in batteries and distributed across the village.

Maintenance becomes a living ritual: fabrics are refreshed with seasonal designs, new stories, and techniques passed between generations. Illustrated manuals and community training ensure that the entire system is locally operable and repairable. Modular and expandable, it is designed to evolve.

TALI-TALI-LAND is a celebration of weaving in every sense—of materials, relationships, knowledge, and climate resilience. It is not just what the land holds, but how the land itself is made, strand by strand, by the people who call it home.

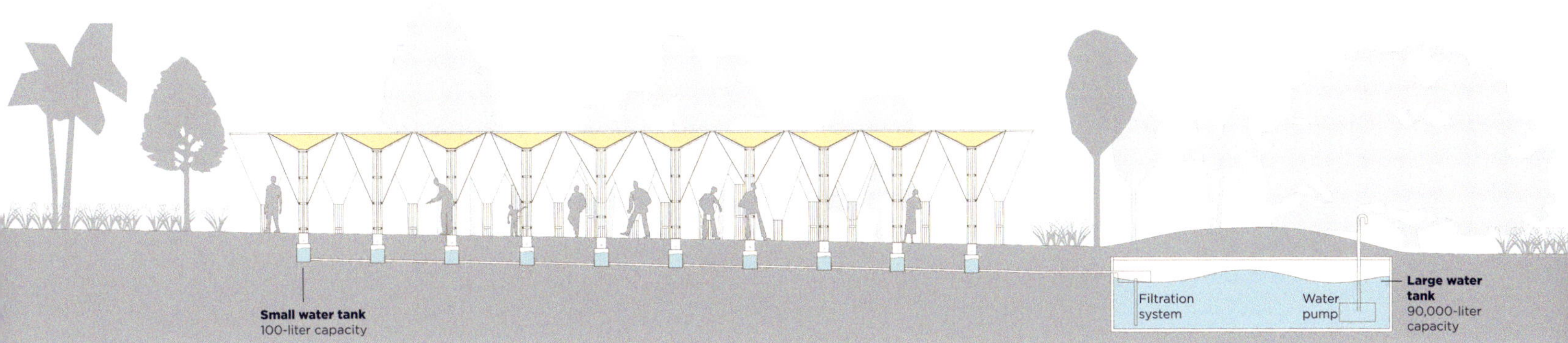

Longitudinal section

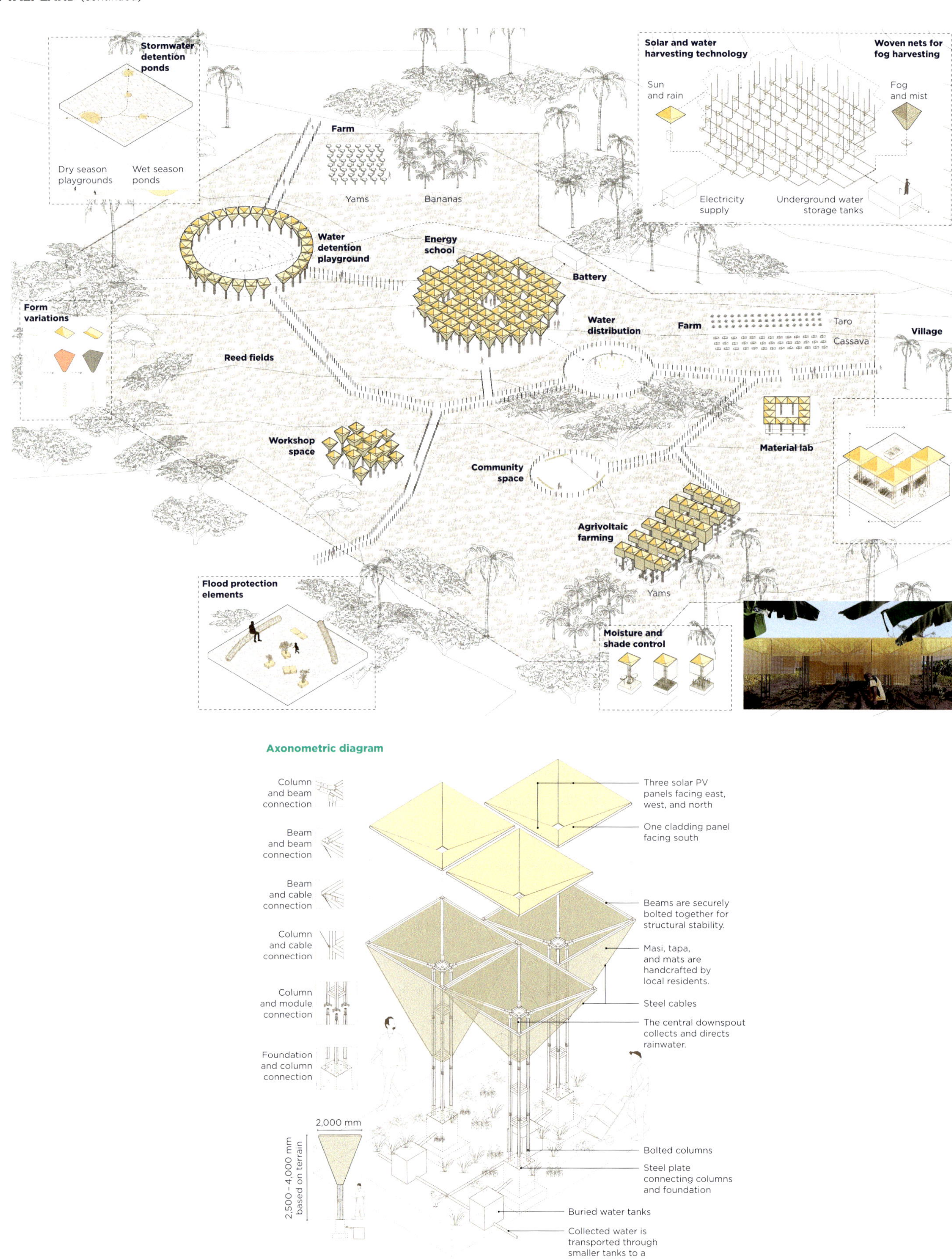
Stormwater detention ponds
Dry season playgrounds
Wet season ponds
Farm
Yams
Bananas
Solar and water harvesting technology
Woven nets for fog harvesting
Sun and rain
Fog and mist
Electricity supply
Underground water storage tanks
Water detention playground
Energy school
Battery
Form variations
Water distribution
Farm
Taro
Cassava
Village
Reed fields
Material lab
Workshop space
Community space
Agrivoltaic farming
Flood protection elements
Yams
Moisture and shade control
Axonometric diagram
Column and beam connection
Beam and beam connection
Beam and cable connection
Column and cable connection
Column and module connection
Foundation and column connection
2,000 mm
2,500–4,000 mm based on terrain
Three solar PV panels facing east, west, and north
One cladding panel facing south
Beams are securely bolted together for structural stability.
Masi, tapa, and mats are handcrafted by local residents.
Steel cables
The central downspout collects and directs rainwater.
Bolted columns
Steel plate connecting columns and foundation
Buried water tanks
Collected water is transported through smaller tanks to a central storage tank.

Installation begins on the textile windbreak elements.

Water harvesting nets can be designed to introduce colorful elements into the landscape.

Module design

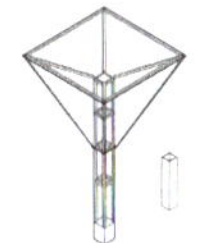

Base structure
Cold-formed hollow section steel modules

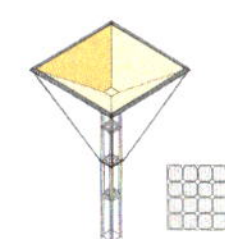

PV panel
Tinted photovoltaic panels mounted on top for energy generation.

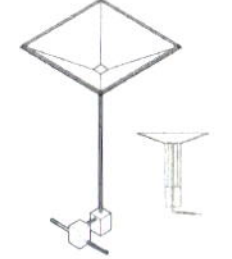

Water collection
Solar panels double as rainwater catchment surfaces.

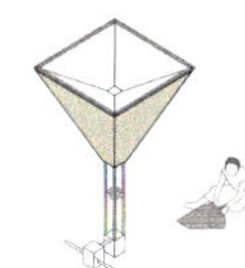

Fabric/mat envelope
Mats and traditional fabrics (masi, tapa) are woven by local residents.

Formation of energy space

Energy infrastructure
Each module functions as a self-contained energy system.

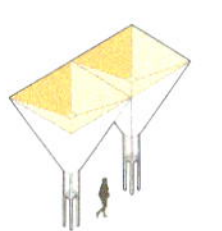

Energy art
Multiple units transform infrastructure into art.

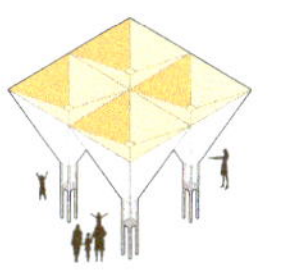

Water pavilion
As it expands, the water pavilion creates space for communal gathering.

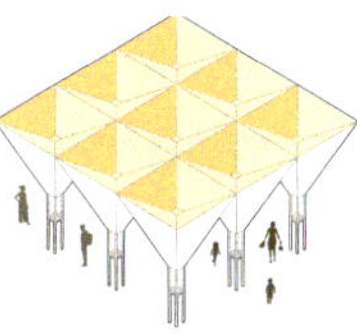

Energy space
Multiple energy modules assemble to create a shaded, functional space for community activities.

Configurable arrangements

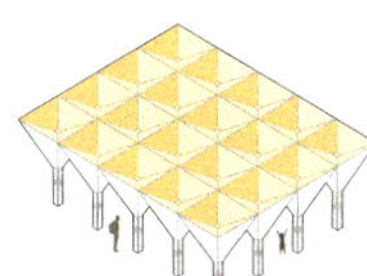

Aligned grid
A gridded arrangement allows for scalable, orderly growth.

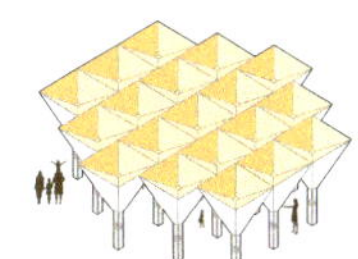

Offset grid
Modules arranged on a shifted grid create dynamic spatial variation.

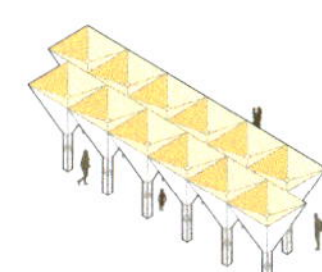

Elongated
Modules extend horizontally across the landscape, inviting residents to explore.

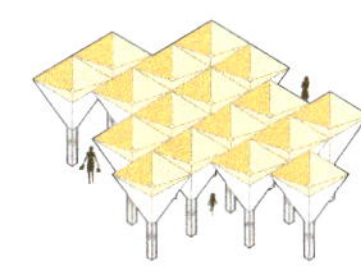

Random
Modules are placed in response to community needs, creating an organic form.

Solar Waves

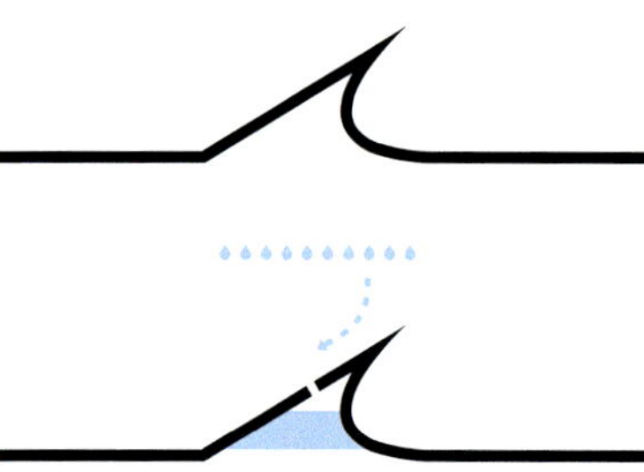

Photovoltaic panels collect sunlight and channel rainwater through gaps to internal tanks.

DESIGNER: Antonio Maccà

TECHNOLOGIES: solar photovoltaic, battery energy storage, rainwater harvesting and storage

ANNUAL PRODUCTION: 120 MWh of electricity, 300,000 liters of filtered water

DESIGN TEAM LOCATION: Italy

Solar Waves rises from the Earth like the sea itself — three-dimensional solar sculptures shaped by wind and water, capturing light by day and glowing softly at night. Inspired by the ocean swells surrounding Naviti Island, the artwork transforms waveforms into active, inhabitable infrastructure — gathering sun, channeling rain, and offering shelter from heat and storms.

Each sculpture is a curved, aerodynamic shell that blends into the terrain. Sloping white metal surfaces support photovoltaic arrays designed to conceal their technological function beneath a custom high-transmittance nano-film. These crests fold into the land, creating public spaces where the community can meet, rest, and reflect. Like waves frozen mid-motion, they suggest both power and calm.

Beneath the tilted surfaces, rainwater is collected and stored in integrated tanks housed within the wave volumes themselves. These internal spaces are multipurpose, serving as water reservoirs, shaded gathering places, or sites for cultural activities and artistic performance. As a landscape intervention, *Solar Waves* becomes a living amphitheater shaped by light, sound, and community use.

The modular system includes sculptural forms in three scales, each with distinct curvatures and energy profiles. Some are optimized for east–west solar exposure, others for north-facing maximum yield. Their orientations and inclinations vary in response to site conditions and community energy needs, making the system inherently flexible and expandable.

Solar Waves offers a poetic translation of ocean strength into grounded infrastructure. It is a place where art, nature, and technology meet to reimagine the relationship between the sea and the land it shapes.

Solar Waves is a destination artwork, a monumental gesture whose monolithic white form distinguishes itself from the landscape.

The Arc of Nature

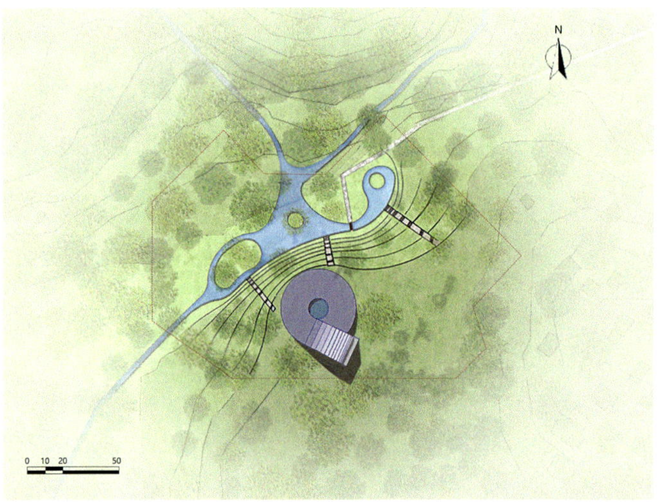

Site plan

DESIGNERS: Liu Panpan, Gulyasman Abdurahman, Liu Chang

TECHNOLOGIES: solar photovoltaic, battery energy storage, rainwater harvesting, soil-based water filtration, underground cisterns

ANNUAL PRODUCTION: 108 MWh of electricity, 150,000 liters of filtered water

DESIGN TEAM LOCATION: China

Perched atop Marou Village, *The Arc of Nature* offers a quiet yet powerful statement about the unity of people, landscape, and the elemental forces that sustain life. Inspired by bonfire rituals and reverence for natural harmony, the design takes the form of a circular pavilion — an architectural embrace that gathers light, collects water, and offers a new vantage point overlooking the village and horizon in all directions.

The structure's elevated platform is topped with a canopy of photovoltaic panels that mirrors the terrain and traces the paths of the sun and clouds across the sky. The platform is a place of gathering and reflection, offering views of the mountaintop and the village below. As seen from the water, the artwork stands as a beacon, a recognizable symbol of sustainable tourism.

Beneath the pavilion, a recessed water pool anchors the design, its basin collecting rainwater that flows from the sculpted roof and from seasonal mountain runoff. This water is filtered and circulated through a soil-based system that mimics natural hydrological processes, replenishing landscape features and supporting community use.

The circle was chosen intentionally: a form with no beginning or end, it evokes infinity, inclusivity, and the continuity of human and ecological systems. Built from durable materials that balance beauty with performance, *The Arc of Nature* functions as a visible nexus of infrastructure and culture, where tradition informs design and sustainability becomes an experience.

Community members engage with the pavilion not just as a utility but as a civic space — a site for ceremony, education, and daily life. As the sun powers light and life and water flows quietly beneath, *The Arc* becomes a living symbol of coexistence.

A stepped stormwater detention area filters rainwater and creates a dynamic foreground for the artwork.

The landmark seems to merge with the sky at midday and glows like a lighthouse as the sun sets over the island.

The Arc of Nature (continued)

Solar panels
Floor
Girder
Stairs
Pillar
Pool and bonfire pit

Solar panels
Energy
Water
4.5 m
Valve
Water circulation system
Water pump
Mountain water collection

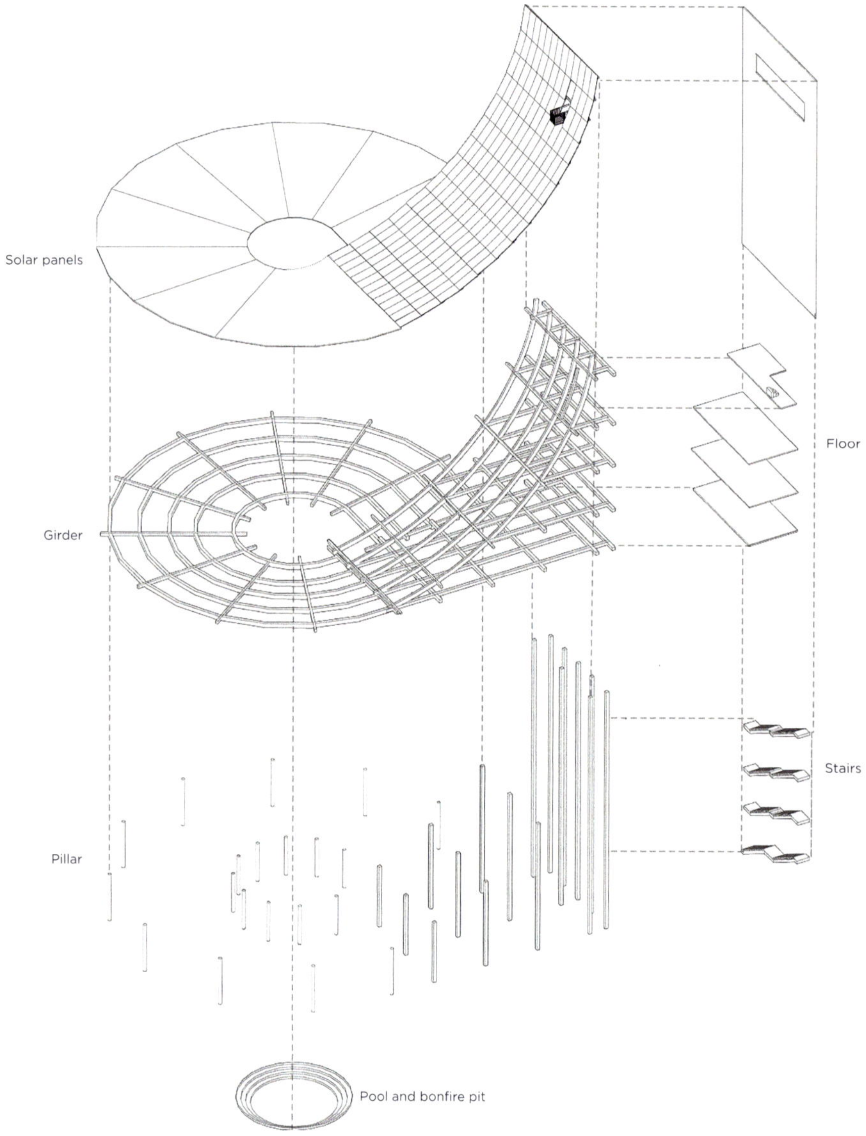

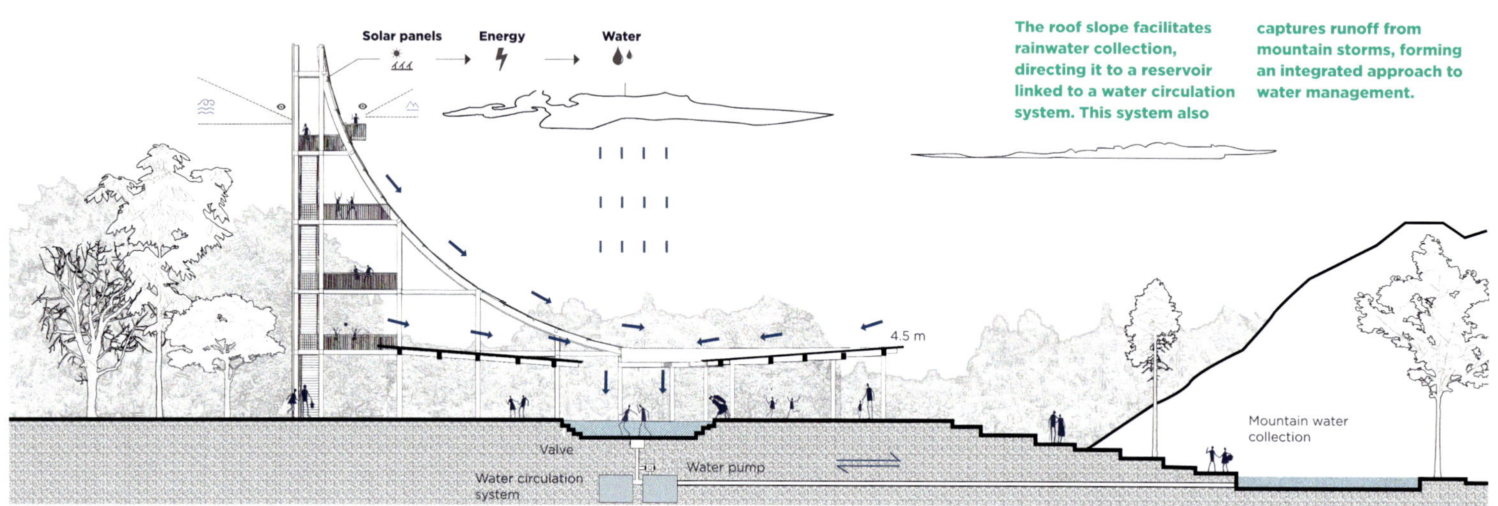

The roof slope facilitates rainwater collection, directing it to a reservoir linked to a water circulation system. This system also captures runoff from mountain storms, forming an integrated approach to water management.

The shaded spaces beneath the canopy are enjoyed by both visitors and Marou residents.

Seen from the foothills of Vatu Rua, the artwork stands as a monument to resilience.

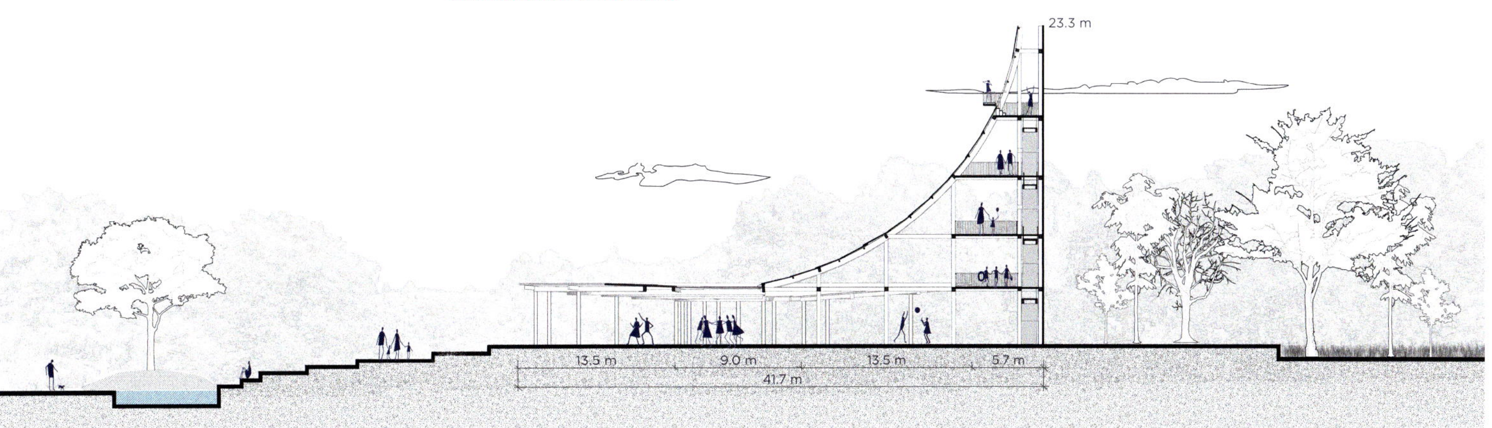

Just a Roof

DESIGNERS: Flóra Fanni Imre, Gergely Bence Bodnár, Tamás Gombos

TECHNOLOGIES: solar photovoltaic, battery energy storage, rainwater harvesting, filtration, and storage

ANNUAL PRODUCTION: 70 MWh of electricity, 30,000 liters of filtered water

DESIGN TEAM LOCATION: Hungary

A variety of activities take place beneath the shade of the roof canopy.

At the southern edge of Marou Village, a simple form rises — a pitched canopy, modest in gesture but generous in spirit. *Just a Roof* transforms renewable infrastructure into a public asset, creating energy while offering an open, shaded space for gathering, celebration, and everyday life.

Elevated on a structural frame of locally harvested bamboo, the canopy tilts north at 16 degrees to capture the sun's path. Beneath it, a wide, uninterrupted plane of shelter stretches across the site — inviting a range of uses that emerge from community need rather than prescriptive design. It may host market stalls, musical performances, lessons, or simply provide a quiet retreat from the midday heat. The space is intentionally undefined, open to adaptation, and made to belong to those who inhabit it.

The structure is enriched by woven bamboo cladding that wraps the solar panels and hides technical components from view. This layer serves both functional and cultural roles, protecting sensitive elements from wind and sun while referencing vernacular craftsmanship. Sunlight filters through occasional voids in the canopy, casting patterns that animate the ground below.

Rainwater is collected through the cladding system and stored in discreet ground-level tanks, ready for domestic or landscape use. All materials are selected for longevity and low-maintenance care. The bamboo is treated with natural preservatives, the PV system is easy to monitor, and maintenance routines are designed to be learned and led by the community.

By combining low-tech resilience with quiet architectural beauty, *Just a Roof* becomes a living classroom, a climate shelter, and a civic commons. Through its simplicity, it models a future in which renewable energy is not hidden or industrial, but celebratory and shared.

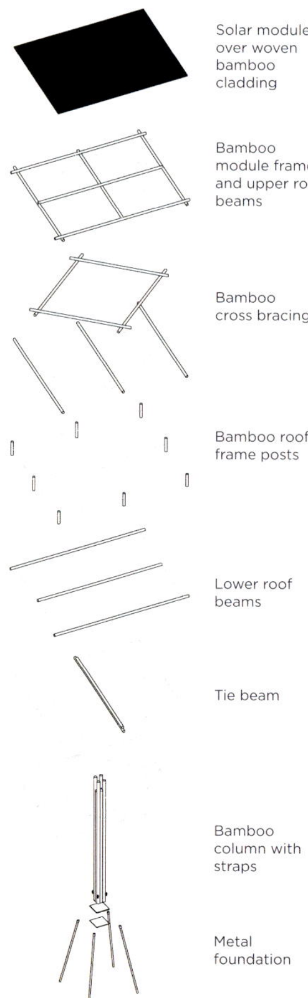

The roof is angled 16° to the north to optimize solar exposure.

The Cloud

DESIGNERS: Martin Rein-Cano, Carsten Schmidt, Olya Cherniakova, Francisco Claisse, Mayank Gupta, Alexander Hartway, Manuel Lacerda, Lakshmishree Venugopal, Moritz Szekely (TOPOTEK 1 with Transsolar)

TECHNOLOGIES: solar photovoltaic, battery energy storage, rainwater harvesting and filtration, flexible membrane water storage

ANNUAL PRODUCTION: 300 MWh of electricity, 2.2 million liters of filtered water

DESIGN TEAM LOCATION: Germany

Site plan

RIGHT: The aerial view reveals *The Cloud*, an amorphous and diaphanous form in the landscape.

The Cloud drifts above the landscape like a suspended dream, at once grounded and ephemeral. Shaped by a modular grid and guided by natural forces, it forms a porous canopy of photovoltaic panels and flexible rain-harvesting vessels, a sacral place of water, sun, and shared space.

Constructed primarily from bamboo, *The Cloud* uses local materials and low-tech assembly methods that are accessible to the community. The lightweight structure rests gently on the land, rising and spiraling outward from a central gathering space. Its form evokes coral growth — incremental, responsive, and inherently local. The largest volume houses an open hearth for storytelling and community interaction, while smaller chambers create thresholds, shaded nooks, and flexible zones for rest, reflection, and play.

The PV panels are positioned both horizontally and vertically, with orientations that follow the arc of the sun from east to west, distributing energy generation across the day. These dark, tessellated surfaces catch light like wings, while their integrated flexibility allows wind to pass through, reducing structural stress. Suspended beneath, translucent water vessels collect and store rain, using their weight to anchor the bamboo grid to the earth. Gravity assists with passive water distribution from the vessels to a 140 m^2 reservoir for filtration and distribution.

Every detail is shaped by simplicity and purpose. Ropes, wooden pegs, and bolts tie the structure together. Its porous form resists high winds and allows filtered light to dapple the ground below. From a distance, it appears like a drifting cloud, shifting in light and meaning depending on one's vantage point.

Inside, the experience is immersive and serene. Columns dissolve into the canopy, and the boundary between built and natural blurs. As the structure gathers sun and rain, it also gathers people, creating a quiet monument to resilience, emerging like mist from many intersections of intention.

Detailed sections

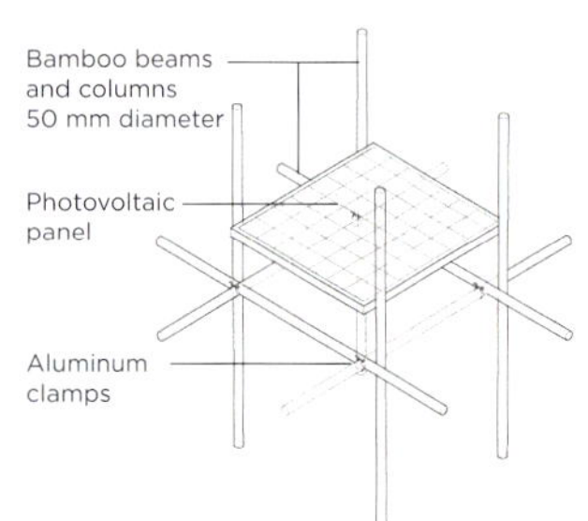

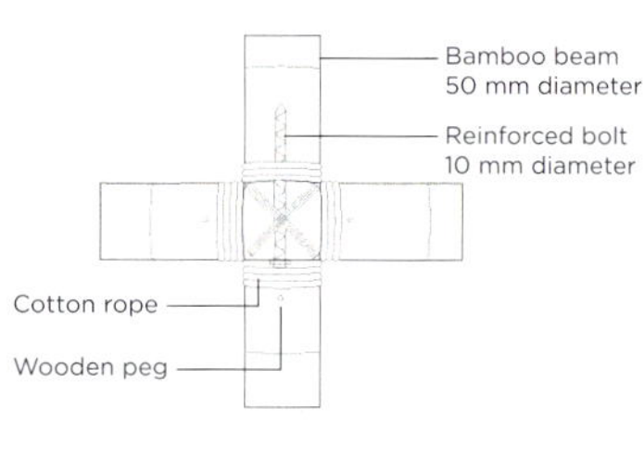

The interconnected matrix is a robust structure that allows wind and light to pass through, creating interesting visual effects.

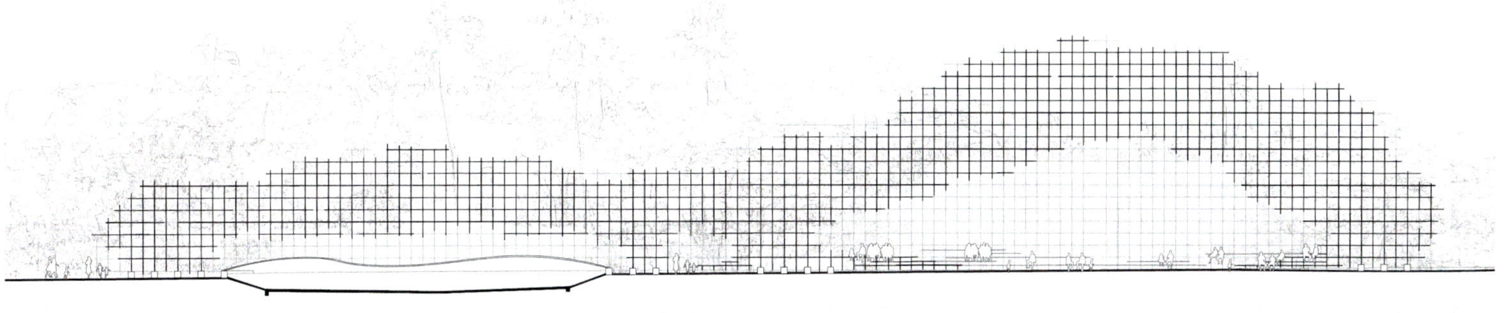

East–west section

Solar Pavilion for the Community

DESIGNERS: Csongor Csepregi, Tas Szabó, Soma Urbán, Zóra Vida

TECHNOLOGIES: modular solar photovoltaic with rope-adjusted panel tilt, battery energy storage, rainwater harvesting and storage

ANNUAL PRODUCTION: 120 MWh of electricity, 500,000 liters of filtered water

DESIGN TEAM LOCATION: Hungary

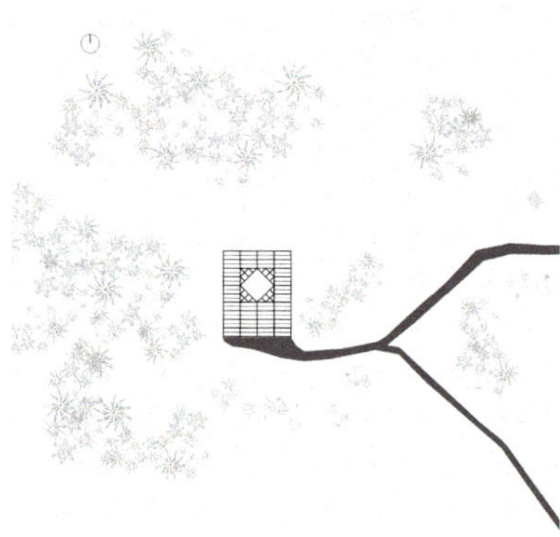

Site plan

RIGHT: Small logs are bundled together to create bench seating around a central space used for performance and celebration.

Framed by triangular bracing and crafted from locally sourced coconut palm timber, *Solar Pavilion for the Community* is an elegant synthesis of renewable energy and shared civic space. Set lightly on the land atop adjustable ground screws, its modular 6.4 m × 6.4 m grid allows for phased expansion, growing in rhythm with the needs of Marou Village.

The structure is a celebration of adaptive simplicity. Solar panels mounted across the roof are adjusted monthly by a rope-and-pulley system, optimized for changing sun angles throughout the year. The timber frame is joined by traditional mortise and tenon, while locally woven natural fiber shades wrap around the canopy, cooling the interior and infusing the structure with cultural identity.

Beneath the canopy, logs arranged as benches and tables create a setting for gatherings, markets, performances, and rainwater storage. The space shifts easily between informal everyday use and formal village events. Its openness invites participation; its geometry speaks of both seafaring heritage and practical resilience.

The pavilion's energy system powers essential infrastructure through underground, low-voltage distribution lines. Battery energy storage ensures continuity during overcast periods or at night, and all components are designed for maintainability with basic tools and training. Clear visual markers on the structure guide the solar angle adjustments, anchoring routine maintenance in accessible practice.

Community members are central to every stage, from design conversations to construction and long-term stewardship. The system's beauty lies not just in its elegant simplicity, but also in its ability to foster ownership and participation.

The *Solar Pavilion* is a modular structure offering clean energy and communal space to Marou residents.

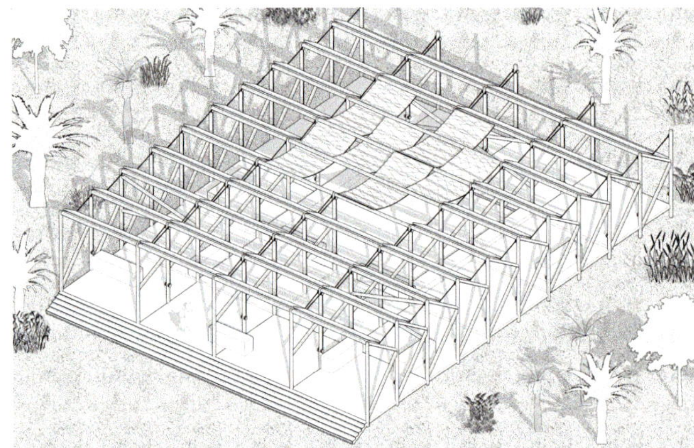

Axonometric drawing

Section

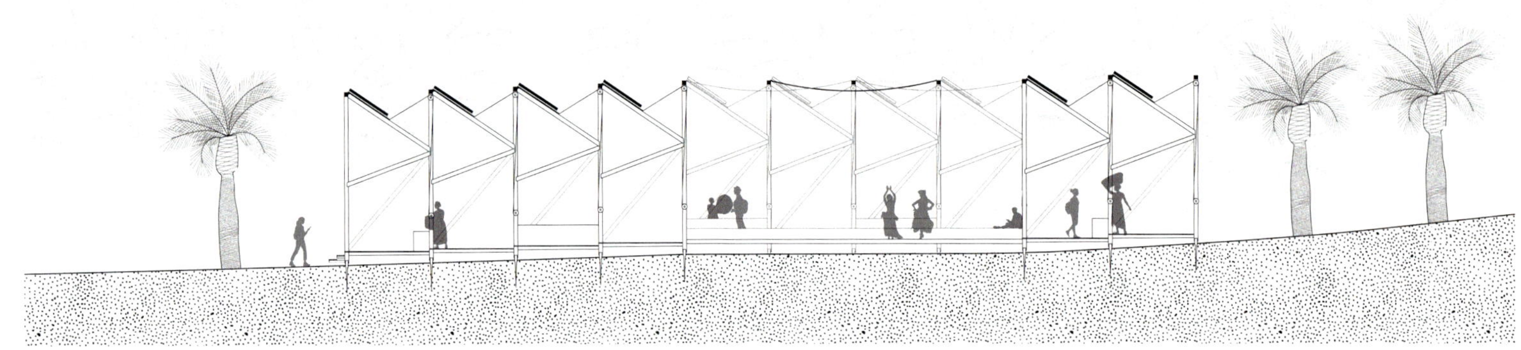

From the south, the solar modules are entirely concealed behind the roof structure.

The structure supports solar panels that can be manually adjusted with a pulley and rope system to optimize efficiency.

View of the *Solar Pavilion* from above

A view over the central space offers a glimpse of the solar modules from the north.

Solar Forest

DESIGNER: Daniel Cueto Mondéjar

TECHNOLOGIES: vertically-oriented semi-transparent solar photovoltaic modules (similar to Lumos), battery energy storage, rainwater-harvesting, underground cisterns

ANNUAL PRODUCTION: 120 MWh of electricity, 450,000 liters of filtered water

DESIGN TEAM LOCATION: Belgium

RIGHT: The rainwater harvesting island pavilion is visible through the forest of photovoltaic modules, which blend into the surrounding landscape.

Solar Forest envisions a landscape where infrastructure floats gently across the terrain — an open, adaptive system of solar trees and rainwater islands that weaves energy generation, water collection, agriculture, and gathering into a unified, low-impact mosaic. Rooted in the aesthetics of Fijian masi textiles, the design translates cultural patterning into spatial organization in a 6 m × 6 m triangular grid.

Bifacial semi-transparent solar modules are placed vertically to create a "Solar Tree." This vertical orientation liberates ground space while preserving the same solar collection area, allowing crops such as cassava or yam to grow in harmony with the installation. Rather than maximizing output, the energy system is designed around balance — serving social, ecological, and productive needs simultaneously.

Complementing the solar trees are circular rainwater islands: platforms that host social interaction while capturing and storing water in partially buried 5,000-liter tanks. These quiet oases create shaded gathering points within the grid and help regulate water supply throughout the dry season.

Together, the trees and islands form an "energy landscape" where the ecological footprint is soft and the spatial language is open-ended.

The system balances energy production with ecological sensitivity and cultural integration. It uses local materials, avoids large foundations, and is easy to repair. Community participation in design and assembly fosters long-term stewardship. Visual gaps are preserved around existing trees, and the system's porosity allows light, wind, wildlife, and water to move freely through the site.

Designed to be maintained by the community, *Solar Forest* creates an adaptable and porous infrastructure that merges seamlessly with the landscape and daily life in Marou Village.

Visitors enjoy the sound of rain falling within the water harvesting islands.

Both the Solar Tree and Rainwater Island modules are constructed with a bamboo frame.

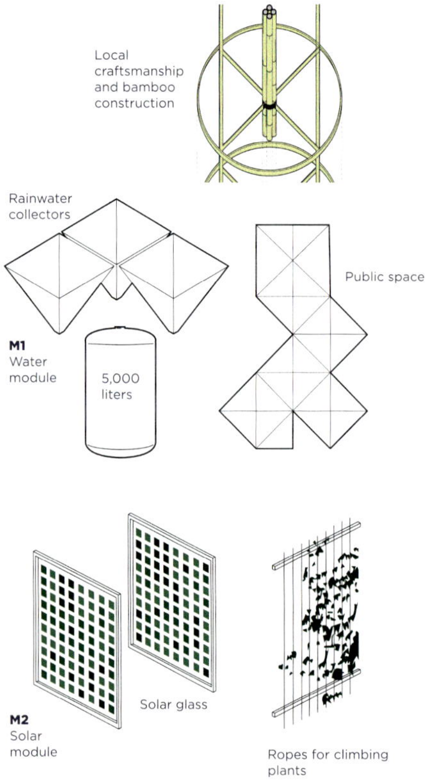

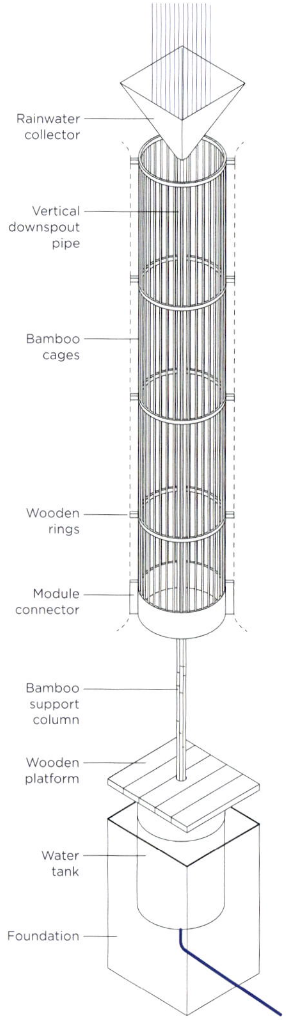

Local craftsmanship and bamboo construction
Rainwater collectors
Public space
M1
Water module
5,000 liters
Solar glass
M2
Solar module
Ropes for climbing plants

Rainwater collector
Vertical downspout pipe
Bamboo cages
Wooden rings
Module connector
Bamboo support column
Wooden platform
Water tank
Foundation

M1
Rainwater Island module

Bamboo structure
Vertical ropes for climbing plants
Bamboo cages
Wooden frame
50% transparent solar panel
Bamboo base structure
Concrete foundation

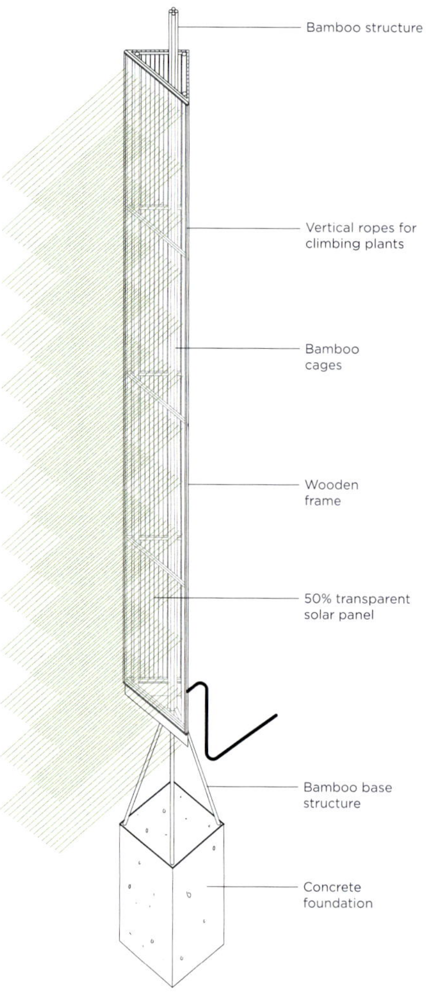

M2
Solar Tree module

10 m tall
Solar panel
Solar tree
6 m
6 m
New functions
6 m
3 m
Paths
New functions

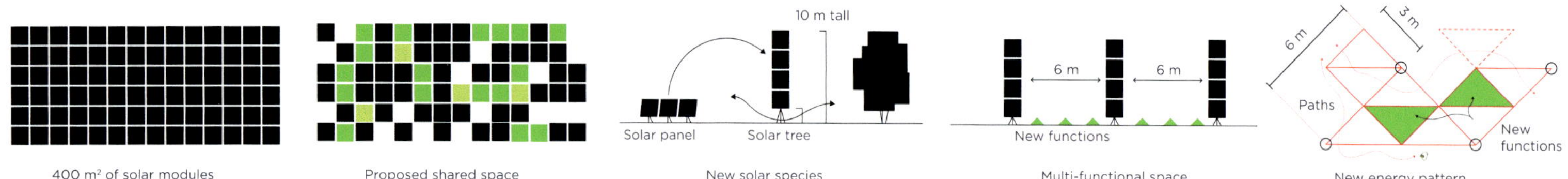

400 m² of solar modules — Proposed shared space — New solar species — Multi-functional space — New energy pattern

The color of the cells shifts in a gradient of greens, transforming the otherwise rigid appearance of the solar panels into a translucent landscape of light, reminiscent of a natural forest.

Land Actuator

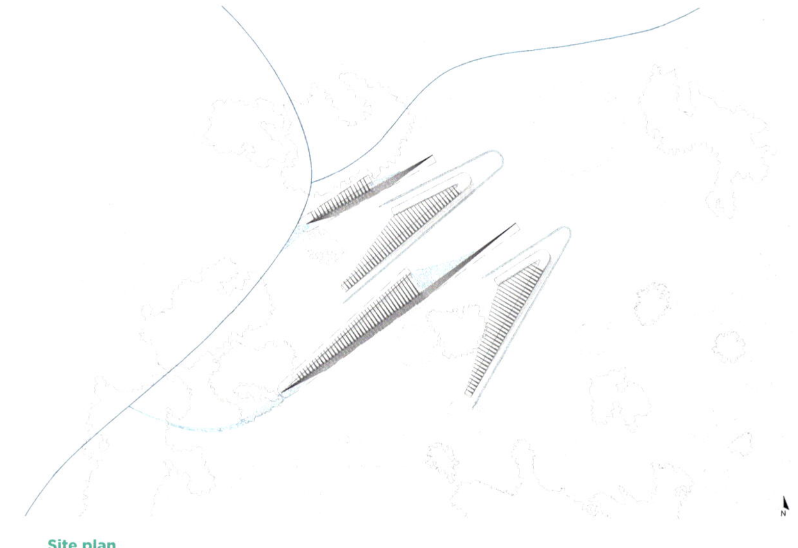

Site plan

DESIGNERS: Sarah Stevens, Hugo Mulder, Sol Macchiavello, Maria Sol Meyer, Carlos Lora (ARCHLABS)

TECHNOLOGIES: semi-transparent solar photovoltaic modules, battery energy storage, fog harvesting, rainwater harvesting, compressed earth cisterns

ANNUAL PRODUCTION: 135 MWh of electricity, 3.7 million liters of filtered water

DESIGN TEAM LOCATION: Argentina

RIGHT: Marou residents care for the solar and water landscape as they do their agricultural landscapes.

Land Actuator is not a single object but an ongoing process—an adaptive system that co-authors stories with the land, the sky, and its people. It begins with earth and bamboo, folded, formed, and fired by sun and storm. Land is carved into positive and negative forms: cisterns are buried, channels flow, and vaults rise, each shaped by compressed earth bricks made from the very soil excavated to create them.

Across this re-formed topography, curving bamboo framed photovoltaic modules are mounted on elegant cradles. The semi-transparent solar panels are designed to pivot with the sun, collect fog at dawn, and close during storms. Repositioned with pulley systems inspired by sailboat rigging, the modules are adjusted by community members to optimize solar exposure, provide shade for crops, and generate cooling mists in times of extreme heat.

The cisterns and reservoirs, with a combined capacity of over 3,700 cubic meters, store water for dry periods and mitigate flooding during storms. The landforms themselves offer refuge during cyclones. Vault interiors stay cool through passive ventilation shafts that also house battery energy storage and carry the power cables from the PV arrays above.

Land Actuator is co-created and co-maintained. Each repair becomes a ritual; each generation adds to its form. It is as much about cultivating knowledge and continuity as it is about producing water and electricity. With every tilt of the bamboo cradles, the village tunes itself to sun, mist, and the fertility of the earth.

Below the fog harvesting nets, Marou residents harvest fresh greens from the garden for dinner.

Steps create a seating area beside the linear reservoir.

The temperature stays cool inside the brick walls of the vaulted cistern.

Kinetic bamboo cradles are controlled by cables and pulleys, adjusting to fit conditions over day and night.

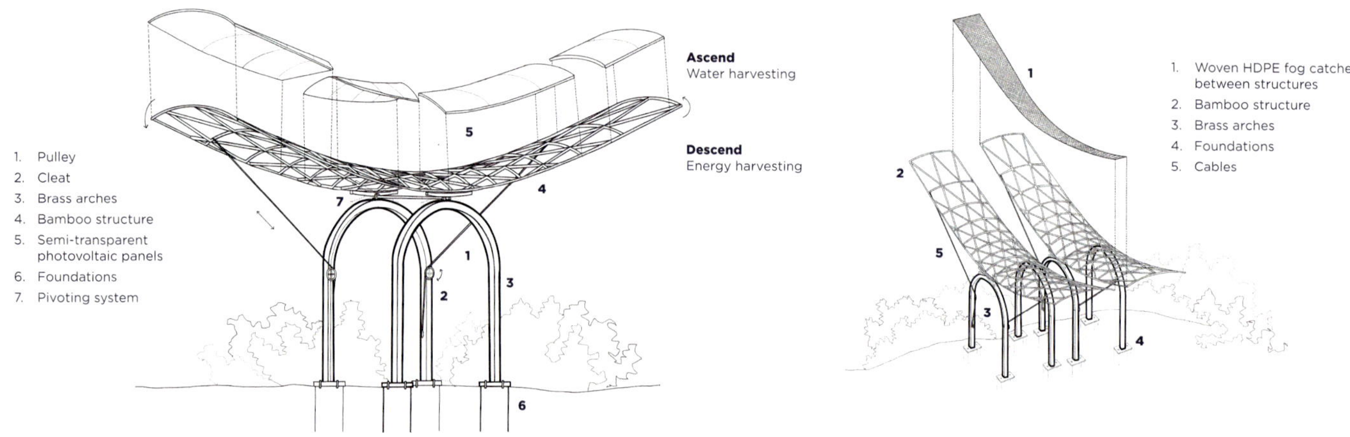

The landforms follow the site's contours and respond to the existing primary vegetation.

Environmentally adaptive structure

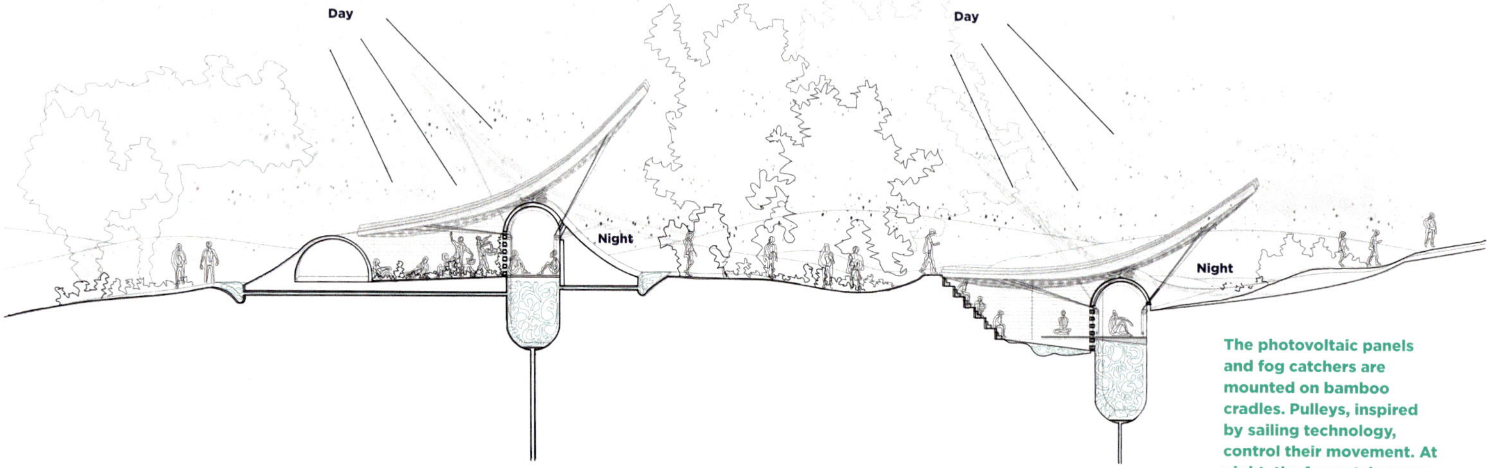

The photovoltaic panels and fog catchers are mounted on bamboo cradles. Pulleys, inspired by sailing technology, control their movement. At night, the fog catchers are hoisted vertically to capture moisture from early morning mist. As the sun rises, the cradles pivot, orienting the photovoltaic panels toward the light to harvest solar energy.

Lowering the solar module on one side and raising them on the other creates spaces of protection and expansiveness.

Na Lomalagi, na Qele, kei na Tamata
The Sky, the Earth, and the People

Visitors soak in the stormwater reservoir.

DESIGNERS: James Tapscott, William Dodge, Lincoln Hancock, Andrew Patterson, Henry Craw

TECHNOLOGIES: solar photovoltaic with submersible cyclone protection, hybrid battery energy storage, passive rainwater harvesting and filtration, reservoir storage, sculptural lightning rods

ANNUAL PRODUCTION: 140 MWh of electricity, 320,000 liters of filtered water

DESIGN TEAM LOCATION: New Zealand

Children play in view of the sculptural lightning rods of the artwork.

Na Lomalagi, na Qele, kei na Tamata — *The Sky, the Earth, and the People* — is not only a phrase, but the guiding principle of this design. It reflects a Fijian worldview rooted in reciprocity between nature and community. In this spirit, the design assembles sunlight, rainfall, and volcanic soil into an integrated system that sustains life and sparks resilience.

At its heart is a sculptural landform that houses a 90 kW solar array, a deep catchment pond, and water storage tanks that collectively address Marou Village's need for clean energy and potable water. The solar panels are arranged in traditional Fijian motifs and, in a radical design move, are safeguarded during cyclones by submerging them in a protective water basin, manually activated via simple taps.

The pond doubles as a social landscape. Planted with Kuta grass, it naturally filters water and creates shaded zones for gathering, play, and reflection. Rainwater is gravity-fed through a series of filters into storage tanks, while overflow returns to existing stream systems.

Three 10-meter stainless steel lightning rods rise above the installation. Designed to visibly flex in high winds, they serve as functional grounding structures and symbolic beacons — mirroring Earth, sky, and water. These rods are outfitted as low-tech warning systems for power and water levels or natural hazards.

The entire system is modular, replicable, and culturally grounded. Sodium-ion batteries are embedded into landscape forms, while underground mini-grids link nearby infrastructure. Operations are designed to be intuitive, training local stewards to read the sky, tend the water, and care for the power beneath their feet.

The artwork comes alive during lightning storms, reminding viewers of the immense energy contained in Earth's atmosphere.

Diagram of major component parts

Vaka ni Lomani
Vessel of Compassion

DESIGNERS: Kaixi Yang, Victor Pineda Torres, Nicc Moeono-Alaiasa

TECHNOLOGIES: solar photovoltaic, battery energy storage, rainwater harvesting, constructed wetland with biofiltration, passive desalination membrane, micro hydro

ANNUAL PRODUCTION: 126 MWh of electricity, 600,000 liters of filtered water

DESIGN TEAM LOCATION: United States, Mexico, Samoa

Custom solar modules in a spiraling Fibonacci pattern create channels that evoke the flow of water.

RIGHT: Water flows from the micro-hydro system into the constructed wetland.

In the heart of Naviti Island, where the mountains meet the sea and the sky cradles the land, the people of Marou wake each day to the rhythm of tide and song. Here, life has always flowed with nature—the rain that nourishes the crops, the sun that warms the earth, the streams that whisper their stories down the slopes. *Vaka ni Lomani: Vessel of Compassion* is born from this connection.

At the heart of the design is a solar pavilion — an open-air gathering place inspired by the Fijian concept of *solesolevaki* (working together) and shaded by a 50 kW solar array. The space serves as a hub for communal life: recreation, dance, ceremony, and collective resilience-building. Rainwater is channeled through a passive desalination membrane and native plant biofiltration beds, after which it makes its way into a 200,000-liter underground cistern. The water supports needs for drinking, sanitation, and agriculture, while the biofiltration beds offer flood protection.

A small hydro turbine, powered by stormwater from a refurbished dam, adds a 15 kW base-load energy source, providing reliable electricity even when solar is low. Additional rooftop solar panels distributed across homes and community buildings extend the generation network, while a 300 kWh lithium iron phosphate (LFP) battery system stores surplus energy for evening use and emergencies.

Together, these technologies form a resilient, decentralized grid that reduces reliance on diesel and enhances local autonomy. Gravity-fed and solar-pumped water systems serve agriculture and fire safety needs, while stormwater management infrastructure mitigates flooding.

Vaka ni Lomani offers a host of co-benefits: reliable power for schools and clinics, support for local fisheries and food production, and a hands-on platform for technical education. Youth help maintain the system; elders help guide it. Together, they ensure the artwork acts as a vessel carrying knowledge forward.

Vaka ni Lomani Vessel of Compassion
(continued)

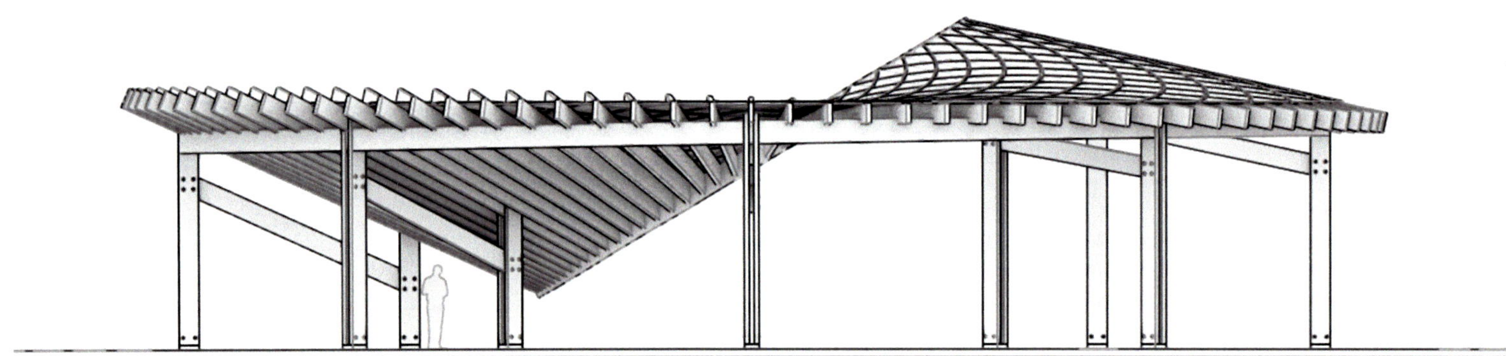

Exploded axonometric

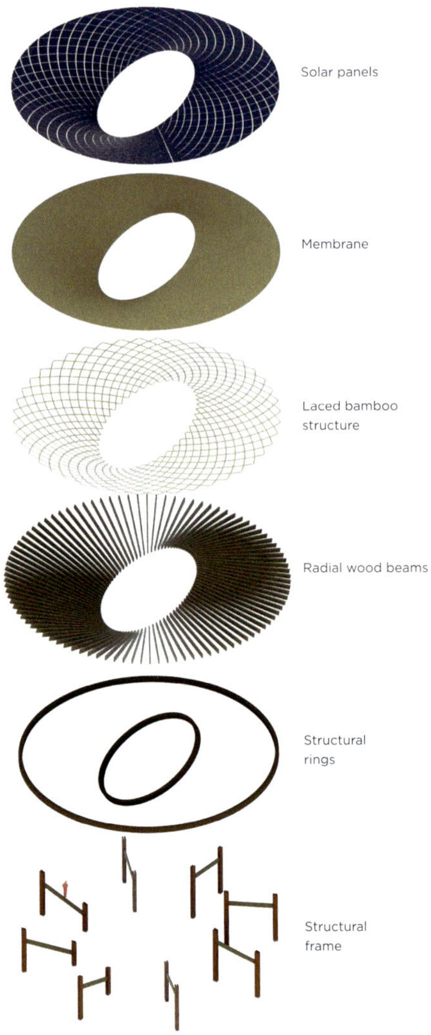

Solar panels

Membrane

Laced bamboo structure

Radial wood beams

Structural rings

Structural frame

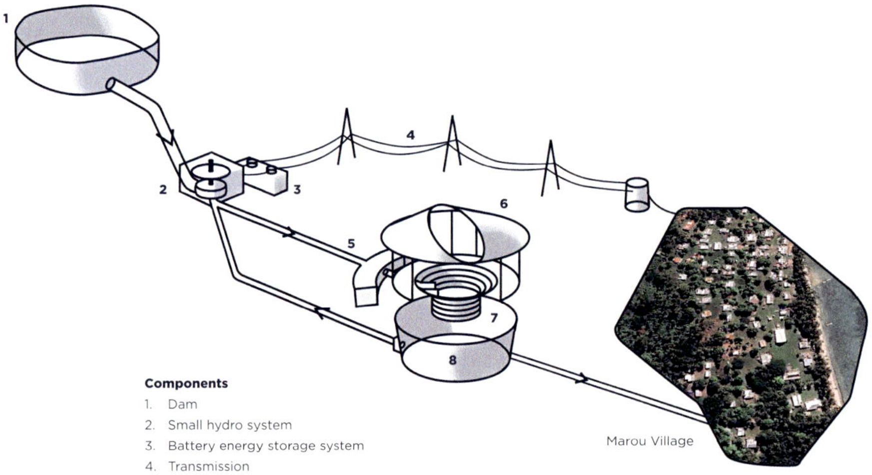

1
2
3
4
5
6
7
8
Marou Village

Components

1. Dam
2. Small hydro system
3. Battery energy storage system
4. Transmission
5. Biofiltration channel
6. Solar structure
7. Filtration system
8. Storage reservoir

The form of the artwork evokes the tanoa—the traditional carved wooden bowl used in the preparation of kava.

Bula Sun

DESIGNER: Caulder Wasmuth

TECHNOLOGIES: solar photovoltaic, battery energy storage, rainwater harvesting

ANNUAL PRODUCTION: 140 MWh of electricity, 1 million liters of filtered water

DESIGN TEAM LOCATION: United States

The solar modules create a pattern of shadows on the platform below.

RIGHT: The dynamic structure stands as a monument to resilience.

Inspired by the seafaring traditions of the iTaukei people, *Bula Sun* unfurls like a fleet of solar sails across the Marou landscape — an elegant energy and water system grounded in community values and cultural memory. Echoing the forms of traditional Fijian vessels, the sail-like structures offer shade, shelter, and a shared space for gathering while producing clean power and collecting vital rainwater.

The installation consists of 244 high-efficiency 410-watt solar panels arranged across four triangular fields and held in tension between a central mast and a large compression ring. The entire composition is supported by a wave-like element that connects the design to the surrounding ocean environment, creating visual harmony with the coastal landscape. The panels are mounted on an aluminum framework engineered to withstand Category 5 cyclones, with wind-permeable design features that allow air to flow safely through the sails. The solar sails shade the ground beneath, creating a welcoming civic space.

The rainwater collection system channels precipitation through integrated gutters to surface grates on the concrete base, and through filters to an underground storage reservoir that can hold nearly 200,000 liters at a time.

Materials were selected for longevity and maintainability in the marine environment: aluminum framing, stainless-steel connections, and a reinforced concrete base and support structure provide structural integrity and resistance to corrosion.

All components are designed to fit on small barges that can access Marou's shore, addressing the critical logistical challenge of material transport to this remote location. The use of standardized, off-the-shelf components ensures both initial construction feasibility and long-term repairability. Community is involved throughout — from early consultations to final installation and ongoing maintenance.

Bula Sun is a landmark that links sea and land, past and future — casting light, catching rain, and reflecting the dynamic spirit of Fiji.

A view from the ground shows the gentle curve of the three planes supporting the position of the circular ring and suspending it in perfect balance.

Solar Leaf

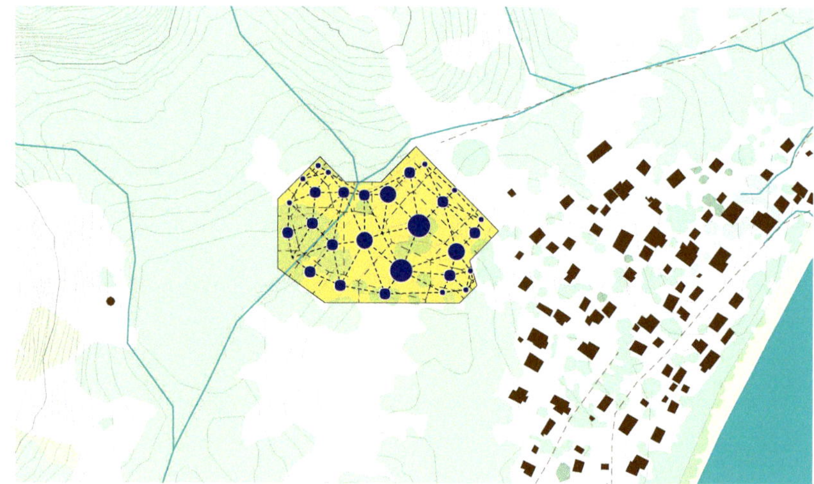

The site plan shows how the various module sizes are connected in a resilient web of energy that flows to the village.

DESIGNER: Iman SheikhAnsari

TECHNOLOGIES: solar photovoltaic, battery energy storage, rainwater harvesting and filtration, above-ground cisterns

ANNUAL PRODUCTION: 120 MWh of electricity, 600,000 liters of filtered water

DESIGN TEAM LOCATION: Iran

RIGHT: ***Solar Leaf*** **is an expressive ecology of solar energy, sustainable water systems, and communal space.**

Solar Leaf unfolds as a regenerative land art installation — an elegant structure that meets the vital needs of Marou Village while offering a poetic expression of sustainability. Inspired by the forms and textures of Fiji's flora and traditional motifs, the design weaves solar energy, water harvesting, and communal gathering spaces into a unified, living system.

The installation incorporates over 75 kW of photovoltaic capacity across biomimetic arrays of varying scales. High-efficiency monocrystalline cells are embedded in custom, leaf-shaped solar modules. Beneath the sculptural canopy, shaded pathways, community gardens, and play areas create spaces for ceremony, learning, and recreation.

Rainwater is collected from photovoltaic surfaces and filtered through gravel beds, nature-based biofilters, and carbon systems. The water is then stored in low-profile tanks or subterranean cisterns, with an annual harvest target exceeding 600,000 liters — bolstering water security in a changing climate.

Energy is stored in lithium iron phosphate (LFP) batteries, calibrated to meet peak daily loads and maintain continuity during cloud cover and nighttime hours. The entire system is engineered for resilience against tropical storms, salt-laden air, and heat extremes, employing durable materials such as bamboo and low-carbon steel.

Beyond its utility, *Solar Leaf* is a platform for community empowerment. Marou residents contribute to its co-design, assembly, and care. Workshops build technical skills in maintenance and operation, while the space supports cultural expression and local enterprise through regenerative tourism, food cultivation, and solar-powered amenities.

Elevations of various configurations of *Solar Leaf*

The leaves can be mass-produced for installations across multiple sites, creating economies of scale for custom solar module production.

The solar structures are designed to blend into the surrounding landscape.

The installation could extend into forested areas while allowing understory trees to coexist under a new solar canopy.

Sky Letters
Letters to the Invisible

Site plan

DESIGNERS: Dai Fen Zeng, Pengyan Wu

TECHNOLOGIES: solar photovoltaic, battery energy storage, rainwater harvesting and filtration, above-ground cisterns

ANNUAL PRODUCTION: 268 MWh of electricity, 1.2 million liters of filtered water

DESIGN TEAM LOCATION: United States

***Sky Letters* takes a creative approach to technology by embedding systems directly into the structural and spatial design. Solar panels become integral to the canopy's form, while the water collection system reinforces its protective and communal functions.**

Sky Letters is an ecological apparatus and poetic structure — part energy system, part communal gathering space. Inspired by the delicate, brush-like blossoms of Fijian rain trees and vutu trees, the design captures water, light, and movement with quiet intelligence. Just as these trees open at dusk to meet the sky, *Sky Letters* opens to the rhythms of Marou Village and its surrounding environment.

The installation consists of 352 monocrystalline solar panels mounted across a modular timber canopy, each module measuring 10 m × 5 m. Together, they form a resilient structure capable of generating more than enough electricity to meet the existing and near future needs of Marou Village. Rainwater is harvested directly from the panel surfaces via stainless-steel gutters and structural rain pipes, collecting nearly 1.2 million liters per year. Water flows into decentralized tanks connected by underground conduits to central storage beneath a community stage.

The structure is composed of locally sourced hardwood beams, anchored to withstand cyclones and storm surges. Elevated trusses and tanks introduce varied spatial conditions, creating platforms for play, shaded zones for shelter, and a central path that gestures toward the mountains. Rain pipes curve overhead, recalling the sails of drua boats and offering both visual poetry and functional resilience.

Each module integrates solar generation and water collection with intentional simplicity: no hidden tech, no unnecessary complexity. The batteries and inverters are stored in protected maintenance rooms, while sinks offer direct access to clean water. The system's parts are repairable with local skills and standard tools, and its modularity allows for phased expansion or adaptation.

Sky Letters is a letter written to the future in light and water — an architectural gesture rooted in culture, shaped by climate, and carried by community.

The installation uses conventional high-performance solar modules and fanning rainwater harvesting downspouts as expressive sculptural elements. The shaded interior, adorned with textiles, serves as a space for gathering and celebration.

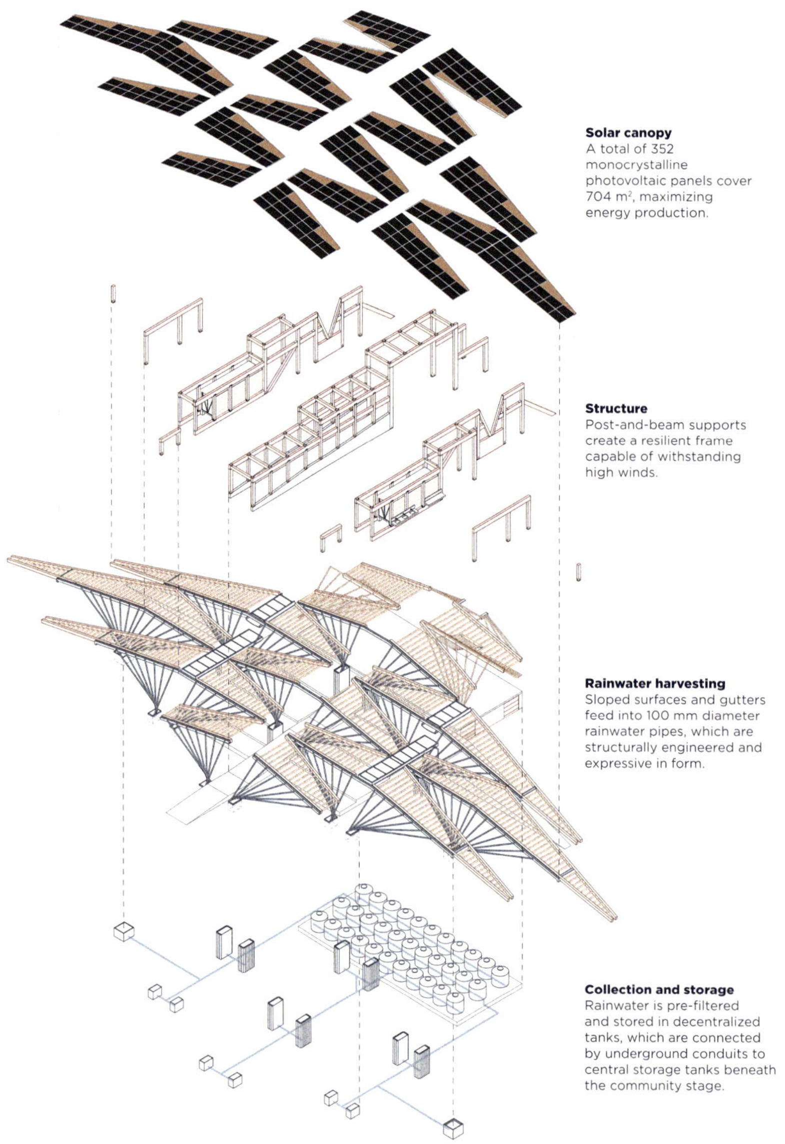
Solar canopy
A total of 352 monocrystalline photovoltaic panels cover 704 m², maximizing energy production.
Structure
Post-and-beam supports create a resilient frame capable of withstanding high winds.
Rainwater harvesting
Sloped surfaces and gutters feed into 100 mm diameter rainwater pipes, which are structurally engineered and expressive in form.
Collection and storage
Rainwater is pre-filtered and stored in decentralized tanks, which are connected by underground conduits to central storage tanks beneath the community stage.

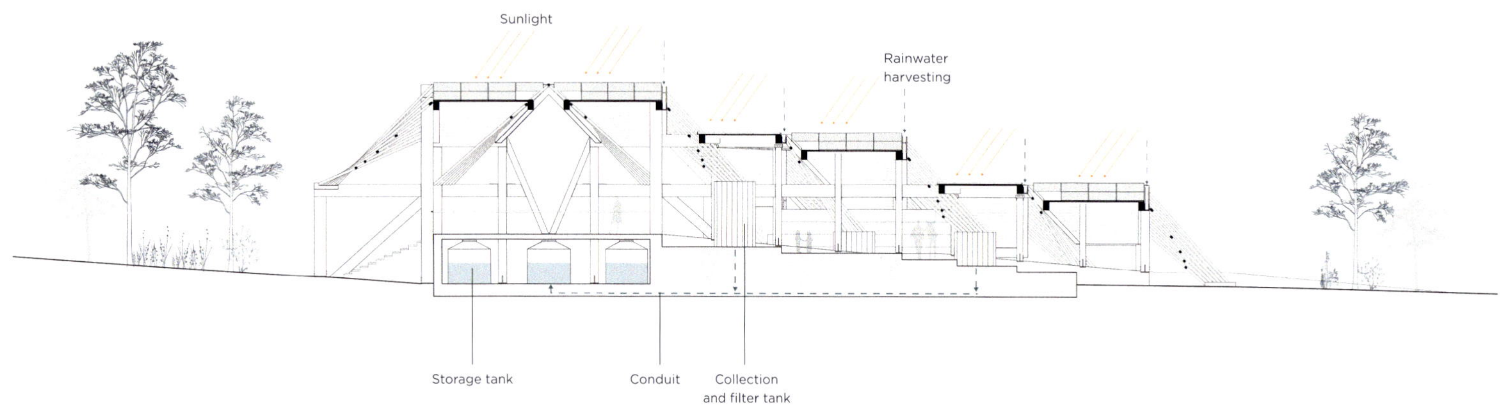
Sunlight
Rainwater harvesting
Storage tank
Conduit
Collection and filter tank

Land Sails

Each year, approximately 232 million liters of rain fall across the Marou Village watershed, with an estimated 28 million liters landing directly within the LAGI 2025 Fiji design site boundary.

DESIGNERS: Karen Curtiss, Mark Myers, Camille Peignet (Red Dot Studio); Lisa M. Farmen, Anika Chakravarti (Aquastry); Henry Gao

TECHNOLOGIES: CIGS thin-film solar photovoltaic, battery energy storage, aquifer recharge, stormwater wetland system, decentralized three-stage water treatment, borehole wells with solar powered pumps

ANNUAL PRODUCTION: 134 MWh of electricity, 8 million liters of filtered water from wetland zone accessed through recharged wells

DESIGN TEAM LOCATION: United States

Land Sails **celebrates Fiji's sailing culture and local knowledge to create an installation of solar sails above Marou Village. The design bridges old and new ways of knowing, offering a regenerative paradigm for progress.**

Sitting quietly on the hillside, *Land Sails* draws from traditional sailing knowledge and land-based practices, merging them with scientific research to generate energy, harvest water, and support habitat for humans and other species.

Land Sails floats above Marou Village like a fleet of migratory birds — solar sails arranged in formation, echoing drua and camakau vessels of Fiji's seafaring heritage. Their triangular silhouettes cast rhythmic shadows across the land, integrating local knowledge of wind, water, and craft into a responsive, regenerative landscape.

Each sail is outfitted with flexible CIGS thin-film photovoltaic panels. Lightweight and shock-resistant, these panels are designed to fold or be lowered in storms, with no risk of microcracking. The fabric is mounted on bamboo or locally sourced hardwood frames, structurally anchored like mangrove roots to resist Category 5 winds. Together, 23 modular sails house 288 panels, generating up to 77 kW of electricity to power pumps, filtration systems, and village energy needs.

The sails shade a new wetland park engineered for aquifer recharge and erosion control. Runoff from Vatu Rua's slopes is fanned across bioswales of native vegetation — slowing water, mitigating flooding, preventing nutrient and soil loss, and creating habitat for pollinators and birds. Below ground, freshwater is directed to boreholes where solar-powered pumps draw it to the surface.

Water is tested and treated through a three-stage system: sediment filtration, arsenic removal, and ultraviolet purification. The result is safe, potable water resilient to climate extremes.

Land Sails creates a living infrastructure of energy, water, and ecology — supporting agriculture, biochar production, and informal gathering under dappled light. The frames are modular and maintainable by local teams. Sails can be folded down or replaced, and the wetland offers long-term stewardship roles for Marou Village residents in ecology, disease prevention, and aquifer management.

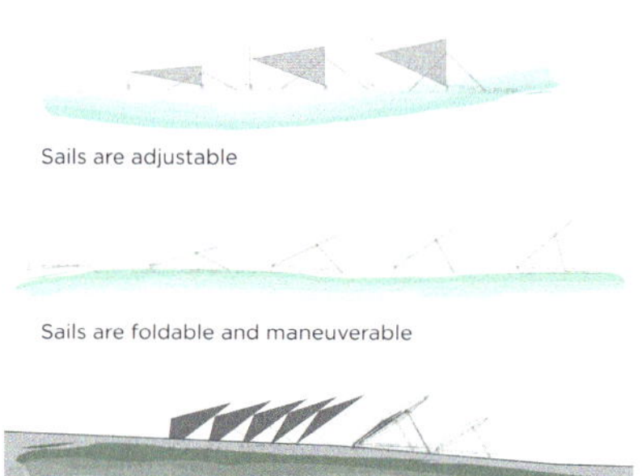

Site section

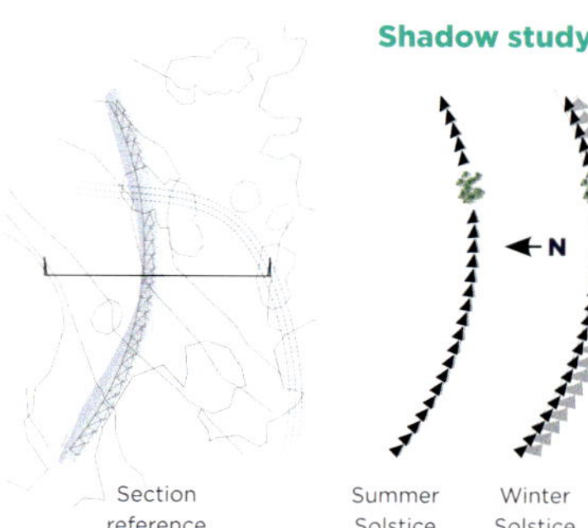

Shadow study

23 modular solar units

The approximately 1.5-hectare percolation area helps retain topsoil and freshwater on the island, reducing stormwater runoff and preventing channel washout.

The system recharges an unconfined aquifer, which serves existing boreholes and prevents saltwater intrusion.

Marou Vula

Shade
Protect the water storage tanks from sunlight with masi patterns using local palm weaving techniques.

Water
Install seven flexible bladder tanks for water storage.

Electricity
Install the custom solar photovoltaic array consisting of 220 modules.

Base
Sculpt the terrain using a small digger to create an 18° slope with an access ramp. Install steps and solar module anchors using locally sourced bamboo half-trunks.

Exploded axonometric view

DESIGNER: Adrien Thivolle

TECHNOLOGIES: solar photovoltaic with custom conducting patterns (similar to Asoleyo Architectural Solar), battery energy storage, rainwater harvesting with fabric-covered bladder storage, erosion control through native planting and coastal composting stations

ANNUAL PRODUCTION: 120 MWh of electricity, 450,000 liters of filtered water

DESIGN TEAM LOCATION: France

Marou Vula draws inspiration from lunar rhythms to shape a decentralized network of energy and water infrastructure across Naviti Island. Its crescent-shaped forms, arranged like moons in orbit, mark a constellation of small-scale, low-tech systems that meet essential needs while celebrating culture, ecology, and community life.

The flagship system, Vula Kaukaua (Energy Moon), combines a solar mini-grid with rainwater harvesting. Photovoltaic panels are arranged in crescent arcs to optimize solar gain throughout the day and reduce the need for battery energy storage. The solar modules themselves are produced with custom patterns created by the community. Rainwater flows into lightweight bladders protected by palm-woven covers. These units are designed for affordability, low maintenance, and ease of installation using local skills.

Each moon-like node is multifunctional, supplying drinking water, irrigation water, and contributing to food production and erosion control. Structures are built from native soil, palm thatch, and artist-designed elements that incorporate traditional Fijian patterns, blending infrastructure and cultural expression.

Marou Vula is deeply participatory, guided by the Fijian principle of *itikotiko*, or local collective action. Residents co-design and construct the systems, using workshops to pass on weaving, masonry, and agricultural skills. Ongoing education, monitoring, and storytelling reinforce community ownership and intergenerational knowledge transfer.

Crescents are not just symbols — they are efficient, modular units that mirror natural processes and minimize resource use. Each one can evolve over time, forming a replicable model for island sustainability.

Marou Vula is a choreography of infrastructure and identity, woven from sunlight, rainfall, and tradition to support life under changing skies.

RIGHT: The circular solar array of the Energy Moon integrates photovoltaic panels and masi-inspired patterns, creating a community space that blends energy generation with cultural expression.

Vula Kau
Vegetable Moons

Vula Kau are crescent-shaped earth mounds distributed along terrain contour lines to retain rainwater and prevent topsoil erosion around the village. They improve soil quality and support the production of local food for both residents and visitors. This half-moon system has been tested in harsh climates and has proven effective in enhancing soil health and increasing agricultural yield.

Vula Kaukaua
Energy Moon

Vula Kaukaua is a low-tech, low-maintenance system for harvesting electricity and water. Set on a 50-meter diameter sloped terrain optimized to an 18° solar angle, the installation combines standard solar panels with rainwater collection infrastructure, storing up to 450 cubic meters of drinkable water. Built from local earth, precast concrete modules, foldable water bladders, and low-cost standard batteries, Vula Kaukaua is designed for ease of transport and assembly in the remote setting of Naviti Island. It also serves as a social space where people gather to harvest water and share kava.

Vula Taqomaka
Protective Compost Moons

Vula Taqomaka are coastal composting prototypes designed to regenerate soil while resisting shoreline erosion. Each 5-meter diameter moon is constructed from woven bamboo and palm leaves and positioned along the coast. Filled daily by local residents with compostable materials, these structures gradually produce fertile soil that supports stabilizing vegetation. Vula Taqomaka play a vital role in protecting both the land and the coastal grave sites of the ancestors who once inhabited it.

Vula Wai
Water Moons

Vula Wai are permeable micro-dams distributed along the streams of the Marou water basin. Designed to slow water flow, they help recharge the water table and mitigate stormwater flooding that contributes to island erosion. Each Vula Wai measures approximately 4 meters in diameter and 0.5 meters in height. Built by the community using local natural materials, the structures are simple to construct but require regular maintenance.

Vula Korala
Coral Moon

Vula Korala is a larger-scale system with the potential to support coral nursery development, contributing in the long term to coastal protection, scientific research, and sustainable tourism.

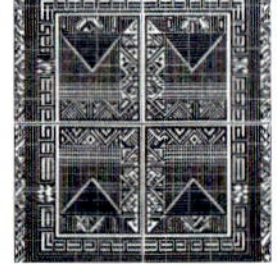
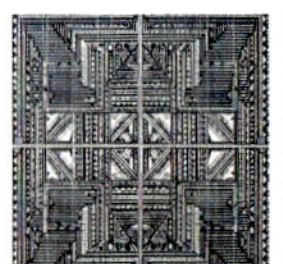
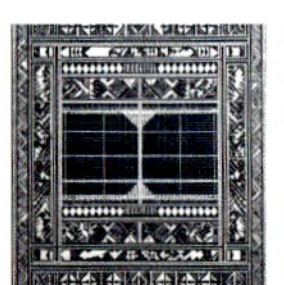
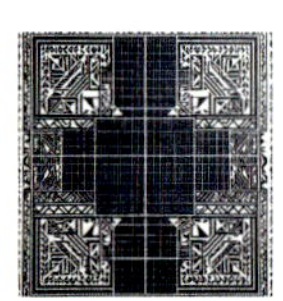

Examples of custom photovoltaic module patterns

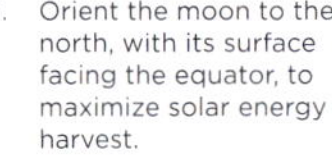

1. Orient the moon to the north, with its surface facing the equator, to maximize solar energy harvest.

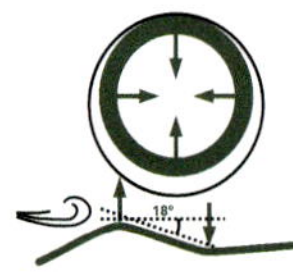

2. Shape the terrain to create an 18° angle and protect the moon from storms.

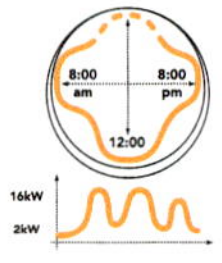

3. Optimize solar panels and battery storage according to Marou Village average hourly consumption.

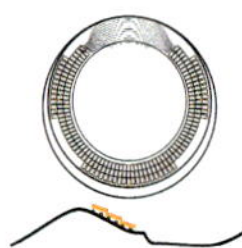

4. Cover the sloped terrain with solar photovoltaic modules anchored on bamboo trunks.

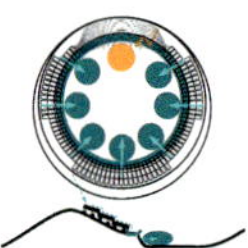

5. Collect and store water in a flexible bladder array, while delivering electricity to the mini-grid and basic battery racks.

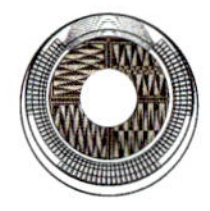

6. Bladders are protected by masi tapa sun covers to limit bacterial growth in the stored water.

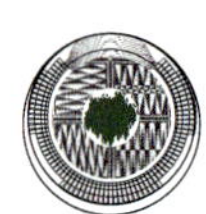

7. Enjoy a central gathering space arranged around a planted garden.

Vula Kaukaua (Energy Moon)

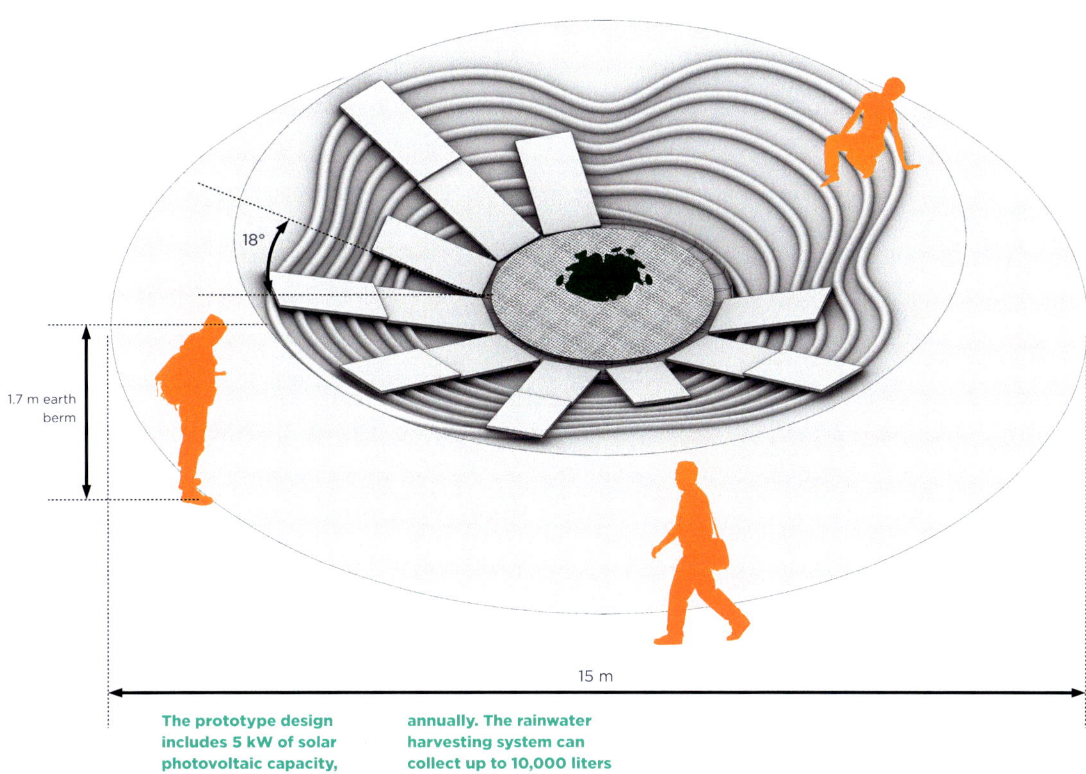

The prototype design includes 5 kW of solar photovoltaic capacity, generating approximately 7 MWh of electricity annually. The rainwater harvesting system can collect up to 10,000 liters per year.

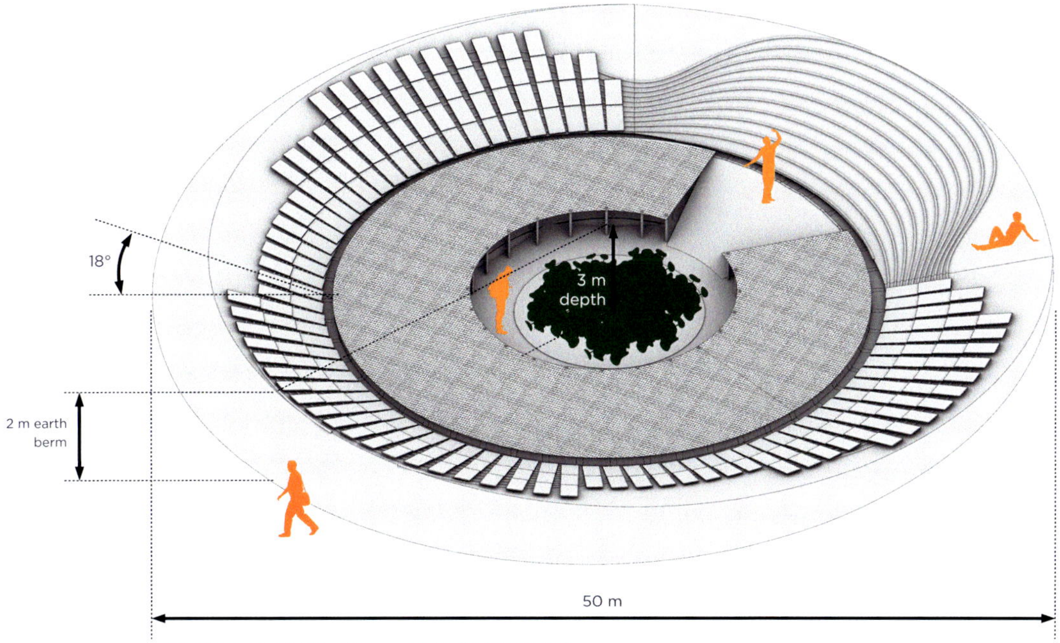

18°
3 m depth
2 m earth berm
50 m

The full-scale pilot design in Marou includes 77 kW of solar photovoltaic capacity, generating an estimated 120 MWh of electricity annually. Integrated rainwater harvesting will provide approximately 450,000 liters of water each year.

Drua

DESIGNERS: Mehrdad Hadighi, Rahman Azari, Hong Wu, Josh Conroy, Hanin Othman, Delaney Minder, John Foreman, Maison Smith, Sarah Renner, Anushka Acharya, Matthew Giarrusso (Penn State Department of Architecture)

TECHNOLOGIES: solar photovoltaic, battery energy storage, biofiltration, aquifer recharge via log dams and timber-constructed water storage vessels

ANNUAL PRODUCTION: 125 MWh of electricity, 4.9 million liters of filtered water

DESIGN TEAM LOCATION: United States

RIGHT: Local rugby players practice in the foreground as the sculptural canopy rises behind them, its undulating timber form blending into the mountainous landscape. Providing shade, renewable energy, and harvested water, the installation serves both community and environment.

Drua brings the wisdom of traditional sailing into dialogue with the future. Drawing from one of the fastest double-hulled sailing vessels ever created, this design uses the form and logic of the drua to weave energy, water, and community into a single regenerative system. Where drua once carried people across oceans, this new vessel helps Marou Village navigate a changing climate, offering resilience by capturing rain, slowing floods, generating power, and sheltering people.

The installation begins in the uplands, where a series of log dams slow seasonal runoff, reduce erosion, and guide water through a rehydrated landscape. This water flows into a bio-retention pond and then into a large-scale biosand filtration system housed in the first of two timber *Drua* hulls. Using layers of sand, gravel, and biological media, the system removes turbidity and pathogens through passive, locally repairable processes.

The second hull stores the treated water — over 4.9 million liters — securing more than five months of reliable supply for the village. Timber construction allows for collective local fabrication, easy maintenance, and long-term stewardship. Together, the hulls form a public deck — a shaded space for ceremony, celebration, and everyday gathering.

Overhead, a fixed 85 kW PV system is mounted on a timber substructure shaped by drua woodworking techniques. It generates enough electricity to meet current needs while providing a margin for future demand. The PV panels also shade the deck and reduce evaporation from the water below.

Drua blends ancestral craft with modern engineering. It is built from knowledge that lives locally, powered by systems that can be maintained by hand. Inspired by a vessel that still speaks to movement and strength, it becomes a new kind of flagship, sailing into a better future.

Set against the backdrop of Vatu Rua, the sculptural canopy arcs over a constructed wetland, integrating energy generation, water harvesting, resilience against flooding, and ecological regeneration within the island's lush landscape.

Reed bed treatment system
Natural sedimentation and biofiltration form the first stage of treatment. Reed beds, planted with native aquatic species, filter out sediment and organic matter through slow percolation across layers of gravel and sand.

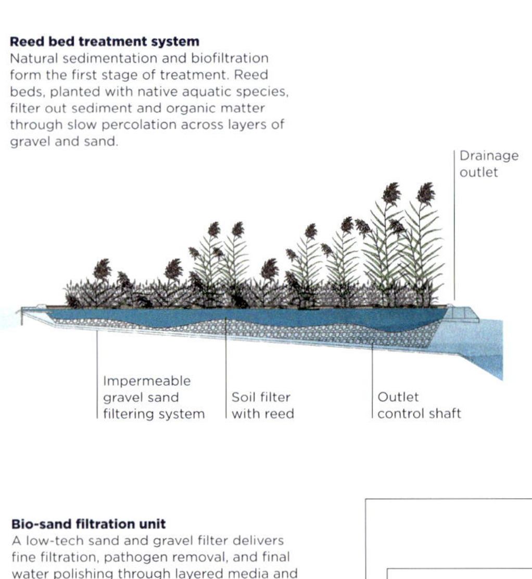

Bioswale pond (hybrid zone)
Following the main reed bed chain, a combined system of flood control, sedimentation, and secondary reed beds slows and buffers water flow. This natural infrastructure enhances filtration, reduces stormwater runoff, and provides an additional layer of ecological treatment through wetland vegetation and microbial processes before the final stage of sand filtration.

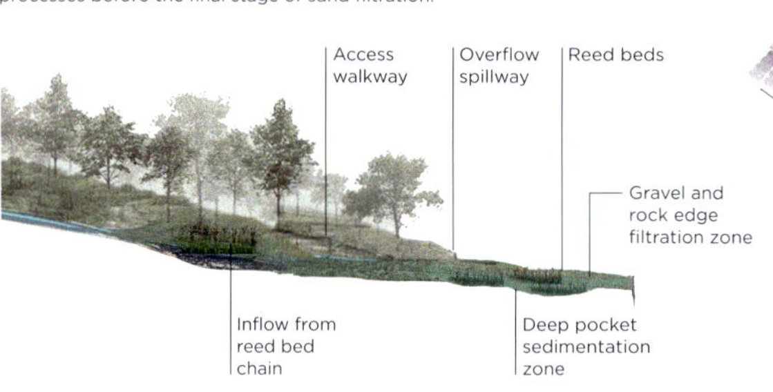

Solar photovoltaic array
A 500 m² photovoltaic system generates renewable electricity to power essential village infrastructure, reduce fossil fuel dependence, and support integrated water-energy resilience.

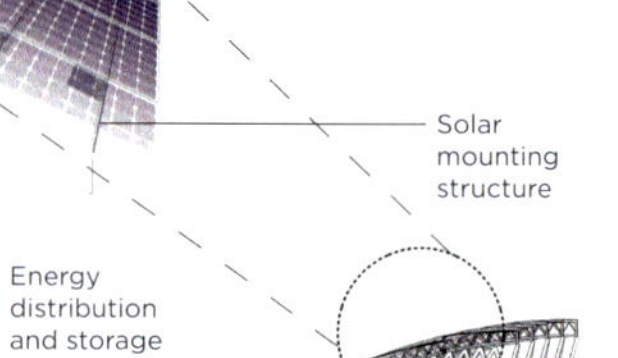

Bio-sand filtration unit
A low-tech sand and gravel filter delivers fine filtration, pathogen removal, and final water polishing through layered media and a biologically active surface film known as the *schmutzdecke*. The system requires no chemicals or external power.

Air gap above water
Prevents overflow, allows for water level adjustments

Diffuser plate
Protects the top of the sand

Standing water layer, clear water (inlet zone)
Keeps biological layer moist and alive

Fine sand layer
Physically removes pathogens and suspended solids

Coarse sand layer
Supports upper sand layers and improves flow distribution

Fine gravel layer
Prevents sand migration and evenly distributes weight and flow

Coarse gravel layer
Acts as drainage base and supports underdrain system

Filter screen

Multi-use pavilion structure
A lightweight wooden pavilion with a concave roof geometry is carefully shaped to maximize solar energy capture and enhance passive climate performance. Photovoltaic panels embedded in the upper roof are angled to collect optimal sunlight throughout the day, generating power for the water treatment system and broader village needs. At the same time, the open, slatted wooden frame channels cooling breezes toward the village, improving thermal comfort in nearby public spaces.

The rainwater harvesting system is a network of precisely positioned gutters and downspouts that capture rainfall from the solar photovoltaic canopy, directing it toward the bioswale pond for filtration, purification, and reuse.

Beneath this shaded canopy, the pavilion creates a welcoming communal area where residents can gather and socialize.

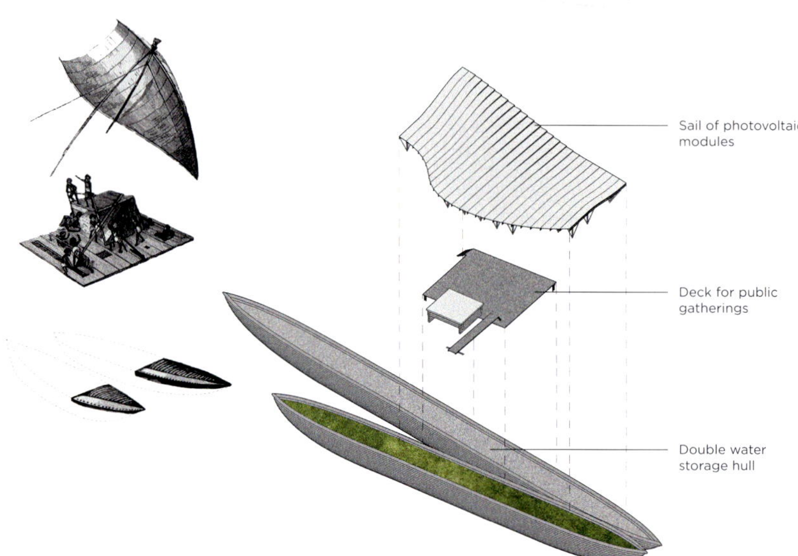

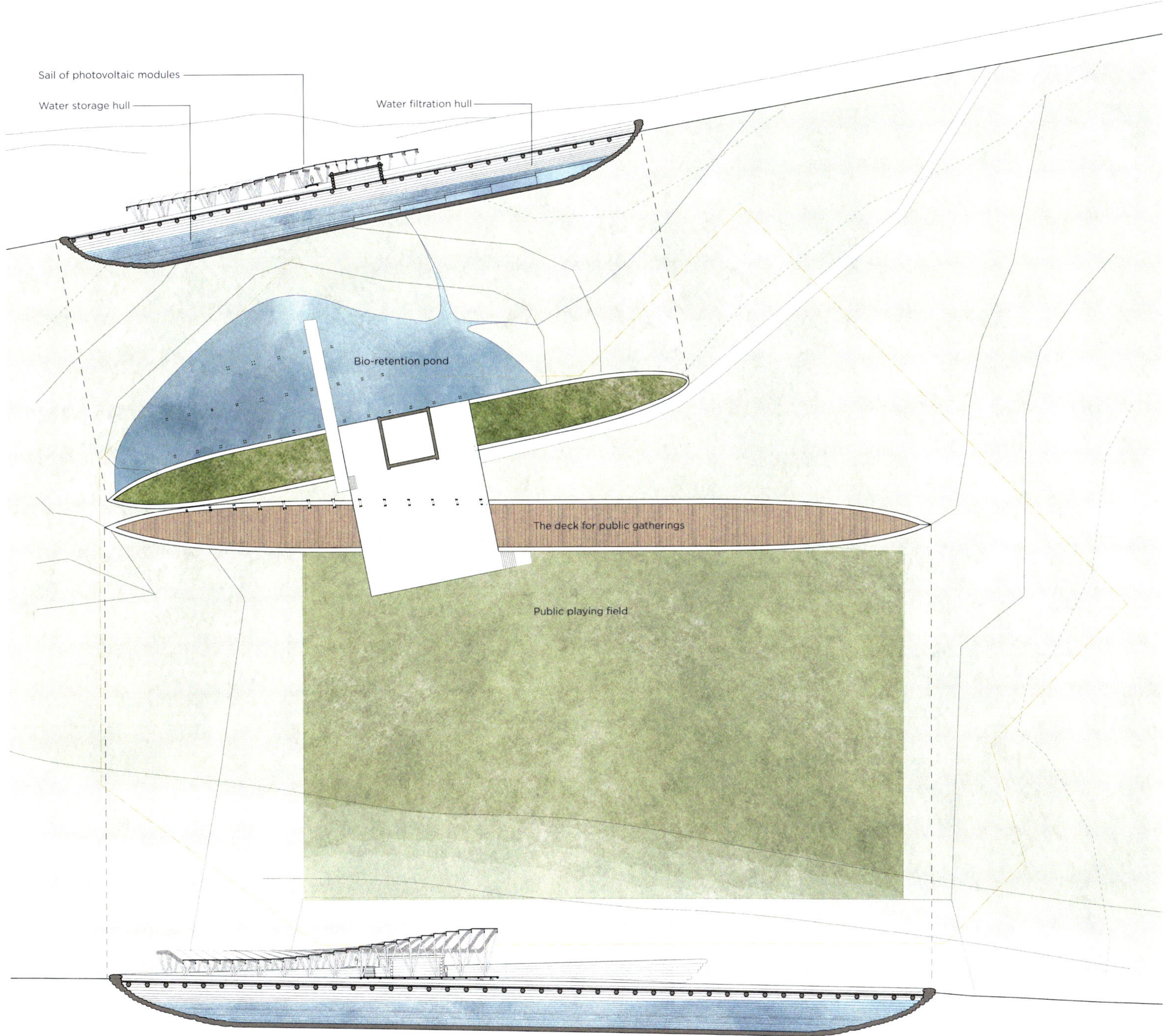
Sail of photovoltaic modules
Water storage hull
Water filtration hull
Bio-retention pond
The deck for public gatherings
Public playing field

Independence

DESIGNERS: Khashayar Ghasemzadeh, Seyede Leila Yousefzadeh Shirazi, Fatemeh Daneshvar, Parimah Nasirzadeh, Seyed Mohammad Erfan Nabavizadeh

TECHNOLOGIES: solar photovoltaic, battery energy storage, modular planter boxes, rainwater harvesting, underground cisterns

ANNUAL PRODUCTION: 250 MWh of electricity, 1 million liters of filtered water

DESIGN TEAM LOCATION: Italy

Inspired by vertical farming and a commitment to soil health and erosion prevention, this raised planting system elevates agriculture off the ground. Each planter features a molded coconut coir liner—breathable, biodegradable, and easily replaceable—supporting clean, efficient growth using collected rainwater.

In *Independence*, sustainability is defined not by permanence, but by how gently a system touches the land. Designed as a raised, modular landscape, this project delivers power, water, and food without excavation or grading, offering a regenerative platform that uplifts the people of Marou while leaving the soil intact.

The system is composed of 105 modular units raised on dry-stacked stone foundations (yavu), each supporting a bamboo-clad solar tower or elevated planter box. Photovoltaic arrays mounted on cyclone-resistant steel frames generate 244 kWh/day, stored in an 860 kWh battery bank built to provide three days of autonomy. The hexagonal solar panels are partially recessed within protective bamboo frames, lowering wind profile and shielding edges from cyclone damage. Local materials — red clay, river stones, natural rope lashings, and bamboo — anchor the structures in place and in culture.

Water harvesting is integrated into each unit. Stormwater is collected via soft canopies and roof drainage into underground tanks or mobile filter carts. A combined storage capacity of up to 1 million liters supports irrigation, cleaning, and emergency supply, with sediment and charcoal filtration ensuring safe use. Overflow paths channel water through planted earthworks to support reforestation and erosion control.

Planter boxes use biodegradable coconut coir liners, geotextiles, and volcanic gravel to grow crops in a low-impact, zero-waste cycle. The raised beds prevent saline intrusion and promote healthy root growth. Coir liners are easily replaced after one or two growing seasons, and all materials—bamboo, melina wood, and coconut fiber—return harmlessly to the Earth.

Independence is built by the people it serves. Its modular, culturally grounded approach allows it to be assembled, maintained, and adapted entirely by local hands. It offers a flexible, future-proof model for off-grid living — one that grows food, captures water, and powers homes, while reinforcing connection to place.

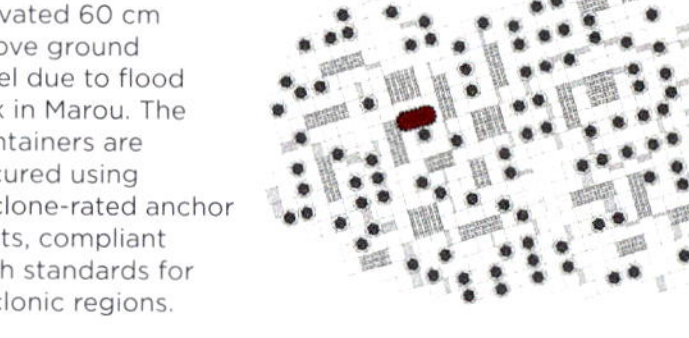

The battery is elevated 60 cm above ground level due to flood risk in Marou. The containers are secured using cyclone-rated anchor bolts, compliant with standards for cyclonic regions.

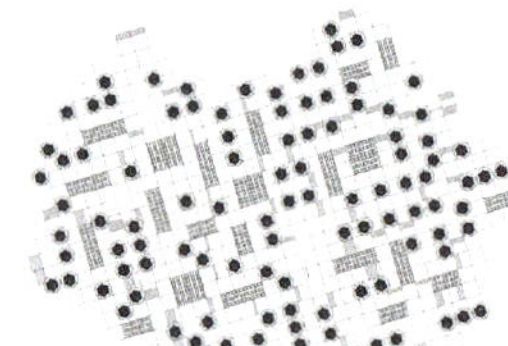

Unused zones are repurposed for sustainable energy generation and regenerative agriculture.

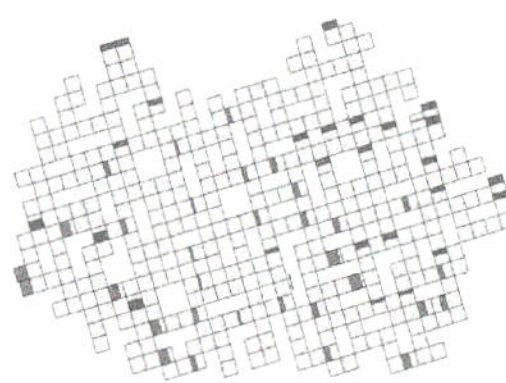

The final grid layout ensures access to all areas of the installation while also shaping spaces for gathering and social interaction.

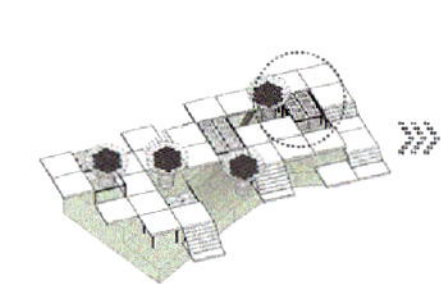

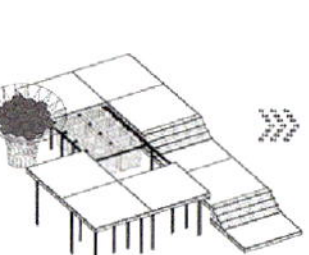

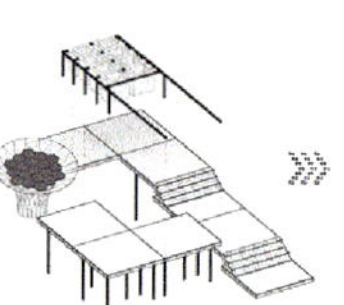

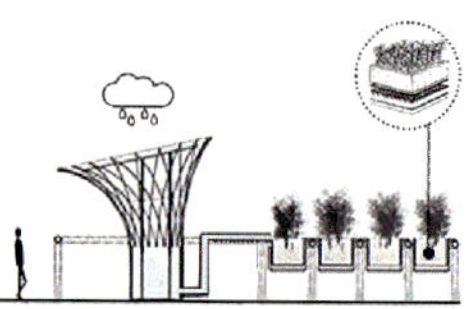

Vanilla Energy

In *Vanilla Energy*, solar arrays are integrated with vertical vanilla cultivation, combining clean energy generation with sustainable agriculture. Rainwater harvesting tanks and shaded community spaces support both ecological and social resilience.

DESIGNERS: Eszter Kardos, Kovács Lőrinc

TECHNOLOGIES: solar photovoltaic, battery energy storage, rainwater harvesting, UV and SODIS water purification, above-ground cisterns, vertical vanilla farming

ANNUAL PRODUCTION: 120 MWh of electricity, 1 million liters of filtered water, 1,000 kilograms of green vanilla beans

DESIGN TEAM LOCATION: Hungary

Vanilla Energy weaves renewable infrastructure with agricultural livelihood, providing an agrivoltaic installation that combines solar energy, water harvesting, and vanilla cultivation under a single modular system. The simple, elegant design delivers clean power and water while offering meaningful employment, sustainable income, and daily engagement with the land.

The system is composed of prefabricated mahogany-framed roof modules tilted at 16° and optimized for solar gain. Each module supports six monocrystalline silicon photovoltaic panels (421-watt each), totaling a 75 kW mini-grid. Solar energy is stored in lithium-ion batteries housed in watertight enclosures, with inverters protected alongside water purification equipment. Rainwater is channeled from panel surfaces into gravity-fed collection tanks with a total storage capacity of 45,000 liters. SODIS purification and optional UV filtration ensure safe, potable supply.

Beneath the solar array lies a commercial-scale vanilla farm. Vanilla vines are grown on vertical supports arranged in a soil-based grid beneath the dappled light of the panels — ideal conditions for the shade-loving plant. A grid of 144 support posts can host 500 vines, producing approximately 1,000 kilograms of green vanilla beans every 8–9 months following the initial establishment period. These yields create an economic engine for the community while promoting biodiversity and soil health.

Each unit can be configured to serve additional needs: dining shelters, rest areas, tool storage, and educational modules for visitors. Assembled side-by-side, the modules form a replicable village-scale system that is adaptable to terrain and growth over time.

Vanilla Energy prioritizes community ownership and low-maintenance design. Timber is locally sourced; workshops train residents in care, assembly, and seasonal cleaning of panels; and maintenance of rainwater and electrical systems are integrated into the farm's daily rhythm.

With every vine and volt, *Vanilla Energy* demonstrates how energy systems can cultivate not only power but also new opportunities.

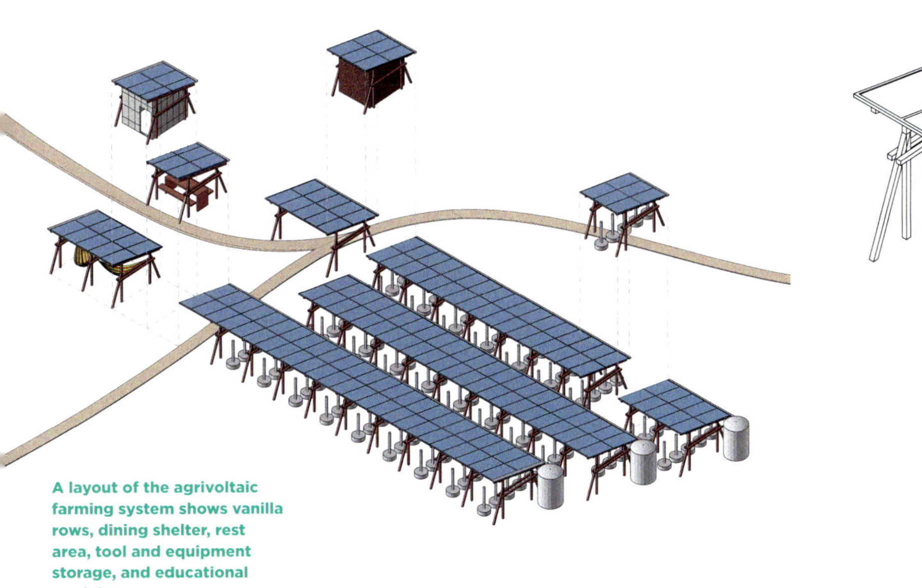

A layout of the agrivoltaic farming system shows vanilla rows, dining shelter, rest area, tool and equipment storage, and educational modules.

One unit

Vertical vanilla farm

Tool storage

Dining area

Rest area

Water intake

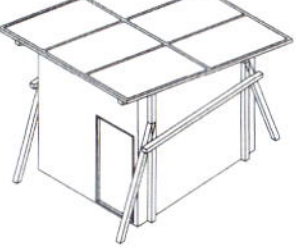

Inverter and battery

Mangrove Bridge

DESIGNERS: Zhida WU, Qihong Wang (WWWorks)

TECHNOLOGIES: solar photovoltaic, battery energy storage, rainwater storage, solar distillation, flexible water storage, community utility resilience hub

ANNUAL PRODUCTION: 120 MWh of electricity, 4 million liters of filtered water

DESIGN TEAM LOCATION: China

RIGHT: Elevated above the floodplain, the linear array integrates solar panels and rainwater harvesting while preserving the natural flow of the watershed. The design unites energy generation, ecological restoration, and climate resilience within the island landscape.

Mangrove Bridge stretches like a living root system between the mountains and sea — a lightweight, elevated structure that captures light, harvests rain, and connects people across terrain and time. Inspired by the adaptive geometries of mangrove roots and the branching networks of coastal wetlands, this biomimetic installation is more than a bridge. It is a community corridor that carries power, water, and people above while restoring ecological flows below.

The tensegrity structure — a dynamic web of steel cables and prefabricated modular frames — minimizes material use while maximizing resilience. Anchored lightly to the landscape, the structure resists heavy winds through pre-tensioned cabling and aerodynamic porosity, allowing wind and stormwater to pass through. A central walkway links public gathering areas, open-air classrooms, farmland, and forest trails, all sheltered beneath a canopy that supports 304 flexible solar modules.

Each of the 32 structural units also functions as a "water stem," harvesting rain into soft-membrane tanks. Excess water flows downhill via gravity-fed yellow pipes into a community utility hub, where solar-powered treatment systems offer clean water, ice production, charging stations, public lighting, and access to digital and financial tools.

Mangrove Bridge is built to be shipped by boat, assembled by hand, and maintained by local residents. Grass mat paving, woven by village artisans, reinforces cultural continuity and offers a platform for storytelling, craft, and commerce. Elevated two and a half meters above ground, the bridge requires minimal excavation and preserves wildlife corridors and hydrology.

Mangrove Bridge is an infrastructure of connection — linking ecology and energy, learning and livelihood, resilience and ritual. It reimagines regenerative infrastructures not as static machines, but as places of participation.

Photovoltaic structures span both water and land, creating shaded community spaces, protected agriculture, and habitat restoration zones.

The lightweight canopy integrates solar generation, rainwater harvesting, and passive cooling, while the elevated design allows for natural water flow beneath.

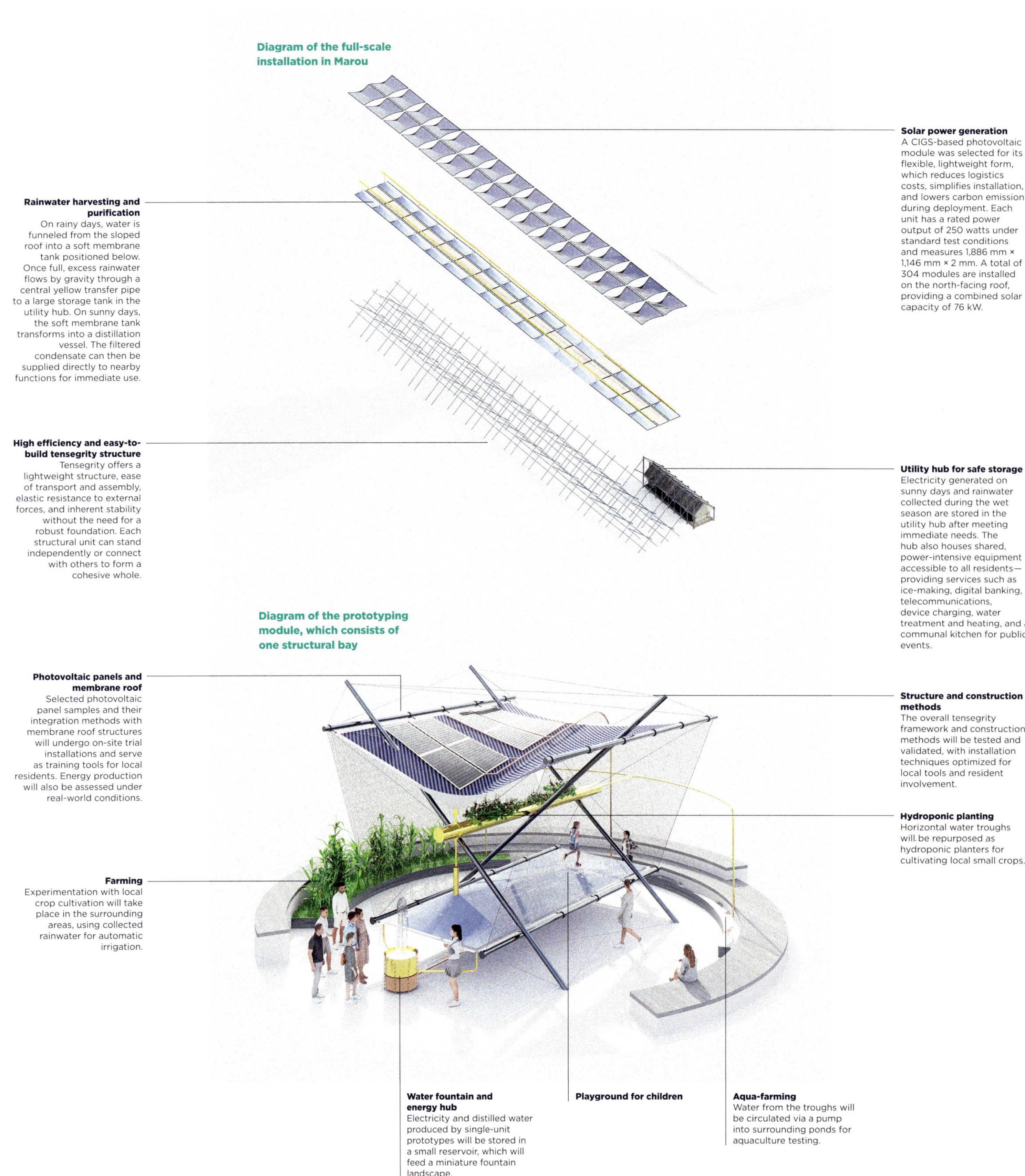
Diagram of the full-scale installation in Marou
Solar power generation
A CIGS-based photovoltaic module was selected for its flexible, lightweight form, which reduces logistics costs, simplifies installation, and lowers carbon emissions during deployment. Each unit has a rated power output of 250 watts under standard test conditions and measures 1,886 mm × 1,146 mm × 2 mm. A total of 304 modules are installed on the north-facing roof, providing a combined solar capacity of 76 kW.
Rainwater harvesting and purification
On rainy days, water is funneled from the sloped roof into a soft membrane tank positioned below. Once full, excess rainwater flows by gravity through a central yellow transfer pipe to a large storage tank in the utility hub. On sunny days, the soft membrane tank transforms into a distillation vessel. The filtered condensate can then be supplied directly to nearby functions for immediate use.
High efficiency and easy-to-build tensegrity structure
Tensegrity offers a lightweight structure, ease of transport and assembly, elastic resistance to external forces, and inherent stability without the need for a robust foundation. Each structural unit can stand independently or connect with others to form a cohesive whole.
Utility hub for safe storage
Electricity generated on sunny days and rainwater collected during the wet season are stored in the utility hub after meeting immediate needs. The hub also houses shared, power-intensive equipment accessible to all residents—providing services such as ice-making, digital banking, telecommunications, device charging, water treatment and heating, and a communal kitchen for public events.
Diagram of the prototyping module, which consists of one structural bay
Photovoltaic panels and membrane roof
Selected photovoltaic panel samples and their integration methods with membrane roof structures will undergo on-site trial installations and serve as training tools for local residents. Energy production will also be assessed under real-world conditions.
Structure and construction methods
The overall tensegrity framework and construction methods will be tested and validated, with installation techniques optimized for local tools and resident involvement.
Hydroponic planting
Horizontal water troughs will be repurposed as hydroponic planters for cultivating local small crops.
Farming
Experimentation with local crop cultivation will take place in the surrounding areas, using collected rainwater for automatic irrigation.
Water fountain and energy hub
Electricity and distilled water produced by single-unit prototypes will be stored in a small reservoir, which will feed a miniature fountain landscape.
Playground for children
Aqua-farming
Water from the troughs will be circulated via a pump into surrounding ponds for aquaculture testing.

The Drua Fleet of Energy

RIGHT: Three solar arrays sit within the landscape. The bold structures integrate clean energy production with shaded community gathering spaces.

DESIGNERS: Claire Benson (SDG Changemakers & OraSoil), Carolyn Hill (Waikato University), Thanh Nguyen (BECA), Supon Manuranga

TECHNOLOGIES: solar photovoltaic, battery energy storage, dual-stream rainwater harvesting, biofiltration, above-ground cisterns, micro-enterprise hubs

ANNUAL PRODUCTION: 183 MWh of electricity, 600,000 liters of filtered water

DESIGN TEAM LOCATION: New Zealand

The Drua Fleet of Energy sails the treetops above Marou like a constellation of ancestral vessels — six towering lateen solar sails inspired by the Fijian drua. Once the most advanced seafaring canoe in the Pacific, the drua now returns as a regenerative force — delivering energy, water, and livelihoods through a modular, cyclone-resilient system deeply rooted in place.

Each sail structure rests on triangulated timber struts and interlocking lattice roofs made from coconut fiber and recycled plastic composites. Dual-glass PV modules (124.2 kW total) power 67 households and two anchor micro-enterprises — a Food Processing Hub and a Fiber Hub — via a smart mini-grid with hybrid inverters, lithium iron phosphate batteries, and load optimization.

Rainwater is harvested from each sail's approximately 100 m^2 roof and filtered for drinking via a dual-stream system: 30,000-liter UV-stabilized tanks for potable water and 150,000-liter stormwater reservoirs for irrigation, fiber processing, and sanitation. Nature-based filtration through coir-lined swales and vetiver grasses improves water quality and recharges groundwater.

At ground level, coconut-based intercropping grids combine staples, like cassava and banana, with botanicals, such as turmeric and lemongrass. Agroforestry supports biochar and essential oil production, while swales, bunds, and contour planting manage runoff and erosion. Processing hubs turn coconut husks into coir mats, ropes, and cocopeat for soil restoration, closing loops and reducing plastic waste.

Each sail hosts a specialized function: energy storage, food production, fiber processing, regenerative tourism, or community gathering. Visitors engage with clean-energy-powered kitchens, water distillation, and craft-making — linking ancestral knowledge to new enterprise.

Managed by a Community Energy & Enterprise Cooperative, the system's governance includes local training, performance-based tariffs, and smart metering.

The integrated systems of *The Drua Fleet of Energy* demonstrate how culturally rooted design and advanced technology can deliver clean energy and water while supporting livelihoods in small island communities.

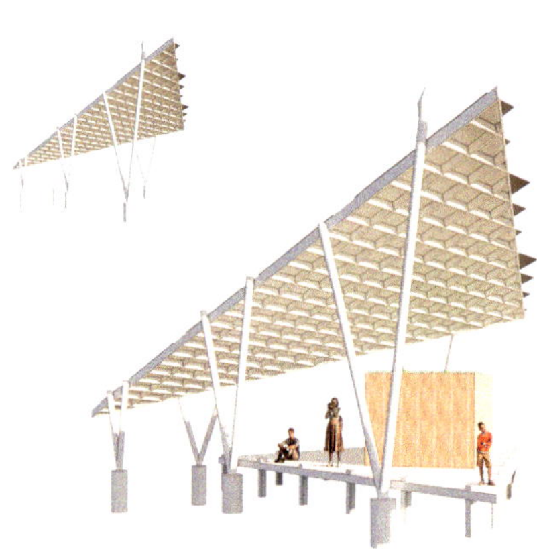

Typical units with solar photovoltaic sail

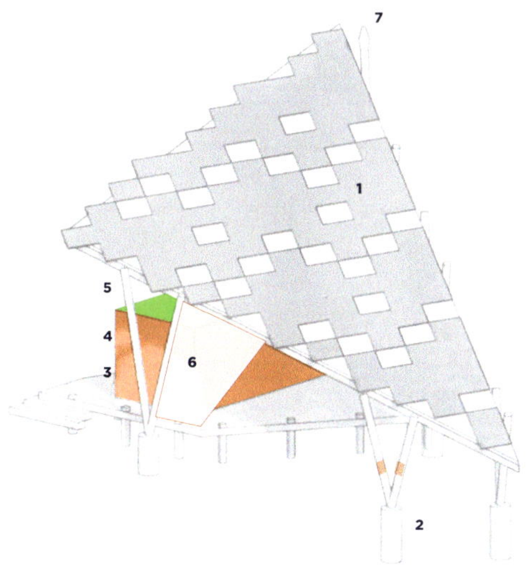

The prototype phase includes constructing a single lateen sail to demonstrate and test the system's integrated functions: solar energy generation, rainwater harvesting, regenerative agriculture, and productive-use enterprise. This prototype unit is designed for disassembly and relocation as necessary.

Key components

1. **Solar sail system**
   Photovoltaic panels are mounted on a solid roof supported by a honeycomb structure. Each solar sail provides an estimated peak output of 20 kW and is oriented to optimize energy production for the specific site. The roof system also collects rainwater, channeling it into the water infrastructure hub.

2. **Main structure**
   The solar sail is supported by a five-post V-shaped timber biocomposite structure with engineered footings designed to suit local soil conditions and cyclone loads. Decorative patterns around the base of each column will be crafted on site by local artisans.

3. **Elevated platform**
   An elevated platform made from biocomposite timber planks supports various production and infrastructure hubs. The raised design also offers flood protection for equipment.

4. **Production or infrastructure hub**
   Various types of prefabricated production or infrastructure hubs can be installed to meet the specific needs of each location. Both the hub and elevated platform can be added at a later stage if required. Exterior panels can be customized with local decorative elements.

5. **Green roof**
   A green roof installed on top of the prefabricated unit provides additional cooling insulation.

6. **Coconut-fiber screen**
   An optional coconut-fiber woven screen can be added to provide additional sun shading. The weaving pattern will be created by members of the local community.

7. **Decorative mast head**
   The biocomposite masthead is 3D-printed and designed to be co-created with the community.

Prototyping diagram

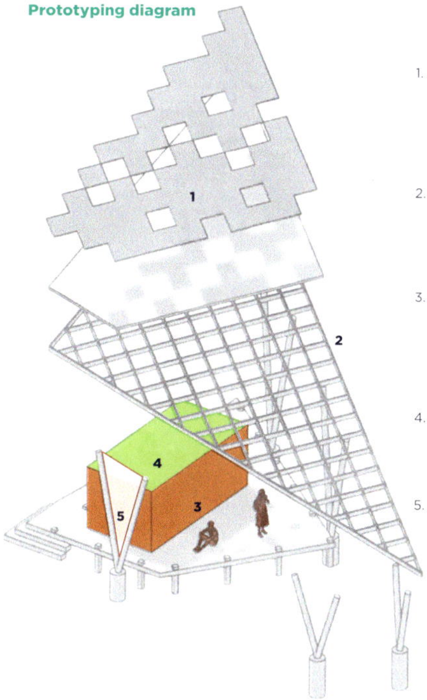

1. One-third of the roof structure is clad in a solar photovoltaic array to test technical performance and supply power to the mini processing unit.
2. A full lateen sail and main structural unit are included to visually demonstrate the full scale of the proposed design.
3. One mini anchor enterprise—either a micro food processing unit or a fiber hub module—is selected through community decision-making.
4. A green roof installed above the processing unit for insulation and coir-based water filtration system.
5. Locally woven coconut-fiber weather screens

10 m × 10 m food forest layout

1. Coconut
2. Banana
3. Papaya
4. Vitiver grass
5. Lemon grass
6. Pigeon pea
7. Bele
8. Chillies, ginger, turmeric, eggplant

Elevation of a typical unit

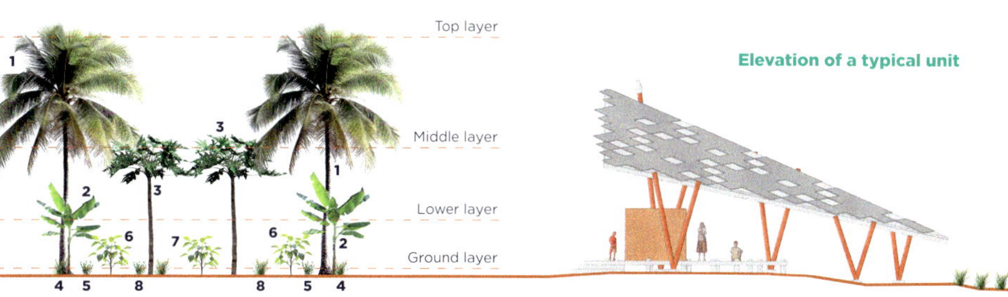

Stormwater swale
Nature-based water filtration system

Vanua Sun-Well
Building Community with Water & Energy

Aerial view of educational module

Perspective view of approach from village

DESIGNERS: Evan Shieh, Dongsei Kim, Clarke Snell, Kendal Eastwood, Elise Park, Lily Kljyan, Anthony Baio (New York Institute of Technology)

TECHNOLOGIES: solar photovoltaic, battery energy storage, rainwater harvesting, UV water purification, above-ground cisterns

ANNUAL PRODUCTION: 183 MWh of electricity, 1.5 million liters of filtered water

DESIGN TEAM LOCATION: United States

RIGHT: ***Vanua Sun-Well*** **creates a multifunctional community space where energy, water, food, and culture converge. Shaded by solar canopies, residents gather to garden, cook, and share daily life, supported by decentralized water and energy systems that foster resilience and self-sufficiency.**

Vanua Sun-Well reimagines the ancient gathering place — the village well — as a modern nexus for energy, water, and communal life. Inspired by the Fijian concept of *vanua* — the unity of land, people, and spirit — this design proposes a modular system of solar-powered rain-harvesting structures that perform essential functions while anchoring collective identity and interaction.

Each unit resembles a branching tree or butterfly in profile, drawing from vernacular Fijian construction: yavu (foundation), lalaga (woven wall), doka (roof), and vakasobuduru (first post). The roof's butterfly form supports photovoltaic panels and directs rainfall into a 4,000-liter food-grade cistern at its base. Shaded cisterns collect between 3,400 and 11,400 liters of rainwater per month, filtered through a passive solids system and treated by a solar-powered UV purifier.

A total of 19 units, arranged in circular arrays, form the complete installation, producing resilient clean electricity and drinking water. Each unit's modular slab foundation contains simple connection points for vertical members, reducing construction time and site disturbance. Foundations are pinned to the ground to resist shear and uplift, and filled cisterns offer additional stability.

Each unit also includes customizable base components for community-determined uses: benches, tables, showers, swings, or storage that transform utility into daily experience. The design encourages local material use, from bamboo screens to native timber, and invites residents to add new features over time.

As the first prototype is built, it becomes the *vakasobuduru* — the ceremonial start of a shared journey. Maintenance tasks, like panel cleaning and cistern checks, become moments of participation, reinforced through community training and celebration.

Vanua Sun-Well is a living network of radiant, rain-fed modules powering daily life in Marou Village.

Vanua Sun-Well Building Community with Water & Energy
(continued)

Exploded axonometric

Solar collection
A single fully-outfitted "tree" produces 10,000 kWh per year.

Water collection
Each cistern will collect 80,000 liters per year and is configurable to provide drinking water with overflow for irrigation and aquaponics.

Modular structure
A prefabricated kit of parts—including a concrete pad with integrated sleeves—enables quick, measurement-free assembly on site.

Customizable bases
Interchangeable base modules are designed to support a variety of social activities, with configurations to be customized by the community.

Community cores
Two central gathering zones are designed to host larger communal activities such as amphitheater events, a central fire pit, playgrounds, or outdoor classrooms.

Complete assembly

Scalability
The design includes expandable zones for community gardening and farming.

Site boundary

N

Existing rainwater swale

Unit configurations

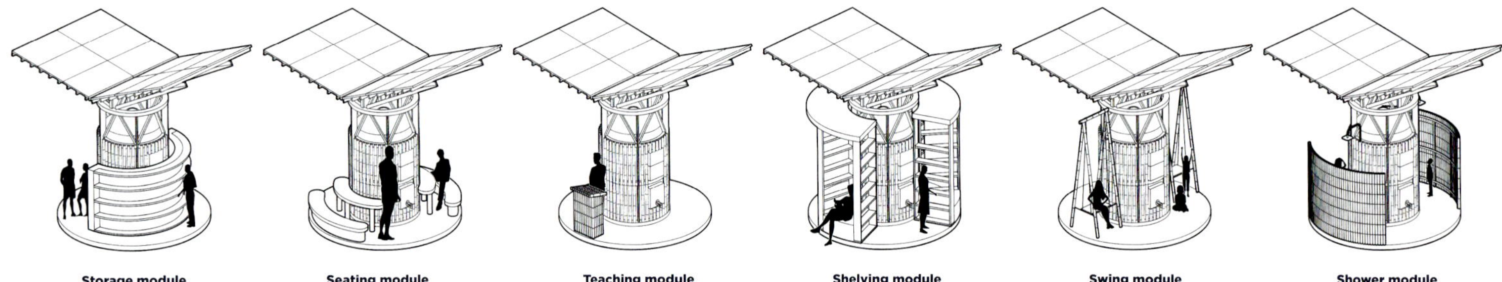

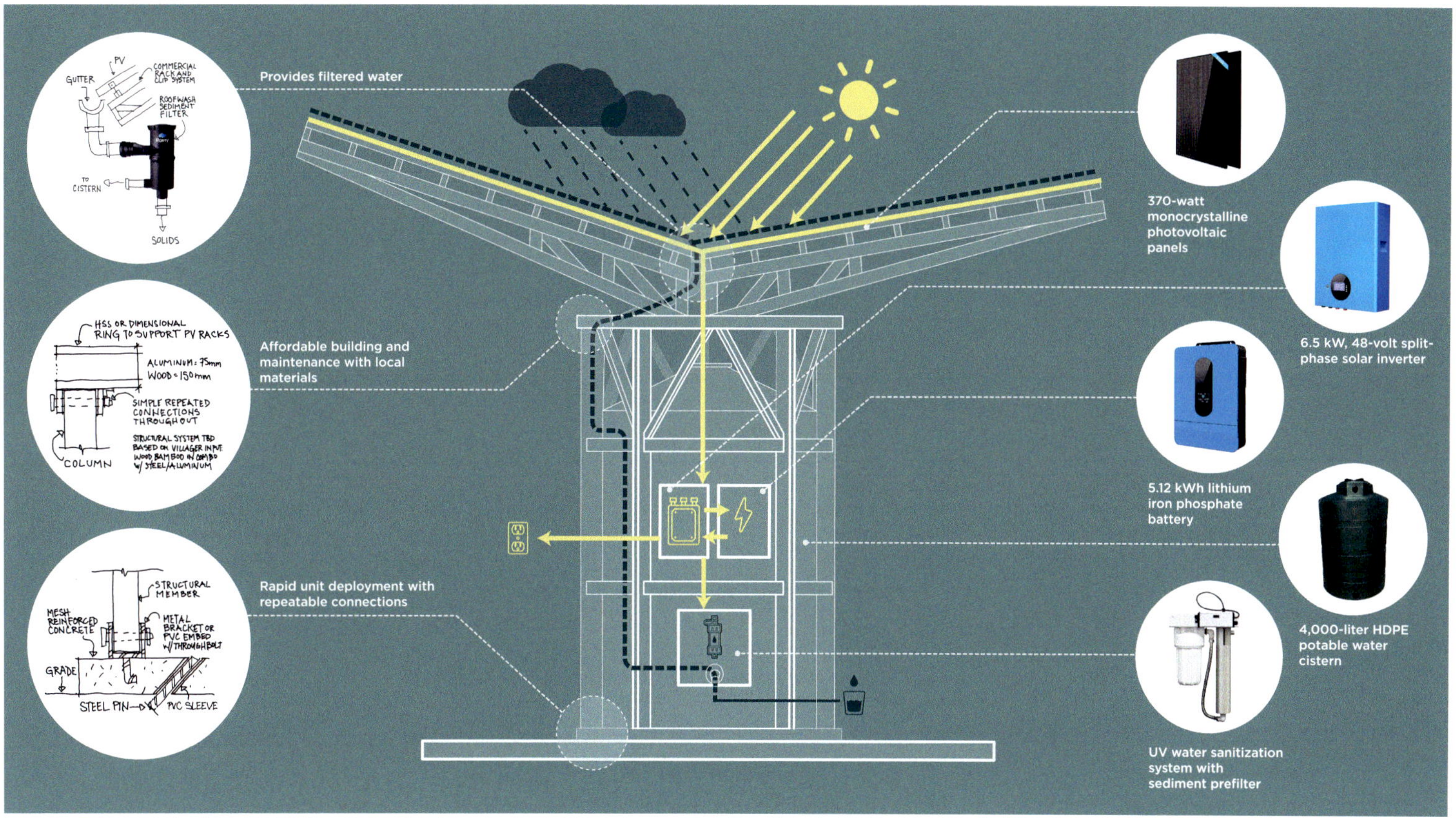

GUTTER
PV
COMMERCIAL RACK AND CLIP SYSTEM
ROOFWASH SEDIMENT FILTER
TO CISTERN
SOLIDS

Provides filtered water

HSS OR DIMENSIONAL RING TO SUPPORT PV RACKS
ALUMINUM: 75mm
WOOD: 150mm
SIMPLE REPEATED CONNECTIONS THROUGHOUT
STRUCTURAL SYSTEM TBD BASED ON VILLAGER INPUT WOOD, BAMBOO OR COMBO W/ STEEL/ALUMINUM
COLUMN

Affordable building and maintenance with local materials

STRUCTURAL MEMBER
MESH REINFORCED CONCRETE
METAL BRACKET OR PVC EMBED W/ THROUGH BOLT
GRADE
STEEL PIN
PVC SLEEVE

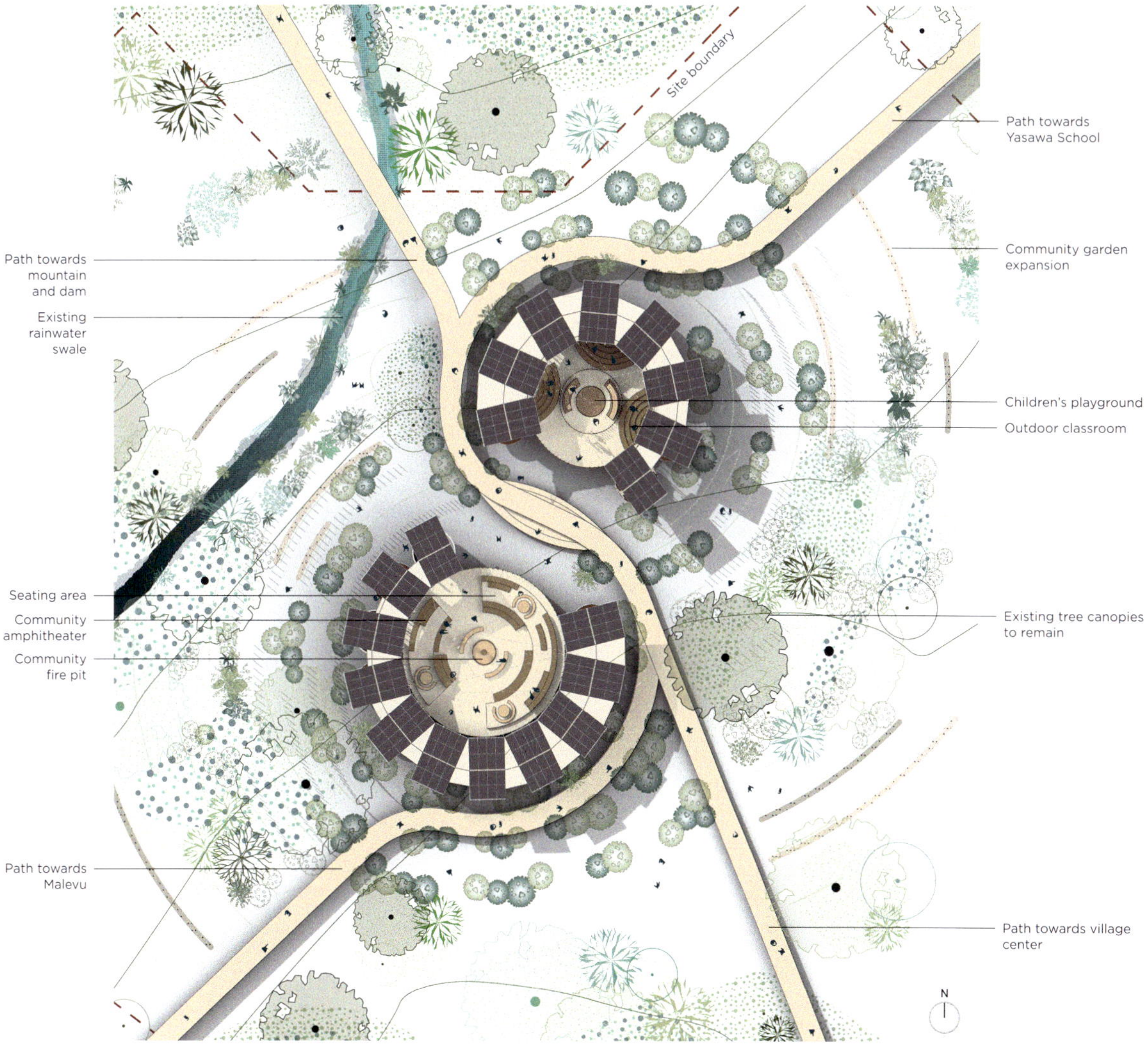

Rapid unit deployment with repeatable connections

370-watt monocrystalline photovoltaic panels

6.5 kW, 48-volt split-phase solar inverter

5.12 kWh lithium iron phosphate battery

4,000-liter HDPE potable water cistern

UV water sanitization system with sediment prefilter

Site boundary

Path towards Yasawa School

Path towards mountain and dam

Community garden expansion

Existing rainwater swale

Children's playground

Outdoor classroom

Seating area

Community amphitheater

Community fire pit

Existing tree canopies to remain

Path towards Malevu

Path towards village center

N

Marou
The Power of Community

The Energy Towers reach for the sky as integrated systems for solar and atmospheric water harvesting.

DESIGNERS: Grigorii Matiunin, Vladislav Larunin

TECHNOLOGIES: solar photovoltaic, fog and rainwater harvesting, helophyte filtration, water storage reservoir, biogas system, thermal sand battery

ANNUAL PRODUCTION: 120 MWh of electricity, 850,000 liters of filtered water

DESIGN TEAM LOCATION: Czech Republic

RIGHT: Rising like woven sails, the Energy Towers honor the collective spirit of Marou through soaring timber forms that harvest wind, sun, and rain. The sculptural structure serves as both energy infrastructure and a powerful symbol of cultural resilience.

Marou: The Power of Community transforms a remote village on Naviti Island into a model for regenerative island infrastructure — one that braids solar power, water harvesting, food systems, regeneration, and cultural gathering into a cohesive, community-led landscape.

At its heart are three Energy Towers inspired by the Fijian bure kalou and traditional sailing forms. Their north-facing facades support photovoltaic panels, while outer mesh surfaces collect both rain and fog. The towers provide indoor spaces for meetings, learning, and celebration, and serve as anchor points for the site's energy and water systems.

Water is harvested from rain, atmospheric vapor, and surface runoff. It flows through a gravity-fed network of ponds where helophyte filters — sand ponds planted with reeds — remove impurities. The ponds double as aquaculture for fish and crabs. Final storage ponds feed into an ozone-based purification system. Purified water supports household use, irrigation, and livestock. Adjacent food gardens grow taro, cassava, greens, and yams, nourished by organic compost and a decentralized biogas system fueled by human and agricultural waste.

Solar panels on the towers and community buildings generate electricity that is stored in thermal batteries for long-term reliability in tropical conditions. While the integrated energy storage can provide electricity throughout most nights, the biogas system powers an auxiliary generator during overcast periods while also producing fertilizer for use across the site.

Construction relies on local knowledge and materials — bamboo, thatch, timber, clay, and stone, assembled with coconut-fiber lashings and glue-laminated framing. Imported components are minimized and chosen for durability.

The entire system is managed by the community through training, workshops, and hands-on engagement. Buildings and landscapes are designed for shared use and adaptation over time.

View to the community center through the fog net

A passenger in a small plane takes a photo of the artwork from their window seat, capturing the sail gestures and the biofiltration pond shaped like the hull of a ship.

Viewed from the base, the Energy Tower reveals its spiraling sculptural form rising toward the sky.

The biodigester housing is inspired by traditional Fijian architecture.

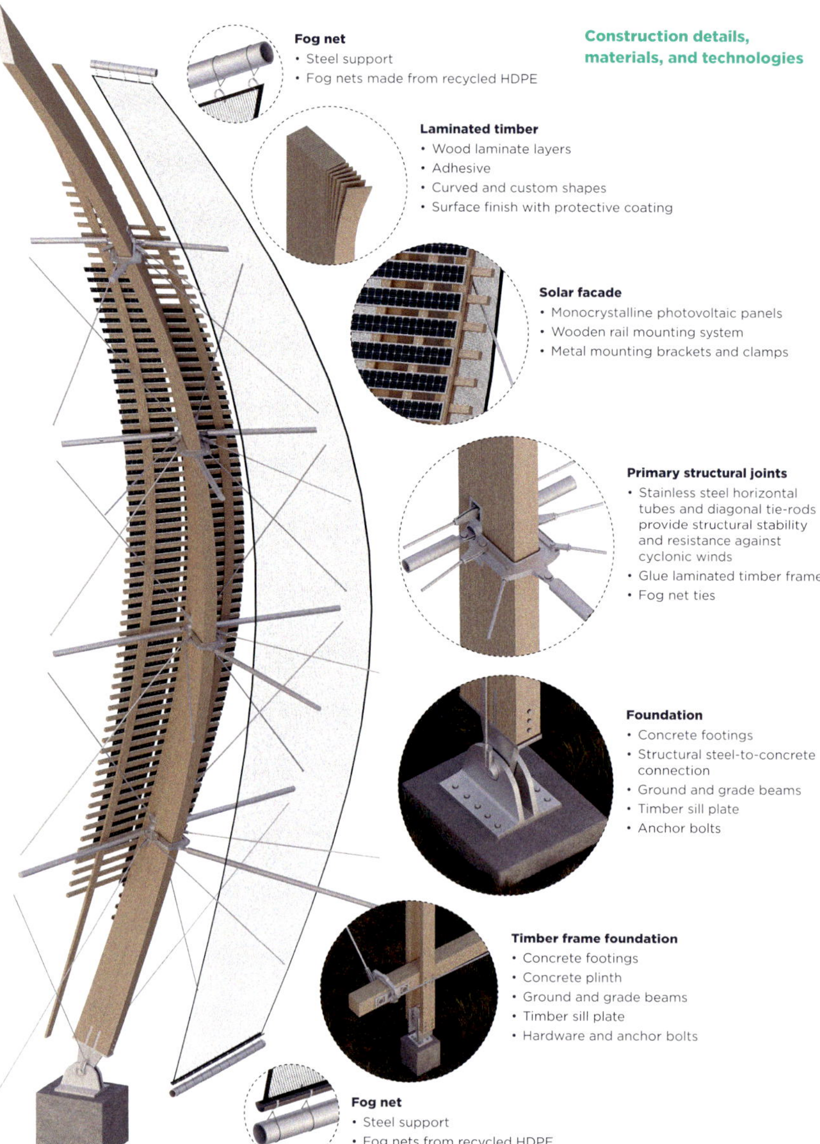

Aerial view with key components highlighted

1. Energy towers
The project's central feature draws inspiration from traditional bure kalou structures and Fijian boats, combining solar energy production and water harvesting in a climate-resilient form. Each tower features a north-facing facade equipped with solar panels, while the outer surface is wrapped in a specialized mesh designed to capture both rain and fog. Inside, the towers offer flexible spaces for community gatherings, workshops, and shelter.

2. Water filtration unit
The ozone-based filtration system makes rainwater safe for drinking.

3. Water storage
The system consists of four interconnected ponds that naturally filter and manage water. The first pond (3.1) integrates a helophyte filter with a fish farm, using wetland plants to purify incoming water. The next two ponds (3.2 and 3.3) support aquaculture and crab farming, extending the system's productive capacity. The final pond stores clean water for irrigation and other non-potable uses. Excess water is discharged through gravity-fed pipes, maintaining a low-energy, self-regulating cycle.

4. Seasonal garden
Designated plots allow residents to cultivate local crops such as cassava, taro, sweet potatoes, bananas, and leafy greens. These fields are irrigated with stored water from the pond system, ensuring resilience during dry seasons. Organic farm waste is repurposed for biogas production or used as feed for animals and insects—supporting a circular system that minimizes waste and strengthens food security.

5. Biowaste
All organic, human, and animal waste is collected and processed on site. Depending on its type and quality, waste is converted into natural fertilizer, used for biogas production, or repurposed as feed for animals and insects—ensuring that nothing is wasted and all resources contribute to the village ecosystem.

6. Insect farm
Insect and bee farms support food systems and biodiversity. Bees aid pollination and honey production, while insects process waste and provide animal feed and fishing bait.

7. Livestock
Pigs and chickens supply eggs and meat, while their waste is reused for fertilizer or biogas, supporting a closed-loop system.

8. Biogas digester
The biogas digester converts organic waste—from animals, agriculture, and households—into renewable energy and nutrient-rich fertilizer, reducing reliance on external fuels and closing local resource loops.

9. Biogas storage
Biogas storage holds gas from the digester, offering backup energy for cooking and lighting when solar power is low.

10. Biogas generator
The biogas generator converts stored gas into electricity, providing an alternative energy source during cloudy days or peak demand.

11. Electricity storage
The electricity storage system uses molten salt or sand batteries to store excess energy, ensuring reliable power supply during the night or during cloudy periods.

12. Public toilet
Public toilets and showers offer basic hygiene, with waste used for biogas energy.

13. Community center
The community center features a solar panel roof and serves as a flexible indoor space for gatherings, education, and cultural activities.

Meke na Mana
The Power Dance

RIGHT: Two *Meke na Mana* sculptures are seen at night, male and female dancers frozen in time and connected through space.

DESIGNERS: Valentina Valero Camargo, Ricardo Andrés Ibañez, Valentina González Moreno, Mario Fernando Ovalle, Juan Mauricio Rodríguez Rivera, Magda Sofía Jiménez Baquero, Diego Alejandro Puentes Aguilera

TECHNOLOGIES: solar photovoltaic, battery energy storage, rainwater harvesting with biofiltration, underground cisterns

ANNUAL PRODUCTION: 120 MWh of electricity, 16,000 liters of filtered water

DESIGN TEAM LOCATION: Colombia

Meke na Mana reimagines architecture as performance — an ensemble of sculptural forms that channel solar energy, water, and cultural memory through movement. Inspired by traditional Fijian dance, the installation transforms choreographic gestures into inhabitable structures that generate power, offer shade, and create space for communal gathering.

Located along the path connecting Marou Village to the foothills of Vatu Rua, the sculptures — abstracted figures of male and female dancers — trace arcs across a symbolic dance floor. These trajectories define plazas, thresholds, and shaded zones for celebration, rest, and reflection. As the figures "move," they also collect: solar panels integrated into their forms generate electricity for the village, while rainwater-harvesting roofs direct water to biofiltration beds and underground tanks. Four male and four female modules form the full array. Together, they provide enough solar energy to meet the needs of Marou's 67 households.

Constructed from lightweight, modular components with simple joints, *Meke na Mana* is designed for local assembly and long-term community stewardship. The system minimizes material use while maximizing spatial impact, elevating sustainability to a performance art.

As people move through the installation, they do not simply observe it — they participate in it. Light, shadow, rhythm, and resources flow together across a site that is both infrastructure and stage. *Meke na Mana* embodies the Fijian concept of *mana* — spiritual power grounded in land, culture, and collective presence.

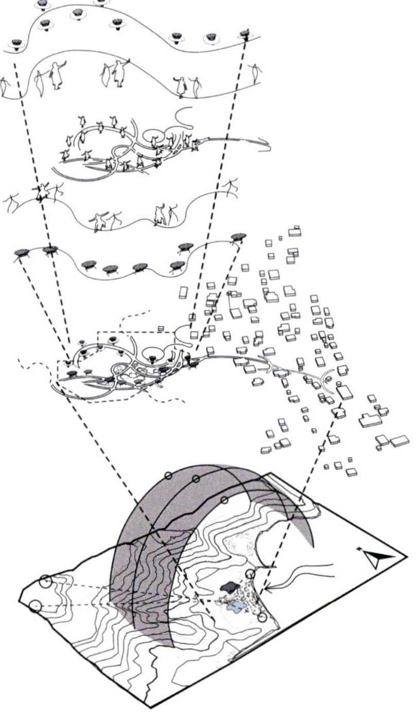

Site placement diagram showing the solar path over Marou Village and the placement of 17 sculptural forms—a composition that spans throughout the design site area.

Inspired by the circular rhythm of Fijian dance, *Meke na Mana* sculptures rise like open petals along the landscape path.

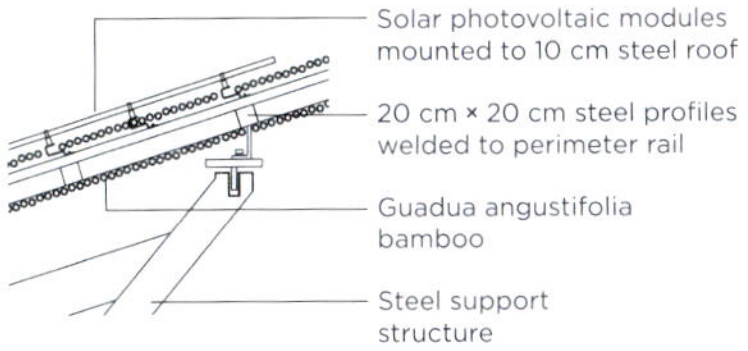

Solar photovoltaic modules mounted to 10 cm steel roof
20 cm × 20 cm steel profiles welded to perimeter rail
Guadua angustifolia bamboo
Steel support structure
Detail A

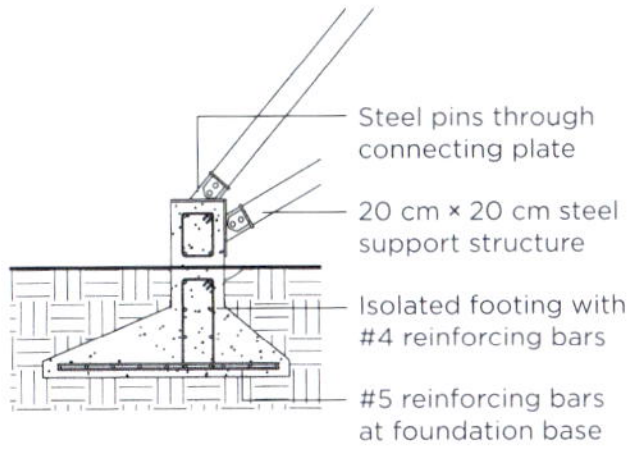

Steel pins through connecting plate
20 cm × 20 cm steel support structure
Isolated footing with #4 reinforcing bars
#5 reinforcing bars at foundation base
Detail B

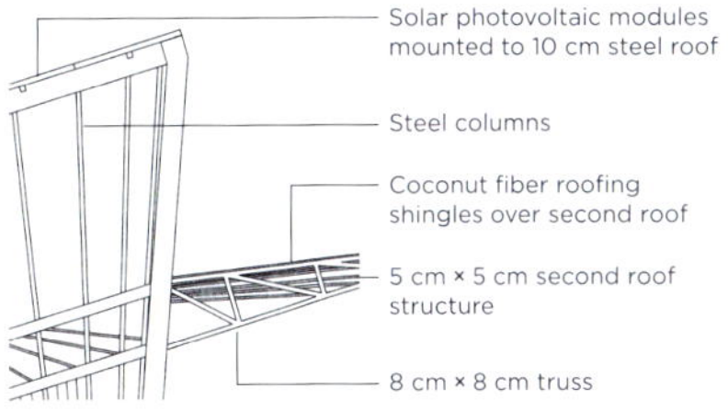

Solar photovoltaic modules mounted to 10 cm steel roof
Steel columns
Coconut fiber roofing shingles over second roof
5 cm × 5 cm second roof structure
8 cm × 8 cm truss
Detail C

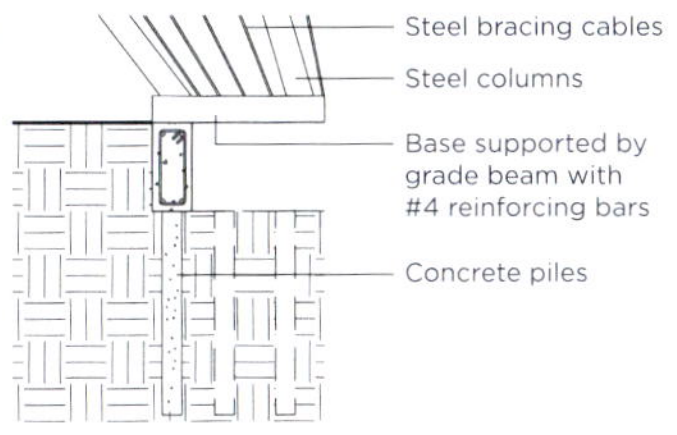

Steel bracing cables
Steel columns
Base supported by grade beam with #4 reinforcing bars
Concrete piles
Detail D

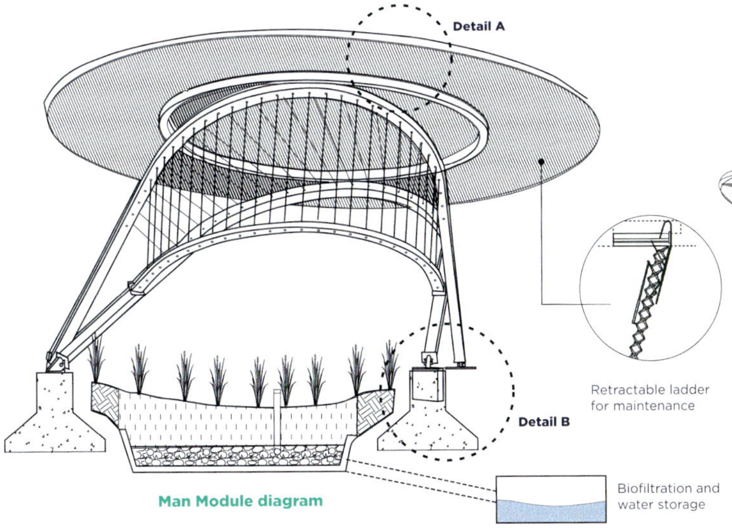

Detail A
Retractable ladder for maintenance
Detail B
Biofiltration and water storage
Man Module diagram

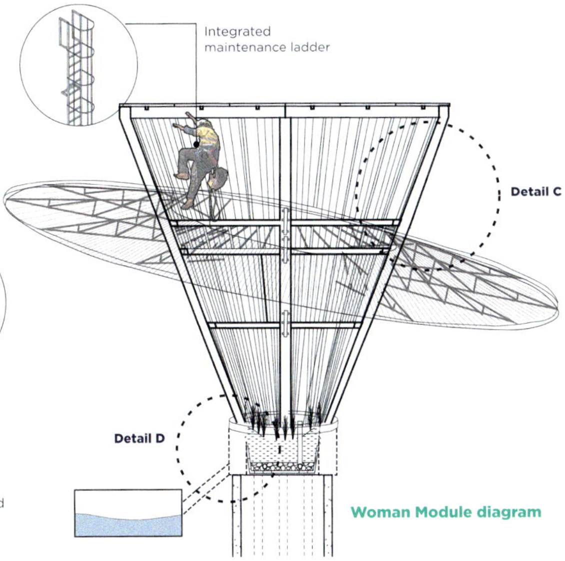

Integrated maintenance ladder
Detail C
Detail D
Woman Module diagram

Construction sequence for Man Module

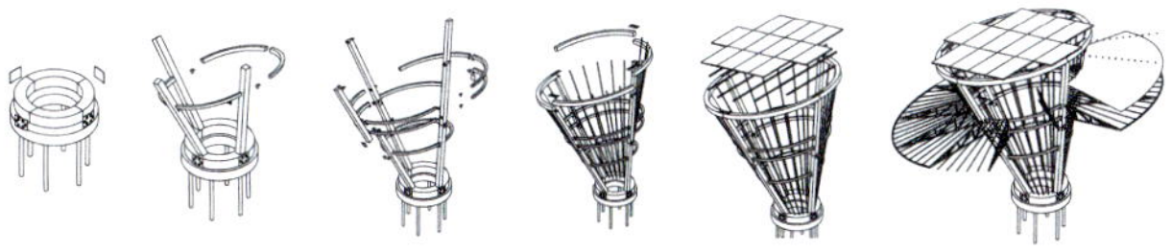

Construction sequence for Woman Module

Navigating Light, Holding Rain

DESIGNERS: Peter Heller, Kunyue Qi, Jisu Yang

TECHNOLOGIES: solar photovoltaic, pumped hydroelectric storage, rainwater harvesting, biofiltration, reservoir storage

ANNUAL PRODUCTION: 250 MWh of electricity, 8 million liters filtered water

DESIGN TEAM LOCATION: United States

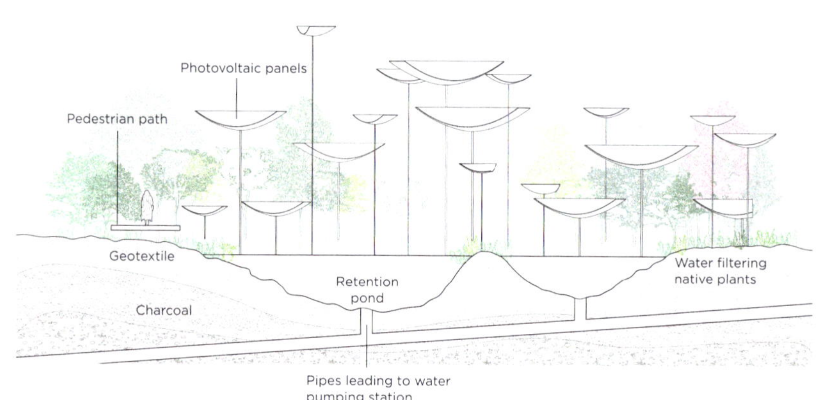

RIGHT: Sculptural vessels rise delicately above the landscape, capturing rainwater by day and glowing softly by night. Floating above reflective pools, the elegant forms evoke sails and celestial navigation, merging renewable energy, water harvesting, and cultural memory.

Navigating Light, Holding Rain is a landscape of movement, memory, and resilience—an energy-generating monument shaped by the celestial navigation traditions of the Pacific and the welcoming ritual of yaqona (kava). Through the poetic language of sails and water, the design honors ancestral knowledge while offering Marou Village a living system of clean power and water.

Ellipsoidal photovoltaic "sails" rise across the site in rhythmic clusters, providing contemporary minimalist interpretations of the geometry of traditional canoe rigs. Mounted on slender masts, these sculptural forms track sunlight by day and glow softly at night with programmable LED edges, echoing constellations used for wayfinding across open ocean. Integrated gutters discreetly channel rain from the sail surfaces to a network of terraced retention ponds below.

The site is designed as a closed-loop water-energy system. A renovated reservoir above the village is transformed into a pumped-storage hydroelectric battery, working in tandem with new lower ponds to balance energy flows. During daylight hours, excess solar power pumps water uphill; at night or during outages, gravity returns it through turbines to produce electricity. This hybrid system supports long-term resilience while drawing on the site's existing topography and hydrological memory.

Rainwater is collected from 5,000 m² of surface area, filtered, and stored in a series of ponds and basins integrated into a terraced landscape. These ponds double as ecological and cultural spaces, supporting native planting, regulating runoff, and inviting play, reflection, and ceremony.

The design's material palette centers on durable, locally viable solutions: geotextile-lined ponds, galvanized steel structures, and native plantings. PV sail modules can be deployed at varying scales from residential to civic. Sails can be fabricated locally, deployed in phases, and maintained by trained community members.

Navigating Light, Holding Rain is a landmark and a recognizable symbol of Marou, welcoming all who arrive by land or sea into a story of regeneration.

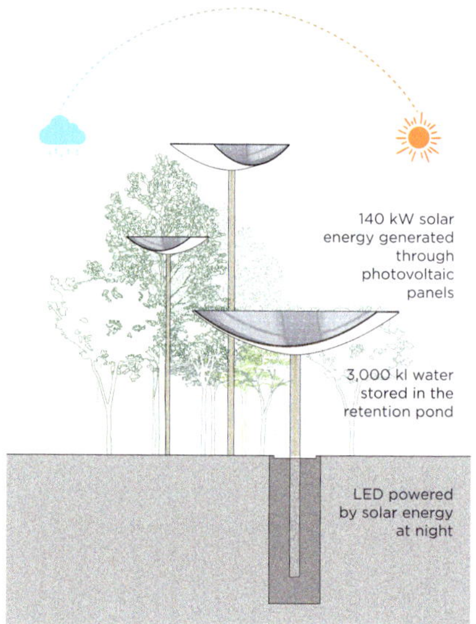

The Flowers of New Life

DESIGNERS: Egor Kiselev, Alexandra Iliasova, Faiz Safin

TECHNOLOGIES: solar photovoltaic, battery energy storage, rainwater harvesting, above-ground cisterns, vertical farming modules

ANNUAL PRODUCTION: 187 MWh of electricity, 180,000 liters of filtered water

DESIGN TEAM LOCATION: Russia

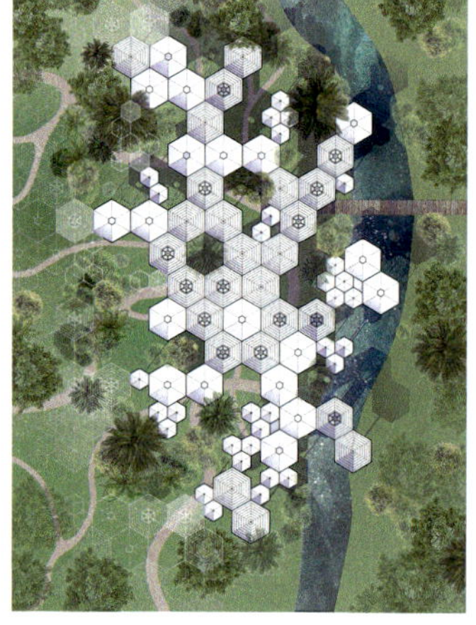

Hexagonal canopies create a flexible system for solar energy, rainwater harvesting, and vertical food production.

RIGHT: Modular canopy structures shelter vertical gardens, edible landscapes, and community gathering spaces. The petal-like forms harvest both rainwater and solar energy, creating a self-sustaining environment where food, energy, water, and community life flourish in harmony.

Emerging like a futuristic garden across the island terrain, *The Flowers of New Life* brings together solar energy, rainwater harvesting, and new forms of modular cultivation in a flexible infrastructure system that is both technological and poetic. Inspired by local flora, architecture, and daily life in Fiji, the installation takes the form of elegant "flowers of the future"—slender vertical stems topped with shallow hexagonal bowls that rotate to catch the sun and rain.

Each flower comes in a standard size of three or six meters in height and is composed of easily assembled mirrored modules. Inside the structure, lightweight metal framing supports embedded solar panels, wiring, and rainwater channels. The bowls act as multifunctional catchments, guiding water through segmented bamboo-like piping to a network of underground storage tanks. These components can be adapted to various slopes and terrains and are designed for fast maintenance and repair.

Some flower modules contain integrated planting trays, "green culture panels," that support vertical vegetation or experimental agriculture. Together, the flowers can be arranged to define public spaces, walking paths, and social zones, transforming infrastructure into a platform for daily life.

The installation is designed as a high-tech yet lightweight intervention. Its visual palette of white aluminum and light gold blends into the Fijian landscape, casting shimmering reflections that change with the wind and sun. Despite its futuristic form, the impact on the soil is minimal—only slender rods meet the ground, allowing the surrounding land to remain ecologically active and visually open.

The Flowers of New Life is at once a technological garden and a living toolkit, a modular system of beauty and function that grows with its people, reshaping the horizon without disturbing the earth beneath it.

Axonometric diagram

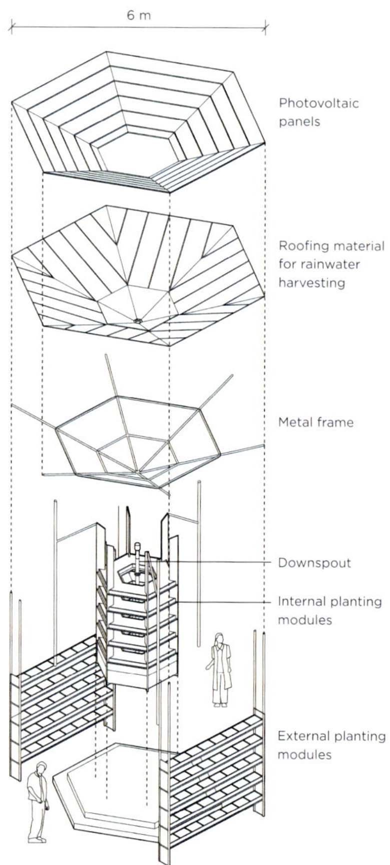

Palm Heart

RIGHT: Seating areas create opportunities for gathering together or resting alone.

DESIGNERS: Evgenia Gruzdeva, Tamila Vedzizheva

TECHNOLOGIES: solar photovoltaic, battery energy storage, rainwater harvesting, UV and RO filtration, above-ground cisterns

ANNUAL PRODUCTION: 113 MWh of electricity, 464,000 liters of filtered water

DESIGN TEAM LOCATION: Russia

A path winding through the canopy

Shaped by the silhouette of the coconut palm, *Palm Heart* blossoms from the land like a flowering canopy of clean energy and water. Each modular "flower" is both functional and expressive, drawing from local architectural forms and vegetation to provide a multipurpose space for community, sustainability, and renewal.

The design centers around a simple but elegant unit: a vertical stem supporting petal-shaped panels arranged in a shallow funnel. These petals are covered in photovoltaic cells, capturing sunlight across their full outer surface. In the center of each module is an opening that collects rainwater, guided inward by the curved petals.

Collected rainwater undergoes a four-stage treatment process: initial filtration with mesh screens, mechanical filtration through porous media, UV disinfection, and optional reverse osmosis to ensure drinking water quality. Solar energy supports daily village life and agricultural activities, with enough output to meet existing needs and expand opportunities. Beyond its technical systems, *Palm Heart* functions as a social hub. Modular seating areas beneath the shaded canopy provide space for relaxation, workshops, and gatherings.

Built with ease of assembly in mind, the structure is designed for rapid deployment using simple connections and sturdy components. Local residents are invited to participate in construction and maintenance, reinforcing community ownership and knowledge-sharing. A tourism component featuring local artisan workshops offers an additional revenue stream and educational outreach.

The natural canopy opens up to allow the solar canopy to flourish.

The sculptural forms of the funnel-shaped solar modules

Sun + Rain Network

Set against the backdrop of Vatu Rua, the *Sun + Rain* Columns rise above the landscape, illustrating their integration with the landscape.

DESIGNERS: Colin Davis, Michael Lucy, Hannah Merrett-Kaufman (Sustainable Life Designs)

TECHNOLOGIES: solar photovoltaic, rainwater harvesting, above-ground cisterns

ANNUAL PRODUCTION: 130 MWh of electricity, 2 million liters of filtered water

DESIGN TEAM LOCATION: United States

Sun + Rain Network is an ecological and sculptural system that transforms Marou's hillside into a landscape of resilience — collecting light, harvesting rain, producing food, and weaving village life together through a local network of solar-power installations.

At the heart of the design is an agrivoltaic facility inspired by tree ferns, traditional boats, and island weaving traditions. The canopy is shaped for solar exposure and rainfall capture. Rainwater funnels to cisterns located near structural columns, storing 2 million liters annually for irrigation and emergency use. The ground below is cultivated with crops nourished by stored water and partly shaded by the elevated solar structure.

Extending from this hub is a sculptural utility corridor — a woven wooden pathway built using invasive or surplus island trees. This living artwork connects the solar site with the village. The corridor functions as a trellis for edible vines, such as Malabar spinach and passion fruit, while carrying electrical and water lines discretely along its length.

Distributed along this pathway and throughout the village are *Sun + Rain* Columns. Each unit adds solar capacity, collects rainwater, and provides charging ports, irrigation, lighting, and spaces for gathering. Columns incorporate local weaving traditions, binding structure and meaning into a cohesive public utility.

The system is expandable, low-maintenance, and designed with community stewardship in mind. Operations are supported by Marou residents through training, maintenance manuals, and a train-the-trainer model that ensures long-term care. A repaired or replaced upstream dam and pond enhance drinking water access and support outdoor aquaponic farming.

The network of radiant canopies and flowing water lines binds energy, ecology, and community together into a living, regenerative landscape.

Bent metal posts

Tension membrane with white top for heat reduction

Up-lights feature cut-offs to prevent light pollution, while down-lights ensure safe illumination along walkways.

Cistern at core of structure

Tension cables are arranged in a pattern inspired by local textile designs, forming a trellis for climbing vines.

Concrete footers are made with low-carbon cement and local aggregate.

Bench

Photovoltaic panels are mounted on a metal frame structure. Panels drain into a cistern via gutters and downspouts.

Tension cables are arranged in a pattern inspired by local textile designs, forming a trellis for climbing vines.

Gaps between solar panels allow light through for growing crops below.

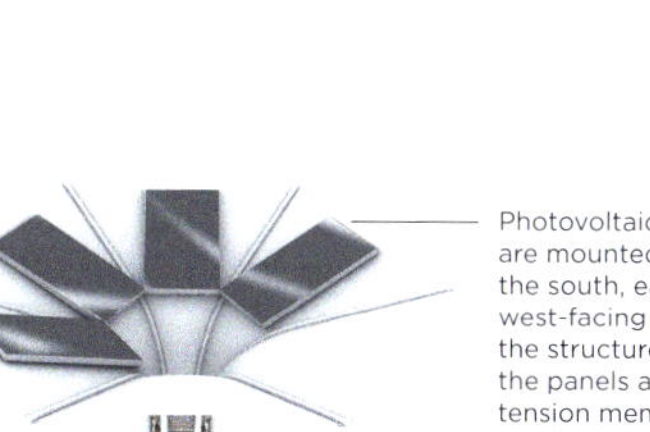

Photovoltaic panels are mounted on the south, east, and west-facing sides of the structure. Both the panels and the tension membrane are designed to channel rainwater into a central cistern.

Arrays of Vanua

The pitched roof is oriented to efficiently channel rainwater into an underground reservoir where the water undergoes filtration before being pumped to storage tanks for village distribution. Surplus water is carefully managed and utilized within the pavilion — for irrigation, passive cooling, and seasonal transformation of the landscape. During the rainy season, a shallow water feature emerges; in the dry season, it becomes a green strip.

DESIGNERS: Ai Ling Mak, Mohammad Horoub, Alex Yango, Kieve Mercado, Adel Zekri, Wichittra Wuthiboon

TECHNOLOGIES: solar photovoltaic, battery energy storage, stormwater harvesting and filtration, above- and below-ground cisterns

ANNUAL PRODUCTION: 150 MWh of electricity, 2.5 million liters of filtered water

DESIGN TEAM LOCATION: Singapore

Constructed from readily available local materials, the pavilion employs a modular and scalable system that adapts to varied terrains and site conditions.

Sunbeams shine through colorful ceiling panels, letting visitors know that electricity is being generated on the roof outside.

Rooted in the Fijian concept of *vanua* — the deep interconnection between land, people, and spirit — *Arrays of Vanua* is a modular, landscape-integrated pavilion that provides clean energy, potable water, and community gathering space for Marou Village. The design celebrates both natural rhythms and cultural resilience, transforming essential infrastructure into a shared civic platform.

Forty-four modular segments form the sweeping roofline of the pavilion, each shaped with a traditional pitch for optimal solar gain and rainwater collection. The canopy supports 176 monocrystalline photovoltaic panels with the option to expand in the future. Below, a network of hybrid underground and above-ground tanks collects up to 2.5 million liters of stormwater annually, meeting village needs through Marou's 70-day dry season and beyond.

Rainwater flows via gravity into filtration systems and reservoirs, minimizing pump usage and energy demands. Overflow during peak rainfall supports on-site vegetation and seasonal transformation zones: shallow pools and shaded green corridors that create a cool microclimate and invite social gathering. The layout encourages multipurpose use — ceremony, play, education, and relaxation.

Built from locally available materials using simple, low-impact construction techniques, *Arrays of Vanua* prioritizes affordability, maintenance access, and long-term stewardship. A custom-designed rolling ladder provides safe, routine cleaning of sloped PV panels. Below, a recessed utility room houses inverters and water systems, shielded from the elements and easily accessible for maintenance.

Arrays of Vanua is an ecosystem in motion — modular, adaptable, and grounded in the values of shared responsibility and regenerative design.

The installation integrates traditional Fijian architectural forms with modern sustainable technologies.

The winding A-frame solar structure blends into the forested landscape, providing a variety of shaded gathering spaces.

Polycarbonate skylight
The material was selected for its economy, strength, lightweight design, and ease of installation.

Bamboo slat roofing
Bamboo is rapidly renewable, locally abundant, and naturally weather resistant.

Pine wood rafters
Pine is strong, fast growing, and locally abundant.

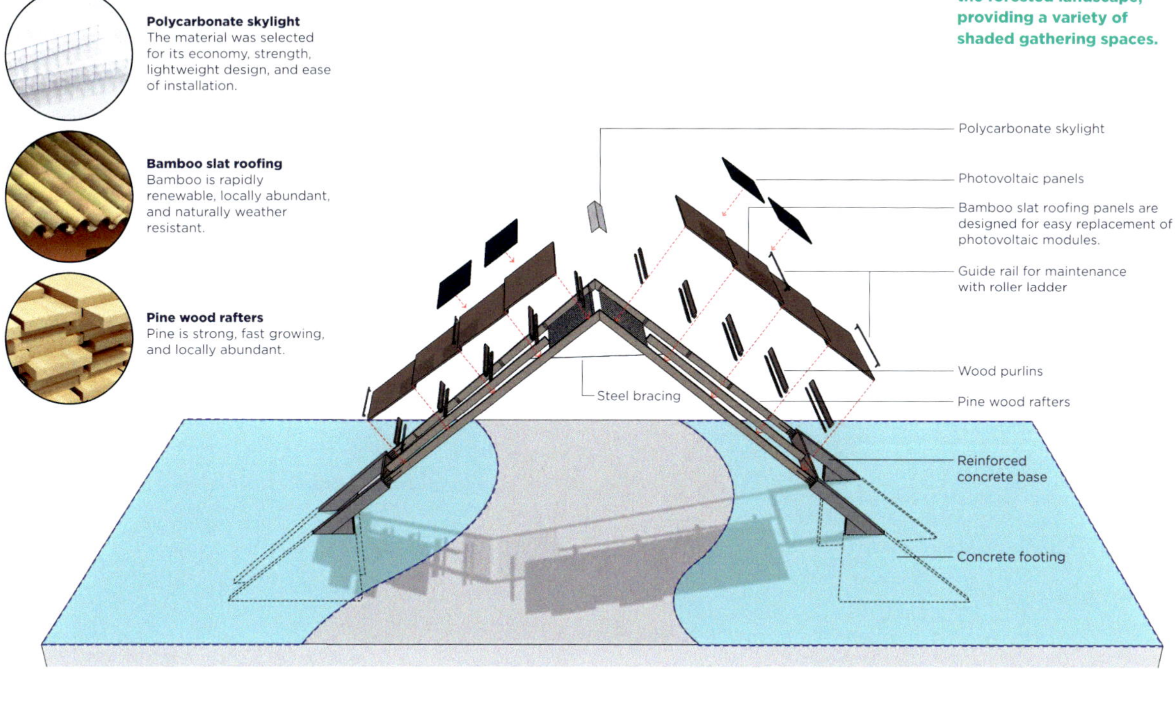

Modular arrangements

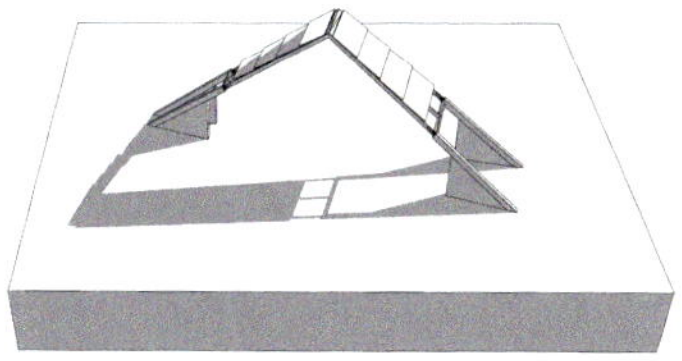

Each module, simple and triangular in form, can be scaled and arranged to suit community needs and site conditions. From this single repeated element, a rich variety of spatial experiences emerges.

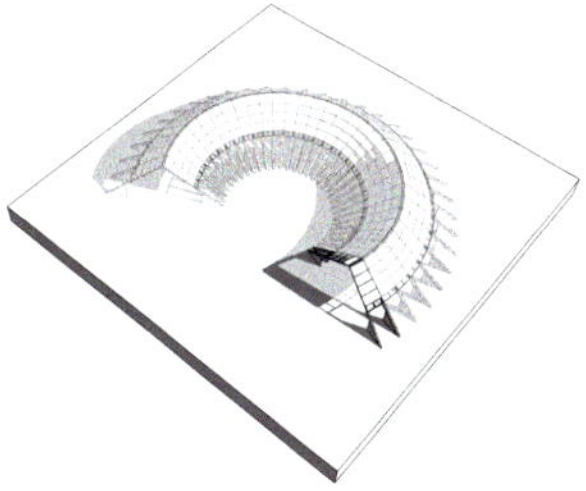

Single module

Circular arrangement

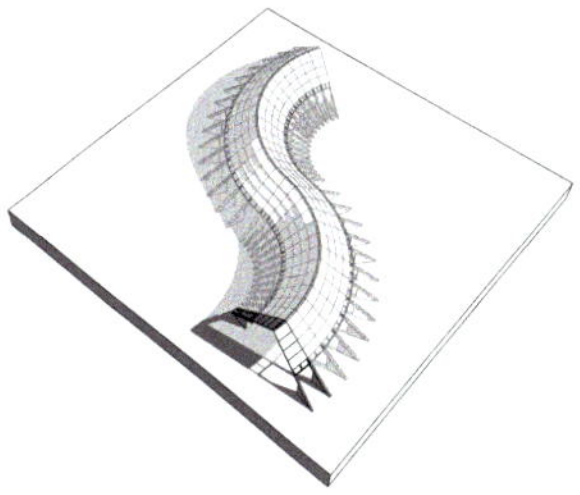

Flowing arrangement

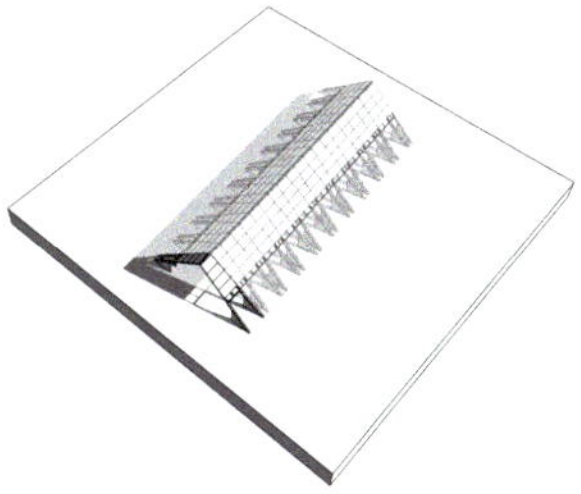

Linear arrangement

The Flow of Life
Currents of Continuum

RIGHT: The mist catcher stands as a beacon at the threshold between Marou Village and the central solar spine.

DESIGNERS: Austin Lim, Phang Lim

TECHNOLOGIES: hybrid solar photovoltaic-thermal (PV-T), biogas, battery energy storage, rainwater harvesting, thermal energy recovery, above-ground cisterns

ANNUAL PRODUCTION: 150 MWh of electricity, 1 million liters of filtered water

DESIGN TEAM LOCATION: Singapore

Marou Village, like many coastal communities across the Pacific, faces rising seas, stronger cyclones, and growing isolation from mainland infrastructures. *The Flow of Life* responds with an integrated, community-led system—an artwork of resilience that merges architecture, landscape, energy, and culture into a regenerative whole.

The Flow of Life unfolds across three interconnected zones: a shaded Gathering Canopy with amphitheater and cultural space; a Nourishing Terrace for farming, cooking, and livestock care; and a Living Reservoir of linked ponds and bioswales that manage water and support biodiversity. At its heart, a modular timber structure, The Spine, rises above flood lines, serving as both cyclone shelter and social hub. A gravity-fed hydrological circuit beneath links all zones, forming a continuous loop of flow and renewal.

A rooftop PV-T system generates over 150 MWh of electricity annually, while also capturing heat for pre-warming water. Lithium iron phosphate batteries store excess power, ensuring continuous supply. Solar dryers preserve food using passive design, and a biogas digester turns organic waste into clean cooking fuel, returning enriched digestate to the soil.

Rainwater is collected via butterfly roofs and filtered through a gravity-fed, multi-stage system into mobile timber barrels that are designed for ease of use and are inspired by traditional water vessels. Agroforestry integrates taro, cassava, yams, bananas, herbs, and leguminous cover crops alongside livestock, creating a symbiotic ecosystem that regenerates the land and feeds the community.

Constructed from low-carbon, locally sourced materials like timber, thatch, rammed earth, and stone, all structures are modular, demountable, and community-maintainable. Passive design strategies ensure comfort, durability, and minimal energy demand.

The Flow of Life is a living framework that invites visitors into a shared experience of tradition and innovation, where sustainable futures are cultivated through the everyday actions of a resilient village.

The sun sets over the outdoor kitchen pavilion as seen across the living reservoir.

Local materials

Thatch
Naturally breathable and lightweight, thatch provides effective insulation and protection when used as roofing material.

Bamboo
Flexible yet strong, bamboo is woven into door screens to allow ventilation while maintaining privacy.

Bark
Soft, fibrous bark is crafted into tapa and masi cloths, offering texture, warmth, and cultural storytelling.

Timber
Dense and durable, timber serves as the primary structural framework, delivering strength and a tactile, organic warmth.

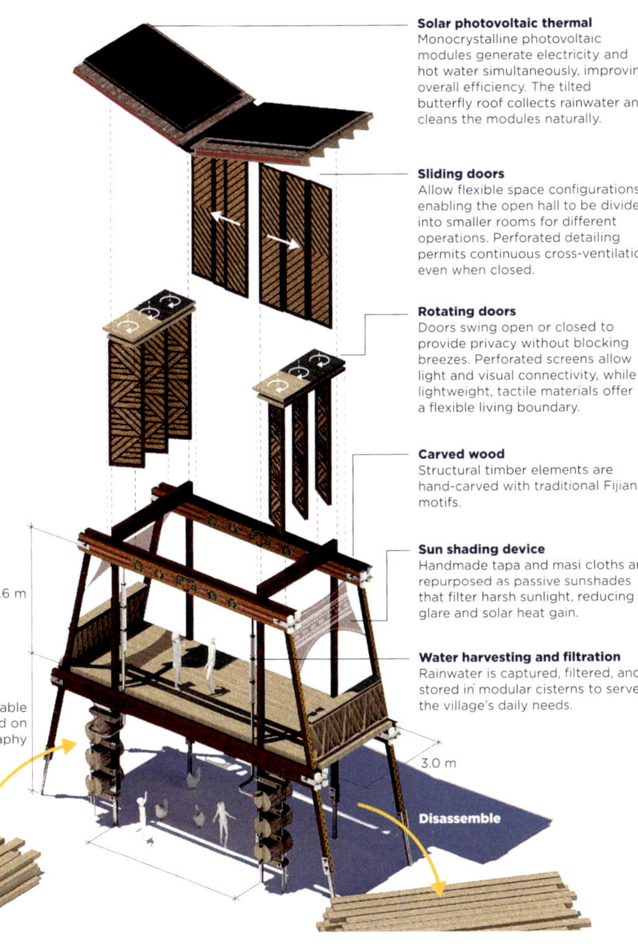

Construction techniques
This modular, low-carbon architectural prototype is designed for community-led regeneration, using locally sourced materials that support reversible construction. Its low-cost, low-maintenance design is adaptable across diverse contexts, featuring a decentralized utility system that scales according to village needs and can be assembled or disassembled as required.

Three mist catcher modules

One homestay module

Three community space modules

One vertical circulation module

Three classroom modules

Two storage and seed bank modules

Aerial view of a complete configuration

1. The Spine
2. Entrance from Marou Village
3. Walking trail
4. Bioswale
5. Playfield
6. Gathering space
7. Kitchen
8. Biogas digester
9. Solar dryer
10. Animal shed
11. Pasture
12. Vegetable farm
13. Water retention pond
14. Fish pond

Vale ni Siga

RIGHT: Visitors gather beneath a woven canopy of light and masi motifs in this immersive cultural space, where Fijian patterns, storytelling, and community knowledge converge within an organic form.

DESIGNERS: Jingxi Peng, Yining Liu, Miyuu Tani, Xiaoyu Li, Robert Brown, Galen Newman, Dongying Li

TECHNOLOGIES: solar photovoltaic, battery energy storage, rainwater harvesting, underground cisterns, planting beds for food and medicine

ANNUAL PRODUCTION: 112 MWh of electricity, 1 million liters of filtered water

DESIGN TEAM LOCATION: United States

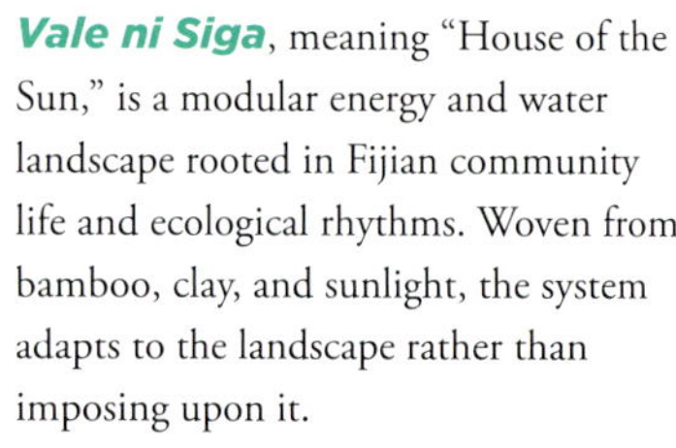

Vale ni Siga, meaning "House of the Sun," is a modular energy and water landscape rooted in Fijian community life and ecological rhythms. Woven from bamboo, clay, and sunlight, the system adapts to the landscape rather than imposing upon it.

Each module fits into a hexagonal network and supports one of three key functions: solar energy generation, rainwater harvesting, or edible planting. Photovoltaic panels are custom-shaped to fit the design, while rainwater is collected from 1,280 m^2 of surface and filtered for household and irrigation use. Medicinal and food gardens are interspersed, enriching the system's ecological and cultural value.

Raised compartments safely house system components. The framework is shaded by a bamboo canopy that evokes traditional methods of construction.

Water gardens, bioswales, and permeable joints create a cool microclimate and manage runoff naturally. Built from bamboo, clay, and rope lashings, the installation invites ongoing care and adaptation by community stewards.

Vale ni Siga is a soft but resilient presence, an evolving structure of regenerative systems that build community through acts of co-creation.

The installation extends toward the village, its sweeping form opening to the north to follow the arc of the sun across the sky.

A Marou resident installs a new solar module into the canopy frame.

Sunlight filters through the multifunctional frame.

The Kaleidoscope of Marou

Visitors explore the installation, encountering works by local artists displayed throughout the atrium. In the background, pale blue pipes distribute water collected by the rainwater catchment system.

RIGHT: Elevated above rainwater-harvesting funnels, the solar modules are hidden from view at ground level, preserving the visual harmony of the landscape.

DESIGNER: Carel Kusters

TECHNOLOGIES: bifacial solar photovoltaic, battery energy storage, reflective surfaces for enhanced solar performance, rainwater catchment, above-ground cisterns

ANNUAL PRODUCTION: 160 MWh of electricity, 1.5 million liters of filtered water

DESIGN TEAM LOCATION: The Netherlands

The Kaleidoscope of Marou is a destination-scale art installation designed to deliver clean energy, safe drinking water, and resilient infrastructure while serving as a cultural landmark shaped by the community. Inspired by Clara von Zweigbergk's Kaleido trays, the design uses modular hexagons as flexible building blocks that residents arrange into meaningful patterns, terraces, and symbols.

Each module integrates bifacial solar panels above inverted rainwater basins that collect runoff into soft pillow tanks. Reflective tarpaulin "umbrellas" below the panels boost energy production and provide shade, while vertical skirts reduce wind load and conceal technical elements without blocking airflow or light.

Available in five sizes, the modules support walking paths, gardens, learning zones, and gathering spaces. Residents use scale models to co-design the arrangement—deciding color, function, and form through a participatory process.

In cyclone conditions, the system enters Tardigrade Mode, lowering modules via remote-controlled winches and securing them with ballast, bracing, and protective barriers to reduce wind exposure.

Constructed from affordable, widely available materials, the installation is replicable and easy to maintain. It offers a model for community-led infrastructure where beauty, resilience, and shared authorship shape the future of island life.

The composition of hexagonal modules is decided by the community.

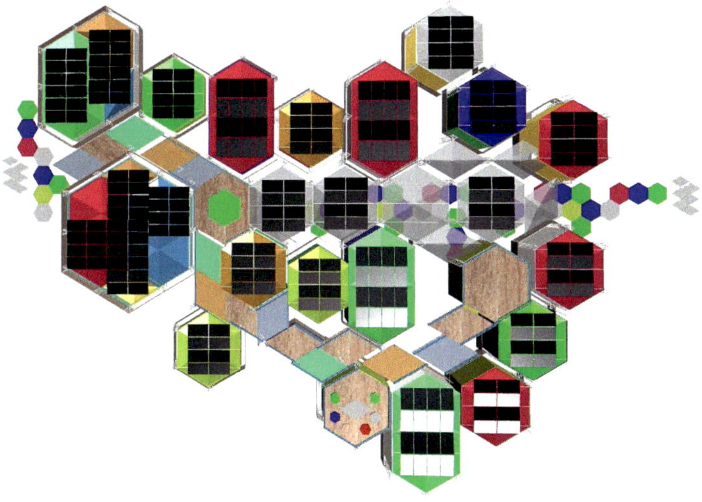

Plug-in Solar Sheds

RIGHT: A network of modular, thatch-roofed structures forms a vibrant village hub, where colorful woven roofs enclose shared spaces.

DESIGNERS: Lily Loveday, Emily Lavoll, Beshoy Daniel, Catty Dan Zhang

TECHNOLOGIES: solar photovoltaic, battery energy storage, modular water harvesting, portable filtration tanks, stormwater retention and irrigation system, underground cisterns

ANNUAL PRODUCTION: 190 MWh of electricity, 1 million liters of filtered water

DESIGN TEAM LOCATION: United States

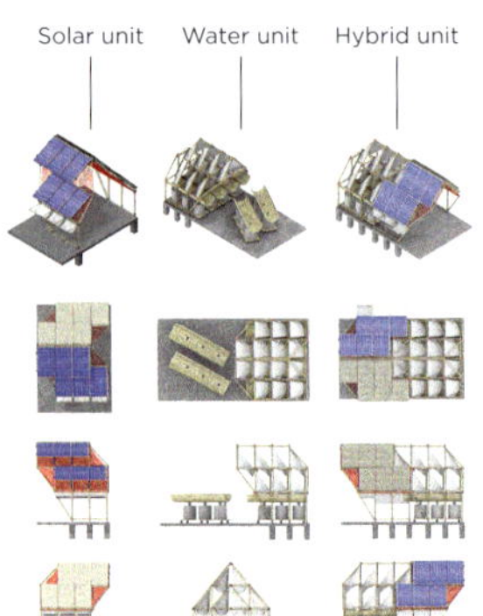

Plug-in Solar Sheds transforms the landscape of Marou Village into a field of modular, multifunctional pavilions—each one harvesting sun and rain while serving as a community gathering place, agricultural hub, or public utility. Rooted in the familiar form of the Fijian vale or bure, the sheds reimagine vernacular thatched structures as solar-powered, water-harvesting nodes that can be clustered, mirrored, and expanded.

Each basic unit measures 4.5 m × 4.5 m × 4.5 m and is configured either as a solar or water module "shed." The solar sheds feature monocrystalline PV panels mounted at optimized angles with tracking capability, providing 120 kW across the installation. Beneath the solar sheds, shaded zones support small crop beds in a mini-agrivoltaic system. The water sheds are equipped with soft sail canopies that direct rainwater into bamboo basins, where it is captured and stored in movable filter carts for daily use. Three carts per unit allow for flexible redistribution and modular storage.

Covered courtyards or open-ended gathering spaces are formed by linking single units in linear or radial patterns. These aggregations scale up to 20 meters in length and 9 meters in height, accommodating markets, recreation, and cultural events. Stormwater is also managed through foundation-level retention systems, capable of storing up to 800,000 liters and feeding irrigation channels.

Locally sourced bamboo, straw, and red palm support airflow, provide filtered light, and offer resilience against wind. Panels are tied with a custom bracketing system that enables rapid replacement and seasonal adjustment. Thatch components are biodegradable and can be composted as fertilizer at end-of-life.

Built to be maintained by the community, *Plug-in Solar Sheds* makes sustainability visible and participatory.

A solar-water hybrid unit

South elevation

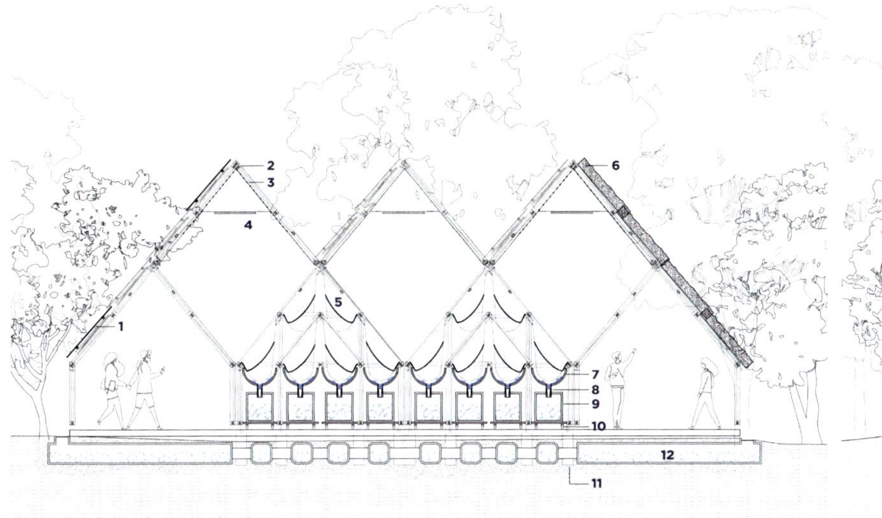

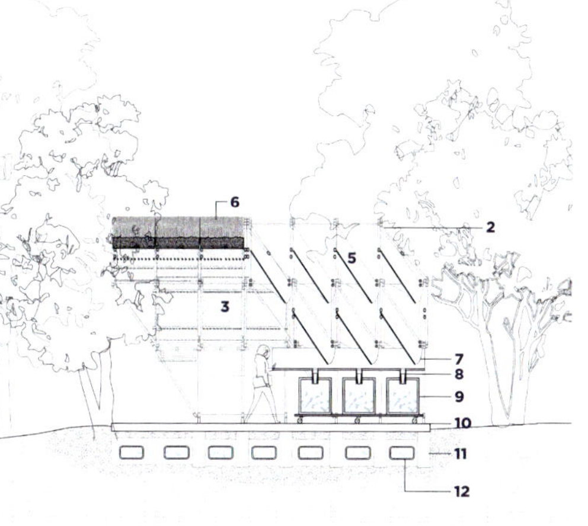

1. Photovoltaic panels
2. Bamboo joint
3. Bamboo backing strip
4. Fixed water collectors
5. Soft sail water collector
6. Thatched panel
7. Bamboo water basin
8. Filter
9. Water tank
10. Movable cart
11. Concrete footings
12. Stormwater retention

Raised platforms with stone perimeters create distributed gathering areas that invite community life to unfold across the landscape.

Solar Vessels

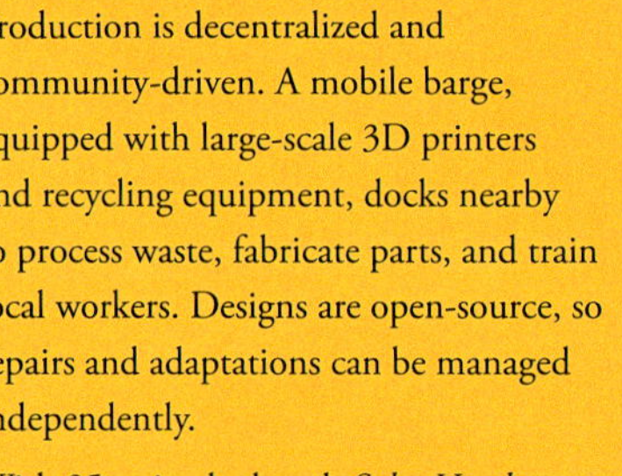

RIGHT: *Solar Vessels* open up to the sky adjacent to the houses of Marou Village.

DESIGNERS: M. Hank Haeusler, Moritz Mungenast, Louis Lamont, Meghan Doherty, Barbara Biggemann Dattwyler, Ivana Kuzmanovska, Farnaz Fattahi, Christopher Bamborough

TECHNOLOGIES: solar photovoltaic, battery energy storage, hydro-pumped energy storage, rainwater harvesting, above-ground cisterns

ANNUAL PRODUCTION: 100 MWh of electricity, 525,000 liters of filtered water

DESIGN TEAM LOCATION: Australia

Solar Vessels transforms one of the Pacific's most pervasive pollutants — plastic waste — into a resource for community resilience. Each modular unit is 3D-printed using locally collected plastic and shaped into a curved form that mimics a floating hull. These vessels house rainwater cisterns, dual solar panels, and a closed-loop "water battery" that stores energy using gravity alone.

During the day, surplus solar electricity powers a small pump that lifts water to an upper tank inside the vessel. At night or during cloudy conditions, the water flows back down through a micro-turbine, generating power without fuel or chemicals. This self-contained system enhances energy resilience while supplying potable water from rain capture.

Production is decentralized and community-driven. A mobile barge, equipped with large-scale 3D printers and recycling equipment, docks nearby to process waste, fabricate parts, and train local workers. Designs are open-source, so repairs and adaptations can be managed independently.

With 35 units deployed, *Solar Vessels* becomes a fleet of regenerative infrastructure, each one autonomously supplying water and energy while expressing local identity. Non-invasive foundations, mosquito-proof systems, and customizable forms ensure long-term sustainability.

This is a future where waste becomes wealth and where energy flows from sunlight, water, and imagination.

Children run through a field of *Solar Vessels*—elegant, amphora-shaped structures that harvest sunlight while echoing the contours of traditional water pots.

The installation brings renewable energy generation into everyday life, blending advanced technology with recognizable cultural forms.

A Place Becoming

RIGHT: The contemporary forms of *A Place Becoming* blend organically with the Fijian island landscape.

DESIGNERS: Z.Y. Liu, Shuai Wang (f-a-n architects)

TECHNOLOGIES: flexible solar photovoltaic membrane, battery energy storage, rainwater harvesting, above-ground cisterns, plug-in pods for food, education, and cooling

ANNUAL PRODUCTION: 115 MWh of electricity, 200,000 liters of filtered water

DESIGN TEAM LOCATION: China

The central pavilion provides space for performances, workshops, markets, and other public events.

A Place Becoming is a modular structure that adapts to the evolving needs of Marou Village. Drawing on principles of metabolism — emphasizing organic growth and adaptability — it integrates solar energy, rainwater harvesting, food production, and shared learning spaces into a living system shaped by the community.

The design begins with a central pavilion: a translucent, wave-like roof made of solar membranes that generate power while shading the open space below. This flexible canopy hosts ceremonies, meals, markets, and workshops. Rainwater is collected and stored in sealed tanks for handwashing, irrigation, and emergency use, while battery energy storage ensures nighttime power.

As the village grows, additional modules can be added — education kiosks, shaded classrooms, cold storage, and farming pods. Construction and upkeep are led by residents, with training and visual manuals that support long-term stewardship. Maintenance becomes part of daily life through school check-ups and seasonal cleaning routines.

Farming pods use composting and organic methods to enhance food security and resilience. Built from galvanized steel and sustainably sourced timber, the structure balances durability with cultural familiarity.

Site diagram

Rainwater harvesting module

Energy Bloom

DESIGNER: Nanxi (Nanncie) Zhu

TECHNOLOGIES: sun-tracking solar photovoltaic, rainwater harvesting and filtration, above-ground cisterns

ANNUAL PRODUCTION: 130 MWh of electricity, 1 million liters of filtered water

DESIGN TEAM LOCATION: China

RIGHT: Petal-like canopies drink in sunlight and touch the sky.

Energy Bloom rises like a living organism — solar towers inspired by sunflowers and traditional Fijian camakau sailboats. Designed to move with the sun and collect rain, the installation brings clean energy, safe water, and shaded gathering space to the heart of the village.

Vertical towers are topped with photovoltaic panels that rotate throughout the day to optimize solar capture. Curved roof forms beneath the panels guide rainwater into pipes for filtration — through sand, gravel, activated carbon, and UV light — before being stored in elevated tanks for irrigation, drinking, and hygiene.

Around the towers, an open-air path weaves between shaded platforms and educational displays, encouraging play, learning, and daily gathering. The layout creates a microclimate of comfort while showcasing sustainable infrastructure in action.

Constructed from bamboo, recycled metals, and timber, the system is modular and lightweight, designed for local assembly and maintenance. Water overflows irrigate nearby planting beds, and integrated shade reduces heat stress.

With room to grow, *Energy Bloom* supports learning, resilience, and tradition under the Fijian sun.

Modular gathering space and dining area

Stretch Point

RIGHT: The site plan illustrates how the installation connects the solar design site through the village and out into the sea, creating a new dock for Marou Village visitors.

DESIGNER: Antti Ahlava, Fredrik Lindberg, Daniel Nowak, Julian Olsson, Katharina Polzin, Kivi Sotamaa, Maria Trojszak

TECHNOLOGIES: solar photovoltaic, battery energy storage, solar thermal, multi-effect distillation (MED) desalination, thermal energy storage, rainwater and seawater harvesting, reservoir storage

ANNUAL PRODUCTION: 315 MWh of electricity, 7 million liters of filtered water

DESIGN TEAM LOCATION: Finland

View down the axis of The Stretch looking out to the sea

Stretch Point bridges the land, the sea, and the future. Composed of two timber-framed buildings — The Stretch and The Point — this design integrates solar energy, water purification, and community gathering into a single infrastructural landscape that connects Marou Village to its farmland.

The Stretch is a 163-meter-long linear structure, roofed with photovoltaic panels and a solar thermal energy system. Beneath its canopy is an open-air corridor housing a water distillation system and storage for energy and water. The timber structure, made from locally sourced wood, is modular, replicable, and designed for community assembly and upkeep.

The Point is a sculptural, freeform building that serves as a community gathering space and emergency shelter. Its curving laminated-timber frame provides contrast to the rectilinear Stretch, symbolizing arrival, refuge, and social connection.

Together, the buildings harvest solar power through a dual system: 75 kW of photovoltaic panels produce 131 MWh per year, while a 100 kW solar thermal system drives a multi-effect distillation system transforming seawater and rain into potable water. Depending on conditions, the system produces 7,500–13,000 cubic meters of clean water annually. A portion of the electricity is stored in batteries and thermal storage, ensuring continuous power and extending the system's power reliability during the rainy season.

Rainwater harvesting is enhanced through terraced planting and demi-lunes — shallow crescent-shaped earthworks that increase infiltration and reduce erosion. Stormwater overflow supports reforestation and soil stabilization, turning the corridor into a green infrastructure spine.

Stretch Point is a demonstration for a world that has exceeded the elasticity of the carrying capacity of nature: stretching materials, systems, and community capacity to power the village, hydrate the soil, and shelter the community beneath a canopy of shared resilience.

The organic form of The Point creates a stark contrast with the rectilinear timber frame of The Stretch.

Section

Tanoa
The Bowl of Life

DESIGNERS: Puya Khalili, Aziz Khalili, Iman Khalili

TECHNOLOGIES: solar photovoltaic, battery energy storage, integrated rainwater harvesting and filtration, underground cisterns

ANNUAL PRODUCTION: 135 MWh of electricity, 732,500 liters of filtered water

DESIGN TEAM LOCATION: Canada

Local materials and expert engineering come together to create a resilient structure that celebrates local culture.

RIGHT: Community gathers under the shade of the artwork.

In Fijian culture, the tanoa is a sacred wooden vessel used in traditional kava ceremonies bringing people together in dialogue, celebration, and communal decision-making. Carved from a single piece of wood with a shallow, circular form, the tanoa represents the heart of Fijian hospitality and collective wisdom. *Tanoa: The Bowl of Life* reimagines this form as a gathering space that collects, transforms, and distributes the natural resources of sun and rain to serve the needs of Marou Village

Positioned along existing village pathways and aligned with community rhythms, the bowl's 27-meter diameter canopy provides 528 m^2 of shaded area beneath its gently sloping form. Constructed from locally sourced structural bamboo and anchored with cyclone-resistant footings, the design merges symbolism and structure. Its aerodynamic profile and open center allow for airflow and pressure equalization, enhancing safety and comfort.

The bowl's interior slope is embedded with photovoltaic panels arranged along a radial curve to optimize solar exposure. Beneath the central structure, batteries and technical systems are housed in a protected enclosure. A 130 kWh daily surplus powers several systems that address specific needs identified by the community: a 5 kW ice-making system that produces 250 kg of ice daily for fish preservation, a community charging station for devices and small batteries, path lighting for nighttime safety, and pumps to distribute harvested water throughout the village.

Rainwater is harvested across the full roof area and funneled into an integrated cistern, where it undergoes a four-stage filtration process before reaching a smaller inspection tank for final clarity checks. Clear filter housings make the system visible and easy to maintain.

The design process includes hands-on workshops with village elders, artists, and youth, incorporating traditional patterns and stories into carvings and surface details. Local residents are trained for construction and maintenance, reinforcing ownership and intergenerational skill-sharing.

At once iconic and pragmatic, *Tanoa: The Bowl of Life* represents a hopeful intersection of tradition, sustainability, and community-led future-making.

LEFT: The aerial view reveals how the artwork is situated in relation to the village it supports, supplying both electricity and water.

RIGHT: The solar modules generate a consistent flow of electricity throughout the day.

Valelaca Rokataki
Prismatic Parasol

DESIGNERS: Michael Kokora, Marcus Carter, Miranda Lee, Jon Marcos (OBJECT TERRITORIES); James Richardson, Chase Rogers (One Hermitage); Nadir Abdessemed, Moritz Muetschele, Valentin Granger, Francisco Gallardo, Mohadese Banaeialishah (Transsolar Klima Engineering); Tony Tsui (noodo lab); Demian Szklar (Oaki Studio)

TECHNOLOGIES: flexible solar photovoltaic, battery energy storage, gravity-fed pumped water energy storage, rainwater harvesting, decentralized freshwater distribution

ANNUAL PRODUCTION: 115 MWh of electricity, 3.6 million liters of filtered water

DESIGN TEAM LOCATION: Hong Kong, United States, Germany, Argentina

RIGHT: The colorful *Valelaca Rokataki* creates a central community space for festivals, events, village meetings, relaxing in the shade, or sheltering from the rain.

Standing twenty-one meters above Marou Village, *Valelaca Rokataki*, meaning "Prismatic Parasol," is a striking solar canopy and overlook tower designed as a beacon of community resilience. Shaped by solar geometry and cultural practice, the structure shelters an amphitheater, collects and stores clean water, generates power, and elevates village life—both literally and symbolically.

The tower's spiral staircase ascends to a panoramic viewing platform, used to watch for incoming storms or returning fishing boats. At night, the illuminated canopy becomes a navigational marker for night fishers, a functional lighthouse woven into the landscape. Below, a stepped amphitheater provides a shaded space for festivals, school events, village meetings, and informal daily gatherings.

The canopy itself is a convex, north-facing form precisely angled to follow the ecliptic path of the sun. Flexible, hydrophobic photovoltaic shingles are clipped to a lattice of locally sourced timber, forming a breathable surface that shades the space below while allowing airflow and resilience in high winds. Rainwater runs off its edges to collection tanks and adjacent mountain catchments.

Integrated with the landscape, a series of hillside reservoirs harvest rain and runoff, doubling as a gravity-fed energy storage system. Excess solar energy powers pumps that move water uphill during the day. This potential energy is later released through turbines at night or during cloudy periods. Smaller, decentralized water collection and filtration stations dot the village path, offering public access to clean water and informal spaces to rest and connect.

Valelaca Rokataki is a new cultural landmark, rooted in local materials and knowledge. It celebrates the intersection of architecture and ecology, ceremony and self-reliance, casting both shade and light as it charts a future of off-grid independence.

Exploring the artwork at dusk as the lights begin to glow

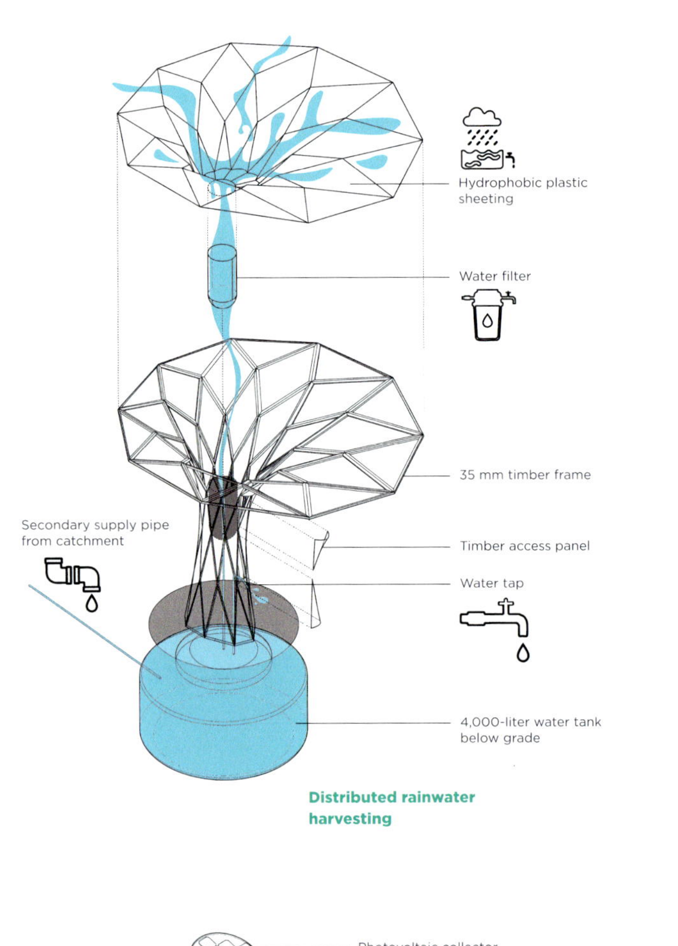

Distributed rainwater harvesting

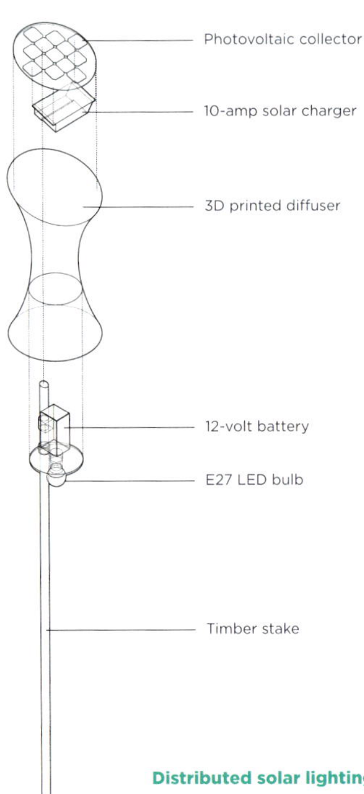

Distributed solar lighting

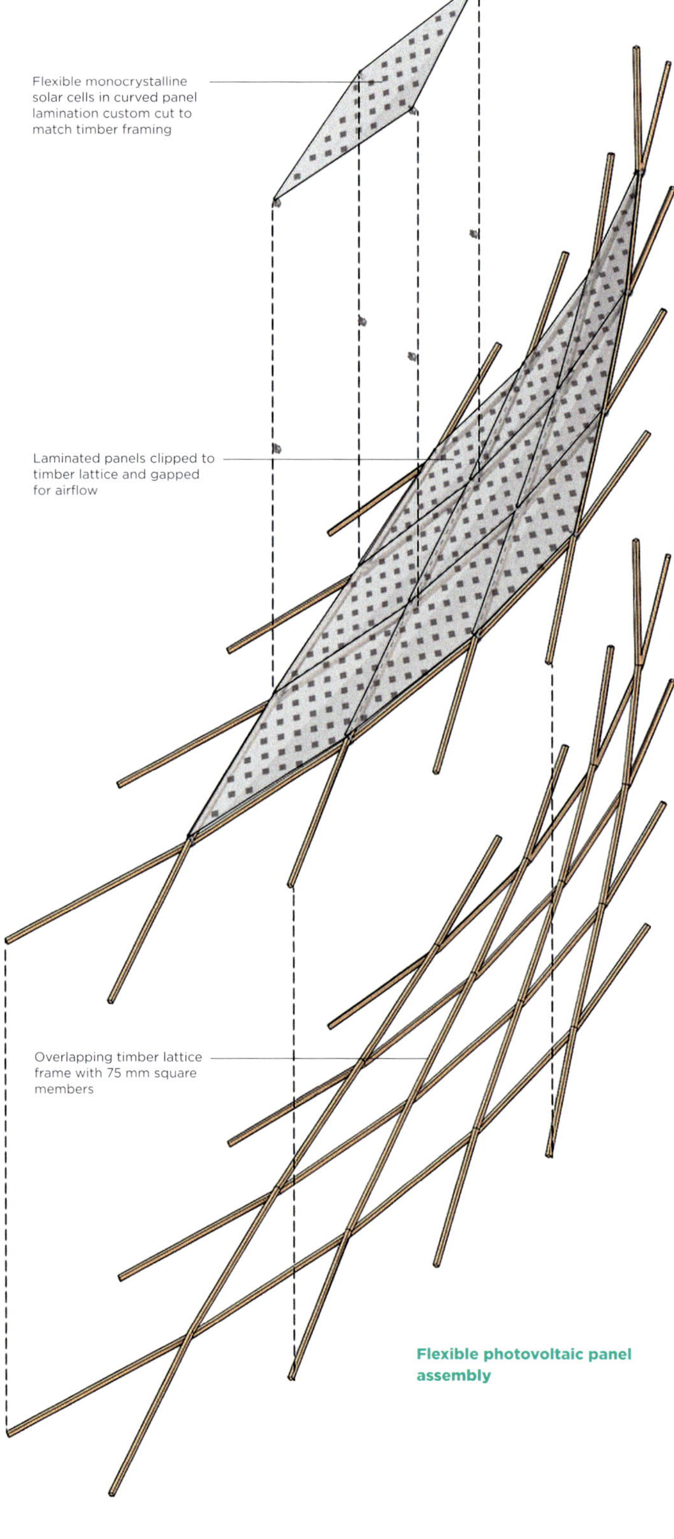

Flexible photovoltaic panel assembly

Beneath a vibrant canopy of filtered light, the community gathers together for music, dance, and storytelling.

Integral to *Valelaca Rokataki* are the distributed solar path lighting and water harvesting elements. An inverted version of the geometry of the main pavilion, they help improve public safety by illuminating village pathways at night and providing distributed access to stored rainwater.

Under One Roof

RIGHT: Aerial view from the south reveals the sculpted, folded geometry of the installation and its spatial organization. North-facing solar modules are seamlessly integrated and hidden from view. The section diagram highlights expansive shaded areas beneath—generous spaces designed for sports, gathering, learning, and rest.

DESIGNERS: Chenyang (Jane) Yu, Haochun Zeng

TECHNOLOGIES: solar photovoltaic, battery energy storage, rainwater harvesting, reservoir storage

ANNUAL PRODUCTION: 330 MWh of electricity, 5 million liters of filtered water

DESIGN TEAM LOCATION: China (Hong Kong SAR)

Sunken public plazas provide overflow rainwater storage. These are discharged early in the dry season and become seasonal spaces for community events.

Under One Roof offers a single, elegant structure that brings together energy, water, and people beneath a simple canopy. Designed as a communal gathering space, it invites Marou Village into a flexible architectural framework, one that adapts daily as a shaded playground, seasonal market, or cultural venue.

A system of steeply angled roofs, tilted at 16° and oriented north, creates a bold and functional geometry. This configuration maximizes solar exposure throughout the year, optimizing energy production for the entire village.

The nearly 4,000-square-meter canopy channels rainwater into an integrated harvesting system. Pipes and gutters follow the roofline, directing water into a collection pond. Seasonal rainfall is stored for irrigation, domestic use, and cooling.

The modular roof structure is constructed from sustainably sourced wood, prefabricated off-site for efficient transport and assembly. Each module is crafted with precision and consistency, enabling quick installation and minimal waste. This approach reduces environmental impact while ensuring the structure remains adaptable and scalable over time.

Maintenance practices are embedded into the design's life cycle, with a community feedback system and educational programming supporting long-term use.

Under One Roof is a statement of unity that is technically sound and socially vibrant. Its open design invites gathering, its solar spine powers the future, and its gently sloping surfaces collect the rain, creating a low-impact, high-utility hub for daily life in Marou Village.

East elevation

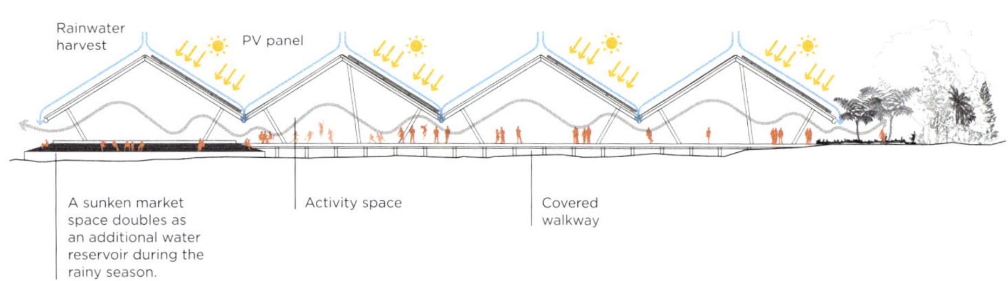

Amphitheater seating surrounds a large public space.

Marou Totem Landscape

RIGHT: The Water Totem mimics the Earth's natural filtration systems, using natural materials and processes to purify water, while incorporating local knowledge during design and fabrication.

DESIGNERS: Eva Perez de Vega, Ian Gordon (e+i studio)

TECHNOLOGIES: solar photovoltaic, battery energy storage, rainwater harvesting, gravity-fed water filtration

ANNUAL PRODUCTION: 104 MWh of electricity, 2.3 million liters of filtered water

DESIGN TEAM LOCATION: United States

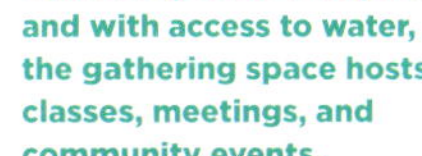

Shaded by solar canopies, and with access to water, the gathering space hosts classes, meetings, and community events.

Marou Totem Landscape is a collaborative project with the people of Marou, combining traditional techniques and natural materials with contemporary design. The result is a modular, tree-like "totem" that collects solar energy and purifies rainwater, offering a low-impact infrastructure rooted in cultural identity.

Each totem is made from a hexagonal timber frame and *bitu dina*, a fast-growing local bamboo. At the top, planter baskets, woven in the style of lovo baskets, hold herbs and act as the first water filter. Rainwater from the solar canopy then passes through layers of natural filtration: coconut coir, loosely woven palm, carbon-infused fibers, and a final ceramic purification system made from local clay. The filtered water is accessed via a faucet at the totem base and stored in a cistern.

Solar panels use smaller, 30-cell modules for ease of transport and maintenance. Connected in parallel, they generate the same power as larger units with less logistical burden.

The design mimics natural systems—drawing inspiration from the rain tree—and is arranged to preserve existing vegetation. *Marou Totem Landscape* is adaptable, scalable, and shaped by local knowledge.

Water harvest detail

Sun capture detail

TAGI LAGI
Plugins for Clean Energy

DESIGNERS: Luisa Ramírez Forero, Luisa Olaya López, Diana Liñán Ariza, Daniel Portillo Hernández, Juan Pérez Alaix, Andrés Ibáñez

TECHNOLOGIES: flexible solar photovoltaic, battery energy storage, rainwater harvesting and biofiltration, underground cisterns

ANNUAL PRODUCTION: 123 MWh of electricity, 4,500 liters of filtered water per module (202,500 liters total for 45 modules)

DESIGN TEAM LOCATION: Colombia

Construction process

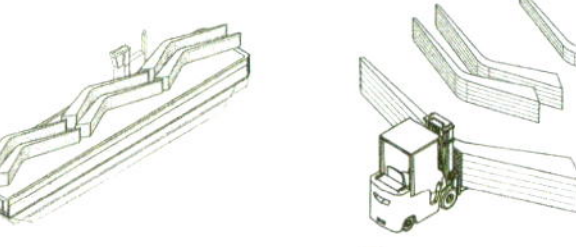

Large components are transported using local barges measuring 4 m × 20 m.

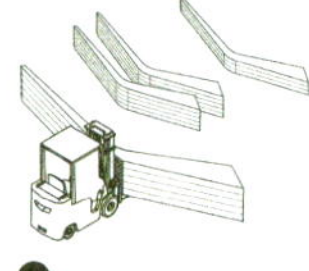

Deliver materials by forklift to the project site.

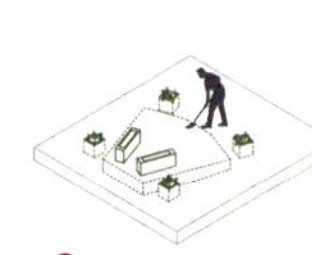

Build foundation for main beams and buttresses.

Lift posts and buttresses. Secure anchor plates.

Bolt purlins to the primary beams.

Fasten natural fiber ceiling with galvanized fittings.

Install bamboo slat ceiling.

Install photovoltaic panels.

Anchor solar panels to beams.

Set planting mesh inside the buttresses.

Use harvested rainwater to maintain clean photovoltaic panels and ensure optimal performance.

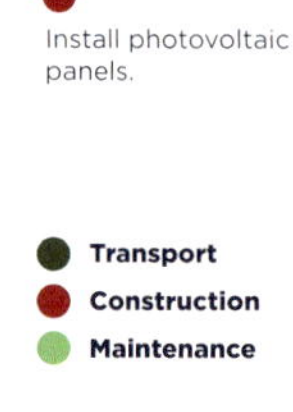

Transport
Construction
Maintenance

RIGHT: Graceful woven canopies arch overhead, offering shade and shelter along a garden path where residents gather, grow food, and share stories—blending traditional craft with contemporary design.

On a remote volcanic island, legend tells of lovers whose tears filled a lake from which the rare tagimoucia flower emerged. *TAGI LAGI* draws inspiration from this flower's layered petals and climbing habit to create a landscape of solar petals that reach for the sun, collect rain, and support community-based agriculture.

Each module — called a plug — is modeled after a petal of the tagimoucia flower and built with low-carbon laminated wood and polycarbonate. Flexible solar panels are mounted on the top layer, tilted northward to capture sunlight efficiently and guide rainwater to integrated channels. The structure is topped with a waterproof canopy and lined underneath with a woven bamboo mat, creating a shaded and culturally resonant space below.

Collected rain flows into gravel-filtered trenches and passive storage ponds. Water is then conveyed by gravity and capillary action to hydroponic beds where edible plants and medicinal herbs are cultivated. No mechanical pumps are needed — gravity does the work.

The system is modular, scalable, and decentralized. Forty-five interconnected petals deliver power for daily village use. Clusters can be added as population and demand grow. Lightweight construction and minimal soil disturbance make it ideal for sensitive landscapes. The artwork is both infrastructure and metaphor — like a climbing vine, it connects land, people, and resources into a resilient network.

Community involvement is integral, from design through construction and maintenance. Residents participate in training workshops focused on solar technology, water conservation, and sustainable agriculture.

TAGI LAGI demonstrates that solutions inspired by natural systems can promote resilience and community well-being in Marou and beyond.

Aerial view of the walking path that meanders through the *TAGI LAGI* modules.

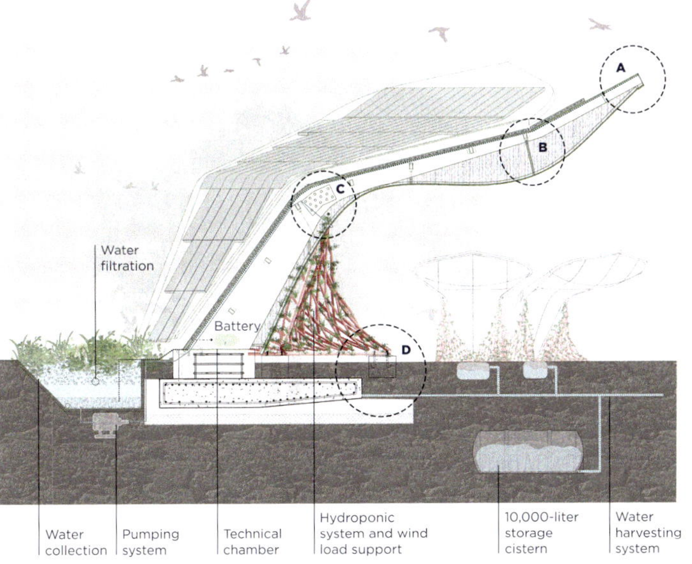

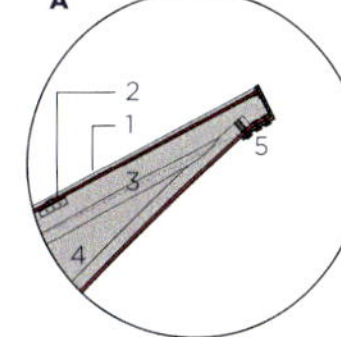

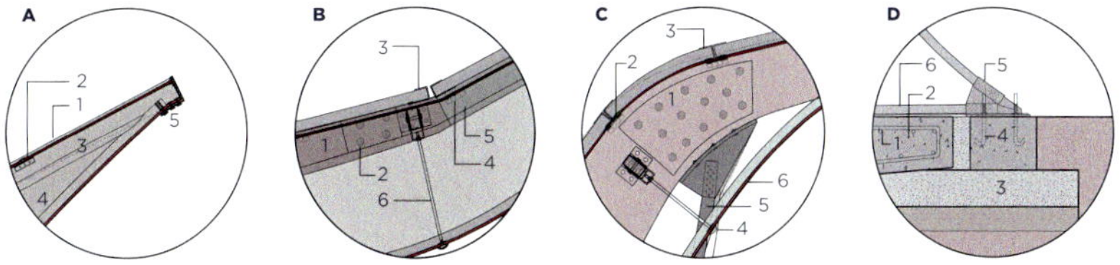

A

1. 4 mm polycarbonate panel
2. Prefabricated steel plates
3. Structural steel ASTM A36
4. Bamboo slats
5. Aluminum blind pop rivets

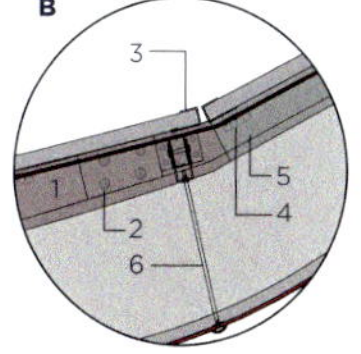

B

1. Prefabricated glue-lam beam
2. Galvanized anchor bolts
3. Solar rail aluminum mounting system
4. Prefabricated steel plates
5. Structural steel ASTM A36
6. Suspended ceiling structural supports

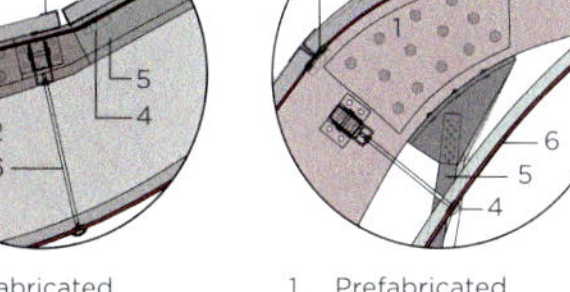

C

1. Prefabricated steel plates
2. Metallic angle
3. Solar rail aluminum mounting system
4. Rubber edge seals
5. 4 mm steel tube
6. Bamboo slats

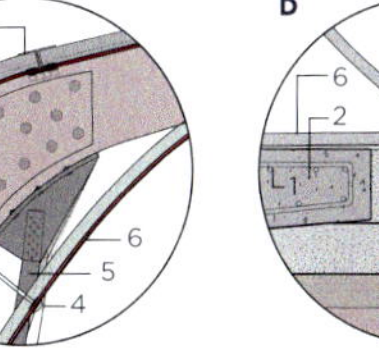

D

1. Reinforcing rod
2. 3,000 psi concrete
3. Concrete base
4. Anchor bolt
5. Steel plates
6. 4 mm steel tube

Threadscape

Children play at dusk in the glow of the vertical axis wind turbine street lamps.

DESIGNERS: Yujin Cao, Doris Qingyi Duanmu, Yiwei Lyu, Liwei Shen, Xi Sun

TECHNOLOGIES: solar photovoltaic, vertical axis wind turbine, battery energy storage, rainwater harvesting, biofiltration, solar distillation, underground cisterns

ANNUAL PRODUCTION: 157 MWh of electricity, 1 million liters of filtered water

DESIGN TEAM LOCATION: United States

RIGHT: Lessons are a common activity under the shade and protection of the Canvas pavilion.

Threadscape is a woven infrastructure, an ecological artwork grounded in the tradition of *tali tali*, the Fijian practice of weaving. Designed for Marou Village, it interlaces solar energy, water harvesting, and cultural space across three architectural scales: Canvas, Patch, and Stitch. Together, they form a living toolkit that adapts to the land, supports community resilience, and celebrates the craft of collective stewardship.

The Canvas, a central land-art pavilion, anchors the system. Its roof supports 120 solar panels generating 157 MWh per year—enough to meet village needs. A network of vertical axis wind turbines supplements the solar array and provides clean electricity during overcast days and overnight while acting as kinetic landmarks across the site. Modular Patch structures extend this system at smaller scales, offering shaded rest stops and localized energy production. The Stitch elements—slender lighting poles and water taps—connect spaces along pathways, creating brief encounters of utility and delight.

Water threads throughout the site. Rain and runoff are collected from roofs and landscapes, filtered through vegetated planters, and retained in biofiltration ponds. The system culminates in a solar-powered evaporation pond, where thermal energy distills water that is stored in a 580,000-liter cistern. During surplus production, ice is generated to support cooling and fish preservation, reducing battery dependence and enhancing food security.

Stitch, Canvas, and Patch come together to form a complete *Threadscape*.

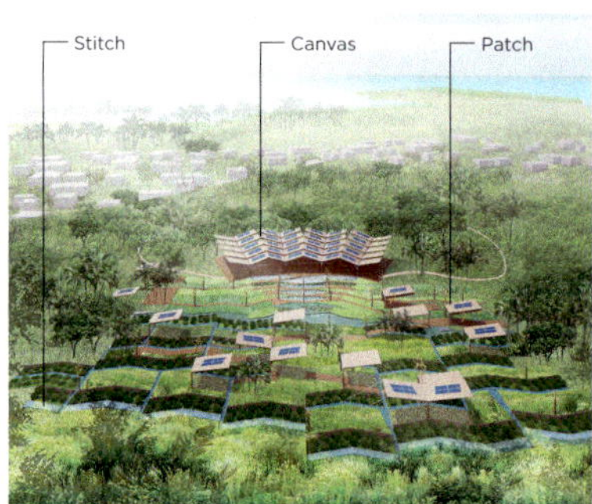

Threadscape also supports ecological restoration. Check dams slow erosion from the surrounding slopes, native plants stabilize the soil, and open ponds mark seasonal abundance. Gathering spaces are threaded into the landscape—amphitheaters by ponds and rest platforms among plantings, inviting ceremony, play, and reflection.

Built from local bamboo, recycled steel, woven textiles, and native fronds, *Threadscape* is low-carbon, modular, and replicable. It is an evolving system woven from light, water, and local knowledge—a landscape that grows with the village, stitch by stitch.

Designed with a systems approach, *Threadscapes* demonstrates the interwoven stocks and flows of energy and water.

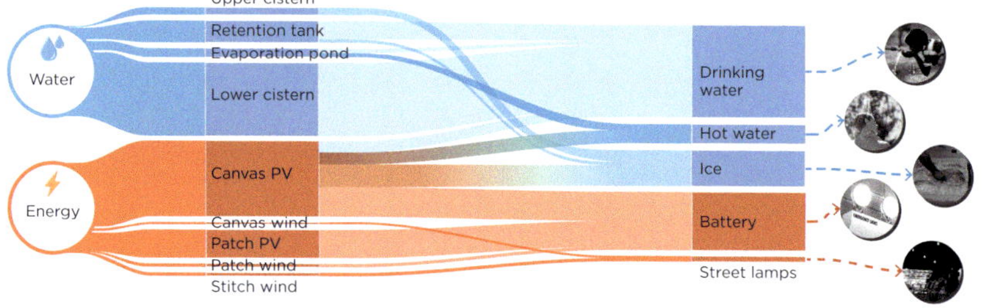

Weaving Marou Village's energy, water, and community threads into an ecological artwork.

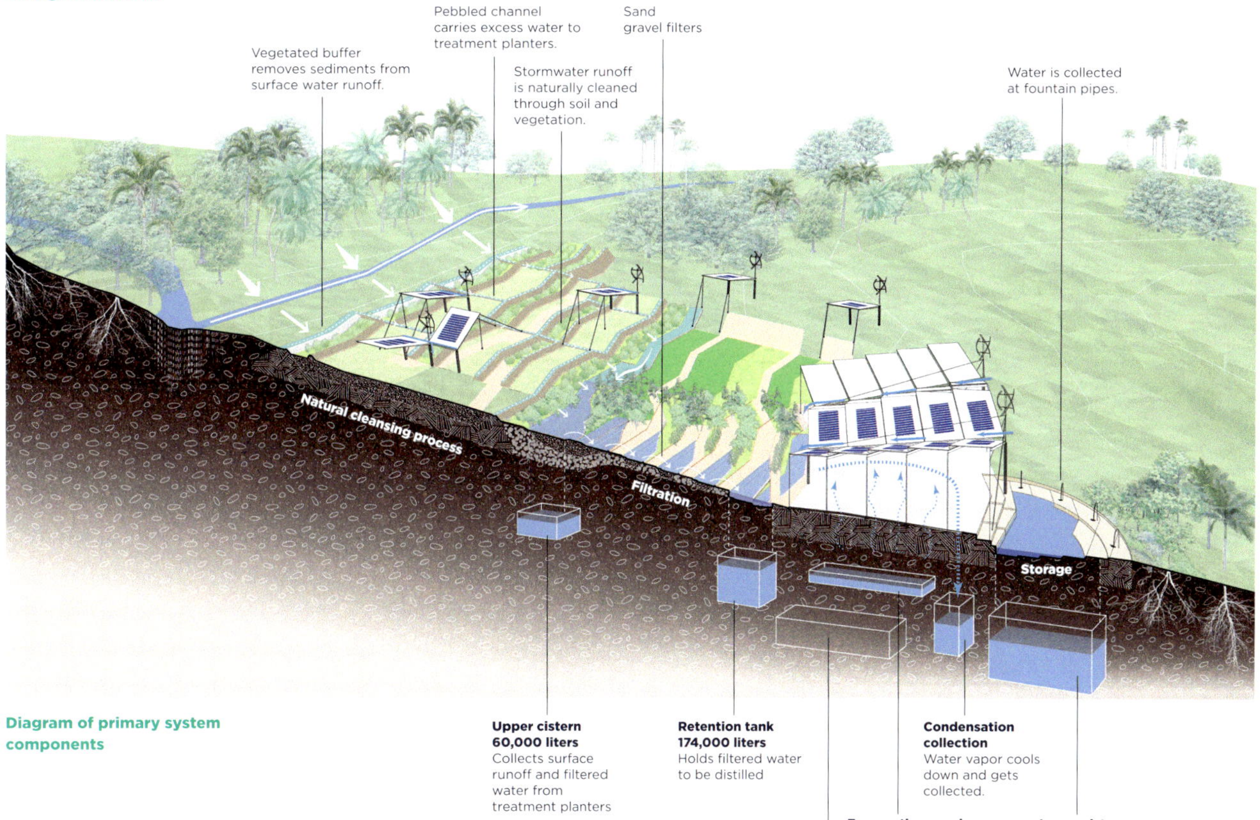

Diagram of primary system components

Vale ni Wai Siga
Aqua Nest Solar Habitat

RIGHT: Triangular solar photovoltaic modules cascade down the sculptural form, creating a striking rhythm of light and shadow. The structure harnesses energy while offering a contemplative space beneath its geometric canopy.

DESIGNERS: Mohamad Rahimizadeh, Fatemeh Rezaei, Mohammad Reza Ghasemi

TECHNOLOGIES: solar photovoltaic, battery energy storage, fog and rainwater harvesting, coconut and algae-based biofiltration, micro-hydro vortex turbine, reservoir storage

ANNUAL PRODUCTION: 135 MWh of electricity, 1.5 million liters of drinking water

DESIGN TEAM LOCATION: United Arab Emirates

Vale ni Wai Siga, meaning "House of Sun and Water," is a regenerative solar habitat that transforms Marou's hillside into a cascading system of energy, water, and agriculture. Drawing from traditional terracing, vernacular materials, and ecological design, the installation weaves light, fog, runoff, and biomass into a closed-loop system.

A bamboo solar canopy forms the central structure, holding 307 photovoltaic panels positioned to reflect the sun's path. Beneath the panels, a network of coconut fiber "veins" filters rainwater as it runs from panel to ground. These fibers double as fog-harvesting nets, oriented to prevailing winds and shaped to enhance condensation. Moisture from air and sky is filtered first by the coconut, then by seaweed biofilters grown in on-site agricultural beds. The result is safe, drinkable water drawn directly from the atmosphere.

At the land's upper edge, a dam slows seasonal floodwaters. Overflow channels feed three small vortex turbines, generating supplemental electricity and irrigating terraced gardens below. These terraces stabilize soil, reduce erosion, and allow for flood irrigation of crops, blending traditional farming practices with modern hydrological design.

The structure is built from locally harvested bamboo and tied with hand-spun coconut rope. Every element — from the algae beds to the filtration lines — is designed for ease of assembly, community maintenance, and circular use. Seaweed cultivation supports both water treatment and nutrition, while local fabrication keeps ownership and knowledge in the village.

Vale ni Wai Siga celebrates the land's rhythms and the community's ability to shape its future. Rain and sunlight become electricity, clean water, food, and shade — woven through a bamboo framework that speaks the language of the land.

Visitors gather in the public plaza at the entrance to the artwork.

The site is terraced into three levels to guide the controlled descent of water, reducing erosion and slowing flow. This design supports traditional flood irrigation techniques, transforming the land into a safe and arable landscape. Above, solar panels are mounted on a spatial bamboo framework that also functions as a dual-purpose system for rainwater collection and purification.

Eco-EnergyScape

RIGHT: The hexagonal modules are nestled into the agricultural landscape just above the village.

DESIGNERS: Sumaiya Rahman Tanisa, Antora Podder, Ryo Abe

TECHNOLOGIES: flexible solar photovoltaic, battery energy storage, rainwater harvesting, fog catchers, above- and below-ground cisterns

ANNUAL PRODUCTION: 260 MWh of electricity, 5.6 million liters of filtered water

DESIGN TEAM LOCATION: Bangladesh

Inspired by the resilience of Fiji's coastal communities, *Eco-EnergyScape* reimagines infrastructure as a living system — uniting ecology, energy, and landscape. The project addresses water scarcity, energy insecurity, and coastal erosion through modular, low-carbon strategies rooted in nature-based solutions and the principles of rejuvenate, coexist, adapt, and grow.

The design features hexagonal modules inspired by honeycombs — efficient, stable forms that support triangular solar panels across a flexible canopy. Each photovoltaic unit generates clean energy while also collecting rainwater, which flows through bamboo channels into underground reservoirs. During dry seasons, fog-harvesting mesh condenses moisture from the air to supplement supply.

Constructed from local bamboo, treated hardwoods, and vines, the system uses simple joinery — twine lashings, notched timber, and stainless-steel joints — that allow it to flex under stress and resist cyclonic winds. All components are modular and easy to repair or replace.

Educational workshops support local fabrication and stewardship, fostering long-term community ownership.

Eco-EnergyScape is infrastructure grown from its environment, collecting from the sky, storing in the earth, and creating shelter in between. Modular, adaptable, and inclusive, it offers a grounded framework for resilience and renewal.

Locals and visitors connect and relax under the shade of interconnected hexagonal modules.

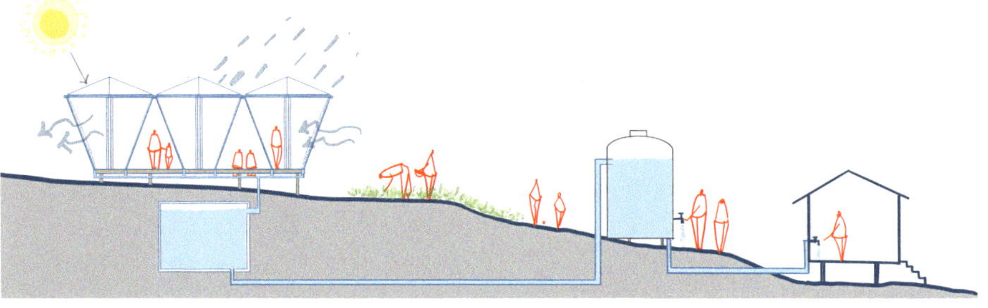

Longitudinal site section

Marou Gathers
A Constellation of Voices, Energy, and Worlds

A view from the tree tops shows the various parts of the system, from rainwater collectors and habitat walls to agrivoltaic farms and solar canopies.

DESIGNERS: Arif Alizada, Aydin Colakoglu, Carmen Beltrán Sangüesa, Chloe Goncalves, Dorothea Joy Mathiopoulos, Feng Yi, Josif Hristovski, Lorenzo Servedio, Nicholas Nolan, Pyeonghwa Park, Rachit Joshi, Shainesh Pillay, Ze Yuan Chao, Dr Patrick Macasaet (RMIT Architecture)

TECHNOLOGIES: solar photovoltaic, hybrid wind and solar systems, water harvesting and filtration

ANNUAL PRODUCTION: 260 MWh of electricity, 1.5 million liters of filtered water

DESIGN TEAM LOCATION: Australia

Marou Gathers envisions an energy-generating landscape that harmonizes with the ecosystems, traditions, and daily rhythms of Marou Village. Inspired by natural systems and Indigenous knowledge, the design integrates architecture, landscape, and infrastructure into a resilient, multifunctional environment.

At its heart are communal structures modeled after the bromeliad flower — each petal-shaped canopy harvesting solar and wind energy, collecting rainwater, and offering shade. Built with bamboo frames and layered polymers, these "petal roofs" symbolize cultural unity and climate adaptation.

Across the site, tensile photovoltaic "solar sails" generate power while forming shaded social zones. A stainless-steel and bamboo Wildlife Wall, patterned after traditional masi designs, fosters native bird habitats by providing nesting space, blending ecology with storytelling.

Parametric bamboo greenhouses support food sovereignty with crops like cassava and guava. Nearby, modular rainwater canopies channel water into underground storage or natural aquifers, aiding watershed restoration.

The Village Energy Station anchors the project, combining hydroelectric infrastructure with civic gathering space.

Throughout the design, land is treated as a shared, living system. Modular, flexible, and culturally resonant, *Marou Gathers* offers a regenerative future where energy, water, food, and community are woven together like the threads of a masi cloth.

Inspired by the structure of the bromeliad flower, the community spaces echo its radial symmetry and form.

TRIvibe

RIGHT: Designed to support the sustainable growth of the local economy, *TRIvibe* provides covered market spaces for the buying and selling of produce grown throughout the Yasawa Islands.

DESIGNERS: Zita Petrák, Alexandra Kurucz, Luca Anna Sápi

TECHNOLOGIES: solar photovoltaic, battery energy storage, UV-treated rainwater harvesting, above-ground cisterns

ANNUAL PRODUCTION: 120 MWh of electricity, 1 million liters of filtered water

DESIGN TEAM LOCATION: Hungary

TRIvibe reimagines the village market as a resilient hub of energy, culture, and connection. Inspired by the structural and symbolic strength of the triangle, the design introduces modular infrastructure that provides solar power, clean water, and shaded space for gathering and exchange.

Each triangular unit is built from recycled timber and corrugated metal roofing, with sloped surfaces that collect rainwater and support photovoltaic panels. The water is filtered via UV treatment and gravity-fed to storage tanks, while the PV panels power lighting, cooling, and charging points across the site.

A total of 48 solar-topped modules generate reliable electricity and shelter daily life. Colorful lamellas add vibrancy, evoking the lively spirit of traditional markets. The modular structures line a new pedestrian path, creating a sequence of shaded stalls, rest areas, and play zones for children along the way.

Construction uses local materials and techniques, and maintenance is designed to be community-led.

TRIvibe is designed to grow with the rhythms of village life, drawing people to Marou for shared exchange, community connection, and mutual benefit.

The modular geometry unfolds into a graceful pathway, weaving visitors through the rhythms of the market.

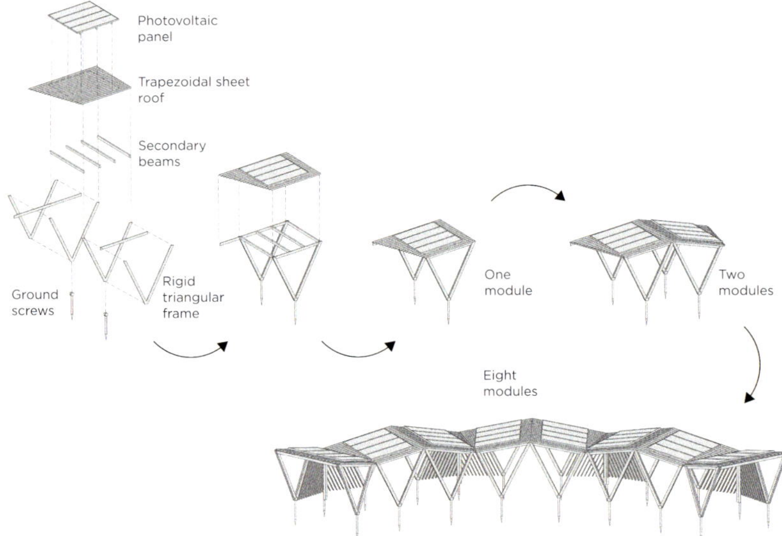

The module is composed of two rigid triangular wooden frames connected by secondary beams. A trapezoidal sheet metal roof spans the top, completing the structural assembly.

Loto Kava Ring

RIGHT: Like a turtle retreating into its shell, the corrugated solar modules can retract into a protective housing during storms, shielding the system from harsh environmental conditions.

DESIGNERS: MiaoShui Huang, JianKun Ye, Ye Ma, JinShuang Chen (MK+ Design Studio); Miao Xu, XiaoFeng Liu, WenXiao Wu

TECHNOLOGIES: solar photovoltaic, battery energy storage, rainwater harvesting and filtration

ANNUAL PRODUCTION: 134 MWh of electricity, 1.2 million liters of filtered water

DESIGN TEAM LOCATION: China

Rooted in the ceremonial traditions of the yaqona ritual, *Loto Kava Ring* creates a gathering place where energy, culture, and ecology converge. At its center, a plaza patterned after the tagimoucia — the national flower of Fiji — anchors the site as an offering, symbolically linking Earth and sky.

Surrounding the plaza is a colonnade inspired by the form of the tanoa bowl. Built with volcanic rock, coconut shell, rattan, and timber, it offers shaded space for community gatherings and supports both village life and sustainable tourism.

On the periphery, a circular photovoltaic array forms a dynamic ring. Each unit contains ten monocrystalline panels, with a combined capacity of 100 kW. In severe weather, the system folds into wind-resistant shells that also house equipment and storage.

Rainwater is collected from the plaza, colonnade, and nearby roofs, filtered through a natural biofiltration system.

Construction is modular and locally accessible, with prefabricated components delivered by barge and installed using hand tools in collaboration with the community. Maintenance is managed by trained local stewards.

Viewed from above, the installation emerges from the landscape as a turtle-shape, a symbol of protection and ancestral memory that makes *Loto Kava Ring* a cultural and ecological landmark.

The view from above reveals the form of the sea turtle.

Koro Coral

RIGHT: A path winds through clusters of *Koro Coral* modules, inviting morning walks as the sun rises over Marou Village.

DESIGNERS: María Paula Ortegón Martínez, David Felipe Torres Ramírez, Alejandra Villamil Camargo, Laura Camila Gómez Roa, Jose Fernando Quintero Jaimes

TECHNOLOGIES: solar photovoltaic, battery energy storage, rainwater harvesting, above-ground cisterns

ANNUAL PRODUCTION: 275 MWh of electricity, 500,000 liters of filtered water

DESIGN TEAM LOCATION: Colombia

Koro Coral brings the ecological logic of the reef onto land. Drawing from the form and function of coral — its role as a climate buffer, habitat, and symbol of resilience — the project offers a terrestrial reef-scape that weaves architecture, culture, and environment into a living infrastructure.

The design uses a modular laminar structure inspired by the layered geometry of coral formations. Each double-curved module is shaped to dissipate wind, maximize solar energy collection, and facilitate rainwater harvesting. When assembled, the modules form larger clusters that rise and fall in height, evoking a stratified coral barrier that meanders across the landscape.

The aerodynamic surfaces are topped with photovoltaic panels and finished in white acrylic to enhance solar efficiency. Beneath, shaded eaves provide gathering space for cultural rituals, performances, and rest. Rainwater is guided into storage tanks integrated within wooden connecting platforms between clusters, minimizing material footprint and optimizing catchment across the site.

Material selection balances durability with vernacular expression: corrosion-resistant steel forms the structural core, while traditional reed and bamboo thatch on the underside invites local craftsmanship and cultural continuity. Cat ladders and a dedicated "control tower" module ensure ease of access and maintenance across the network.

Construction and operation are deeply participatory. Technical training workshops, collaboration with local experts, and iterative feedback loops ensure the system responds to the lived experience of Marou Village. Modular assembly enables flexibility and phased growth. Elevated foundations reduce impact on native flora, and integrated water-flow systems support irrigation.

Koro Coral is a reef above ground — a sheltering, adaptive system that reflects the layered vitality of coral itself. Assembled by many hands and designed to evolve, it offers a model for energy and water infrastructure that grows with the land.

The solar modules collect energy as fog lifts over the foothills of Naviti Island.

A visitor kneels to capture a photo of the artwork in the early morning light.

Sunlight filters through the translucent polycarbonate shells of *Koro Coral*.

Ever Present Naviti

RIGHT: Aerial view of *Ever Present Naviti* reveals a flowing, nature-inspired roofline that integrates solar panels within a parametric bamboo framework, blending seamlessly into the island's lush landscape.

DESIGNERS: Stefi Rescheleit, Eden McGlennon

TECHNOLOGIES: solar photovoltaic, battery energy storage, rainwater harvesting, bioswales, wet pond filtration, above- and below-ground cisterns

ANNUAL PRODUCTION: 118 MWh of electricity, 104,000 liters of filtered water

DESIGN TEAM LOCATION: Canada

Ever Present Naviti is a regenerative landscape that blends energy, water, and agriculture beneath a canopy shaped by nature. Inspired by the pandanus and frangipani—symbols of resilience and welcome—the structure offers a low-impact, high-functioning space that supports community life in harmony with the environment.

The flexible roof stretches across a parametric wooden frame, integrating 400 m^2 of solar photovoltaics. Beneath the canopy, crops such as yams grow in cool, shaded conditions. Rainwater is collected through concealed gutters, filtered via bioswales and rain gardens, and cleaned in a wet-pond system planted with native reeds and grasses.

Built from local vesi hardwood and galvanized steel, the structure is cyclone-ready and long-lasting. Its ETFE-coated solar panels resist salt, wind, and UV exposure, making them well-suited to Fiji's coastal climate.

This is a structure that adapts to people and place—welcoming change, responding to need, and growing over time alongside the community it serves.

Beneath the canopy, edible plants, bioswales, and gathering spaces support daily life in harmony with nature.

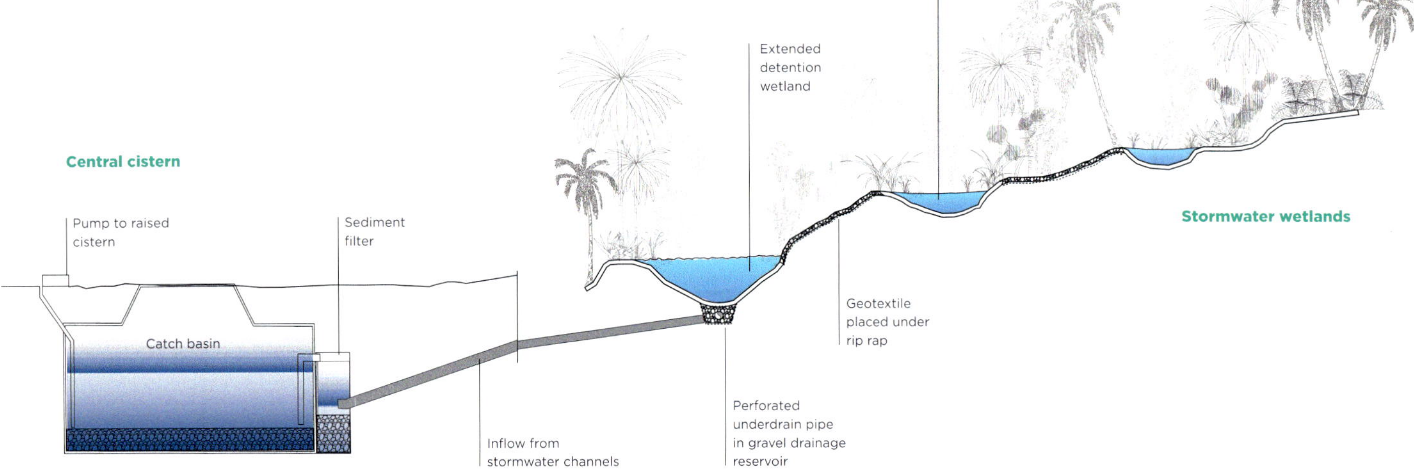

Synergistic Garden

TOP RIGHT: Vertical axis wind turbines with photovoltaic cladding rise from a lush wetland system, integrating clean energy generation with ecological restoration.

CENTER RIGHT: The section shows the alignment of solar wind towers, native vegetation, and water catchment areas in harmony with the natural slope of the site.

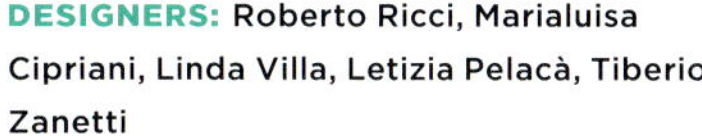

DESIGNERS: Roberto Ricci, Marialuisa Cipriani, Linda Villa, Letizia Pelacà, Tiberio Zanetti

TECHNOLOGIES: solar photovoltaic cladding on vertical axis savonius wind turbine, battery energy storage, engineered wetland, biofiltration, above-ground cisterns

ANNUAL PRODUCTION: 80 MWh of electricity, 1 million liters of filtered water

DESIGN TEAM LOCATION: Italy

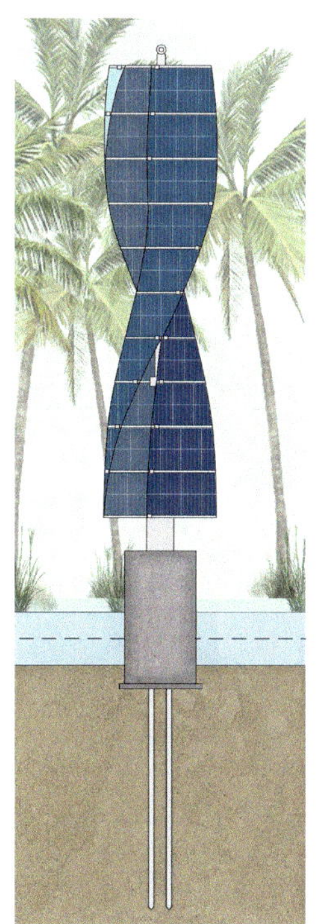

Detail of the tree-inspired wind turbine structure, featuring photovoltaic panels and a minimal footprint to preserve the landscape and allow for localized maintenance.

Synergistic Garden is a regenerative landscape system that unites architecture, agriculture, and energy infrastructure into a self-sufficient model for the Village of Marou. Designed to meet daily water and energy needs without compromising ecological integrity, the project relies on passive and renewable systems shaped by the natural terrain. Basins set within terraced slopes collect seasonal rainwater for use in irrigation and drinking, while vertical axis wind turbines with photovoltaic-coated blades generate power—even in low wind conditions—without harming birdlife or disrupting the visual landscape.

All design elements draw from locally sourced materials, including wood and stone, to minimize the carbon footprint and support the local economy. Basins planted with native vegetation filter water, protect biodiversity, and leave well-irrigated spaces for cultivating staple crops like cassava and taro. The turbine design, refined and tree-like, reinforces the integration of technology with nature.

Pathways throughout the site invite educational tourism while preserving the terrain. A phased implementation strategy, with strong community participation ensures long-term stewardship. Monitoring tools and trained local residents support resilience and autonomy.

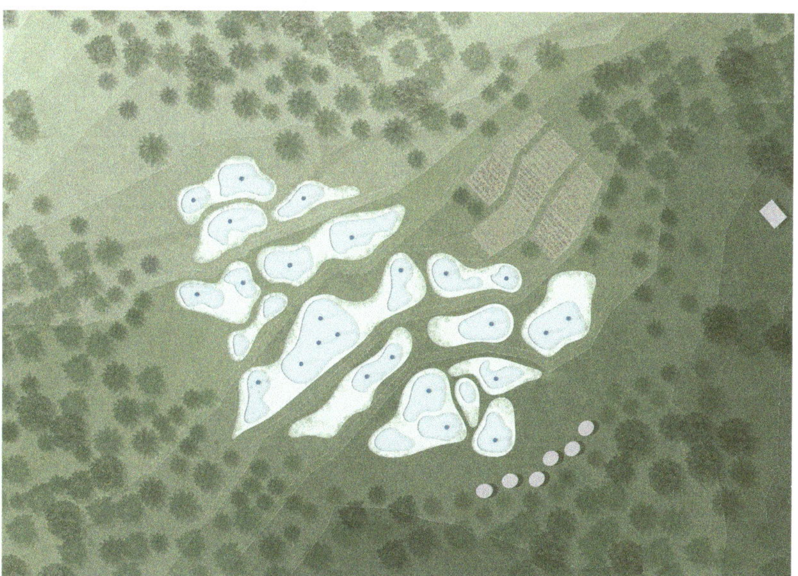

The site plan illustrates the distributed layout of basins, bioswales, and planted terraces designed to slow, filter, and retain seasonal rainwater across the terrain.

Synergistic Garden offers a vision of how human settlements can learn from natural systems, harvesting the energy of the surrounding environment in multifaceted and resilient ways.

The Fifth Element

RIGHT: Community members pass beneath the angular solar canopy of Pavilion One, which generates electricity while providing shade and shelter in the village landscape.

DESIGNERS: Anastasia Lukashchuk, Anastasia Sergeeva

TECHNOLOGIES: solar photovoltaic, battery energy storage, vertical axis wind turbine, rainwater harvesting, atmospheric condensation, food cultivation

ANNUAL PRODUCTION: 156 MWh of electricity, 470,000 liters of filtered water

DESIGN TEAM LOCATION: Russia

The Fifth Element is a modular system of pavilions that brings together clean energy, freshwater, and food cultivation to support daily life in Marou Village. Each structure serves a specific purpose, while together they create a resilient and flexible community hub.

Pavilion One generates electricity from 256 m^2 of solar panels. Pavilion Two harvests rainwater through a large roof catchment system. Pavilion Three combines rainwater harvesting with vertical axis wind turbines that generate additional power. These three structures work in tandem to supply water and energy for various uses.

Pavilion Four is a shaded amphitheater for community gatherings, workshops, and celebrations. The land itself acts as Pavilion Five—a network of food gardens planted with native vegetables, fruits, and herbs that support food security and cultural continuity.

Built using simple angles and standard materials, each pavilion is designed to be assembled and maintained by the community.

The Fifth Element is a place to live, learn, and come together. It grows with the community, powered by sun, wind, rain, and the deep knowledge of people connected to their land.

A view of Pavilion Three shows the integration of vertical axis wind turbines with rainwater harvesting, forming a hybrid energy and water system responsive to local climate conditions.

Pavilion Two is planted with native crops, transforming the landscape into a living pantry that supports food security, ecological education, and cultural continuity.

Sun and Mist Harvest

RIGHT: The compact, pyramid-shaped system combines solar energy generation with fog water harvesting. Wrapped in protective mesh and textile panels, it shields vital infrastructure from wind and debris while channeling sun and mist into clean power and potable water.

DESIGNERS: Violett Birgés, Leona Tekla Hábetler, Sára Magyar

TECHNOLOGIES: solar photovoltaic, battery energy storage, fog harvesting nets with cultural patterning

ANNUAL PRODUCTION: 126 MWh of electricity, 700,000 liters of filtered water

DESIGN TEAM LOCATION: Hungary

Sun and Mist Harvest captures two of Fiji's most generous but underutilized resources — sunlight and moisture in the air — to provide clean energy and freshwater for the Village of Marou. The structure blends cultural expression with ecological function, serving as both shelter and shared gathering space.

The installation acts as an atmospheric water harvesting system, built from local palm wood and wrapped with a canopy of fine mesh decorated with local patterns. As moist air moves through the mesh, water condenses and collects in filtered storage containers below. Rubber expanders hold the mesh taut while absorbing high winds, with a thin upper layer protecting solar panels from falling debris during storms without shading the modules too much.

The solar roof houses 448 m^2 of photovoltaic panels, supplying electricity for lighting, tools, and community programs. The system is decentralized and low-tech, with components designed for ease of repair and maintenance.

Rain, dew, and fog are captured together, helping to stabilize the freshwater supply. Each module can function as a workshop and learning center, supporting education, resilience, and cultural continuity.

Sun and Mist Harvest is a light, resilient framework — one that draws from the air and sky to sustain life on the land.

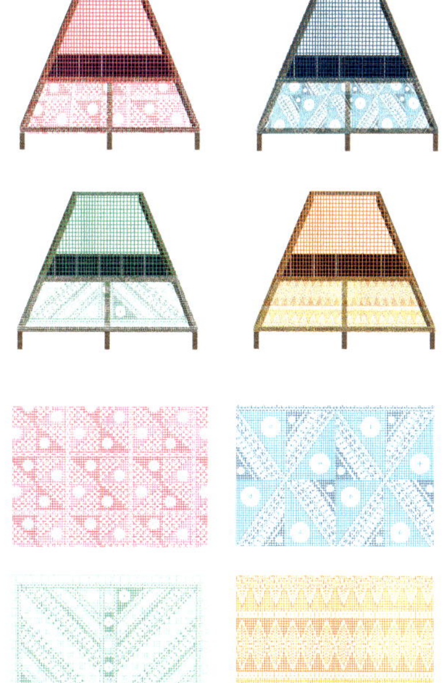

The mesh is adorned with traditional patterns, adding cultural richness that reflects local heritage.

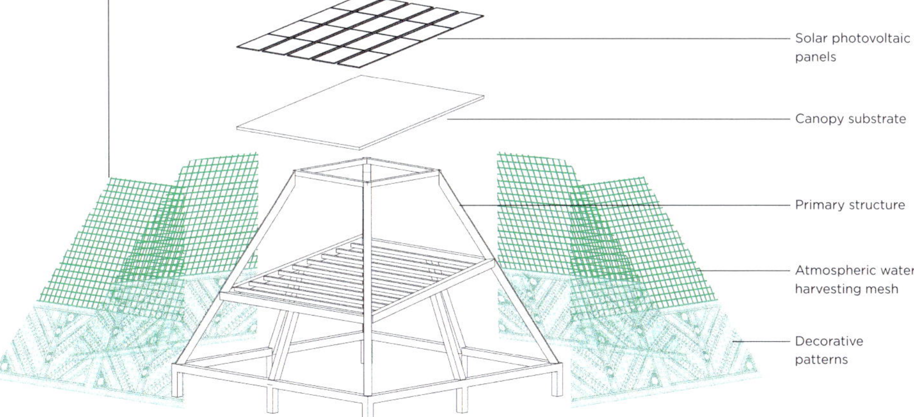

UmbraWell

RIGHT: *UmbraWell* is designed to share land use with agriculture.

DESIGNER: Madison Fraser

TECHNOLOGIES: thin-film solar photovoltaic, battery energy storage, rainwater harvesting with natural filtration

ANNUAL PRODUCTION: 120 MWh of electricity, 680,000 liters of filtered water

DESIGN TEAM LOCATION: United States

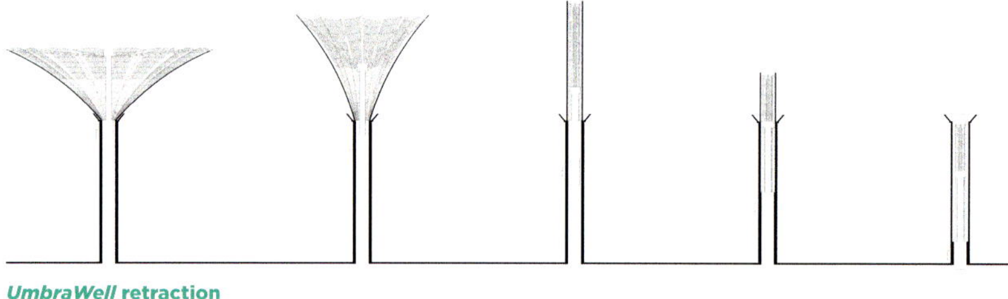

***UmbraWell* retraction process**

UmbraWell is a community-based infrastructure system that combines solar energy, rainwater harvesting, and traditional Fijian craftsmanship. Inspired by the form of an inverted umbrella, each canopy collects water and sunlight while providing shade and a gathering place for residents.

The structure features a woven pandanus surface stretched over a bamboo frame. Rain is funneled through a spout lined with natural fibers and filtered before being stored in underground tanks for household and agricultural use. In storm conditions, the flexible canopy can be collapsed and secured within the downspout for protection.

Thin-film photovoltaic panels are integrated into the canopy's upper surface, generating clean electricity for nearby homes, farms, and solar lighting along village paths. The system is modular and can be expanded or replicated across different contexts.

Local materials — bamboo, coconut fronds, and pandanus — make construction low-impact and familiar. Re-thatching becomes a seasonal ritual, inviting community participation and the sharing of intergenerational knowledge.

UmbraWell envisions a resilient design where technology and tradition work in harmony within Marou Village.

***UmbraWell* axonometric**

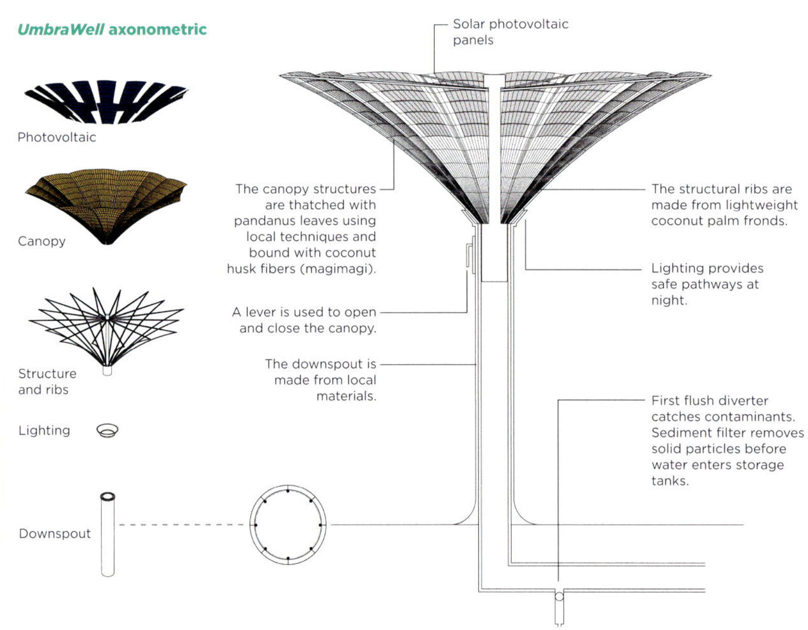

Savu

Inspired by the branching forms of coral, this vibrant canopy structure creates shaded, interconnected spaces beneath a wave of solar-active surfaces—merging aesthetic elegance with renewable energy generation.

DESIGNERS: Kishani De Silva, Jose Aguirre, Yeraz Bandary, Shy-Ann Braceros-Hinau, Davean Cruz, Jade Royer, William Saint (Woodbury University);

TECHNOLOGIES: solar photovoltaic integrated into ETFE, structurally engineered bamboo, rainwater harvesting, bioswales, solar tile pathways

ANNUAL PRODUCTION: 75 MWh of electricity, 113,500 liters of filtered water

DESIGN TEAM LOCATION: United States

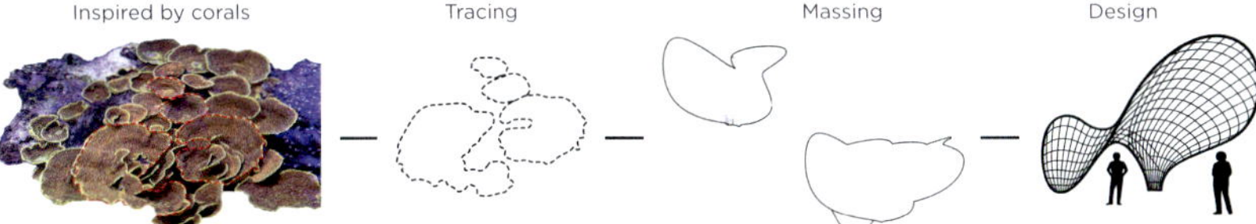

Savu, named after the Fijian word meaning "the edge of a waterfall," is a biomorphic pavilion that gathers solar energy and rainwater while offering shaded space for gathering, rest, and reflection. Inspired by coral formations and forest canopies, the design evokes a living reef system emerging from the land.

The canopy structures, called "Solar Corals," are made from structurally engineered bamboo and wrapped in ETFE skins embedded with colorful solar wafers. These generate electricity while casting filtered light in vibrant patterns across the ground. Rainwater is channeled through bamboo downspouts into underground cisterns, with overflow channeled into bioswales and gardens.

Savu is designed to operate as a decentralized infrastructure system. Water is filtered for irrigation and potable use, while solar tiles along village paths extend energy access. All systems are modular, replicable, and designed for easy maintenance by residents.

Construction uses regenerative, zero-waste materials and embraces a design-for-disassembly approach. The structures are intended to evolve with the needs of the community, eventually returning to the earth.

The installation touches the ground lightly, offering beauty and respite while providing sustainable energy and water resources.

Rainwater harvesting diagram

Filtered rainwater
Main water tank
Overflow tank

Exploded diagram of component parts

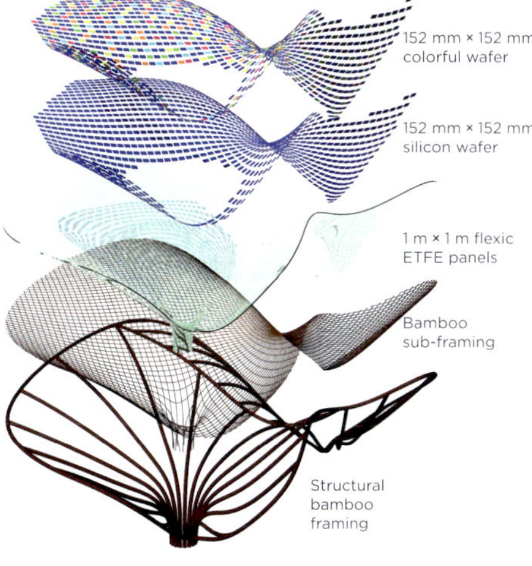

Mataliki

RIGHT: Aerial view of the site layout shows the catchment ponds, the outer ring of solar agrivoltaic canopies, the Pleiades pattern of the inner canopies that shade public spaces, and the pavilion, which houses electrical systems, water storage and treatment, energy storage, and food storage.

DESIGNERS: Giuseppe Orsini, Matteo Rosa, Marzia Carosi, Federico Zelano, Giovanni Ceselli

TECHNOLOGIES: solar photovoltaic, vertical axis wind turbine, salt battery energy storage, rainwater harvesting, wet pond, SODIS water purification, above-ground cisterns

ANNUAL PRODUCTION: 170 MWh of electricity, 5.8 million liters of filtered water

DESIGN TEAM LOCATION: Italy

Site plan

Named after the Fijian word for the Pleiades star cluster, *Mataliki* honors the celestial signals that once guided Pacific navigators. Just as the rising of *Mataliki* marked the start of the sailing season, this design signals a new beginning— uniting renewable energy, water harvesting, and agrivoltaic farming into a resilient community infrastructure.

At the heart of the design is a hybrid mini-grid system combining 80.6 kW of solar capacity with 14 kW of vertical axis bamboo wind turbines. Flexible triangular sails, modeled after traditional Fijian vessels and made from recycled fishing nets, carry 10.6 kW of photovoltaic panels. Additional panels, totaling 70 kW, are arranged horizontally on agrivoltaic structures that provide shade for crops like kava, taro, and bele. The integration of solar and wind smooths fluctuations in production, reducing battery needs by over 35% over solar alone.

A 500 kWh salt-based battery array supports energy storage, offering safety, longevity, and environmental benefits over conventional lithium systems. Power flows are managed by a smart converter, balancing supply from solar, wind, and battery storage to meet community needs, including cultural lighting installations that mirror the Pleiades when viewed from above.

Rainwater is captured through a system of two artificial ponds, totaling over 5,800 cubic meters. One pond supplies irrigation for the agrivoltaic fields, while the other supports domestic needs and solar purification through the SODIS method. Recycled water is stored in rooftop and ground-level tanks, ensuring safe access across the site.

Designed for easy assembly, storm resilience, and low maintenance, the entire infrastructure is modular and largely demountable. Bamboo structures and wind turbines are built to last generations, using dry construction techniques that allow for repairs and upgrades over time.

Mataliki offers a vision of interdependence between stars and soil, tradition and technology, helping us navigate our way to a sustainable future.

The solar canopy modules are designed to be easily disassembled and reassembled to suit the needs of the community and to protect them from damaging winds.

Hibiscus

RIGHT: Aerial view of the *Hibiscus* installation reveals a clustered arrangement of modular petal pods with thatched roofs and integrated solar panels, anchored by vertical axis wind turbines—demonstrating how traditional forms and renewable technologies converge to support resilient, self-sufficient village life.

DESIGNERS: Arianna Vignati, Davide Benvenuti, Piero Fissore, Luna La Volpe, Nellie Nicholas, Samnang Oum, Alessandro Bianciardi, Monica Rossi, Gaetano Cascini, Michelle Douglas, Chi Ryan, Scott Skipworth, Dirk Vos

TECHNOLOGIES: flexible solar photovoltaic, micro wind turbine, battery energy storage, constructed wetland, rainwater harvesting, above-ground cisterns

ANNUAL PRODUCTION: 140 MWh of electricity, 930,000 liters of filtered water

DESIGN TEAM LOCATION: Australia

When the rain comes and the wind howls, the petals close. Like the flower it's named after, *Hibiscus* responds with grace, collapsing gently, protecting what matters, and reopening to the light when the skies clear.

Built from bamboo and shaped by community imagination, *Hibiscus* is a field of modular petal pods — each one a resilient, biomimetic structure that gathers sun and wind, stores clean water, and creates a living, adaptable ecosystem for Marou Village. Beneath their curved canopies, the pods form playful public space and storm-resistant shelter, a dynamic blend of nature and architecture.

The modular shelters display designs co-created with elders and children, evolving each year with new patterns and stories. These textiles and structural skins act as both insulation and expression, blending cultural storytelling with climate-responsive design.

At night, solar-powered lighting illuminates walkways and fish refrigeration units hum quietly beneath the pods — sustaining food, safety, and livelihoods. The elevated platforms support education, arts, and eco-tourism.

Each petal-shaped pod is designed with a mechanical system integrated into both the poles and the curved roof, enabling the entire structure to collapse gently in response to environmental threats.

Textiles are refreshed through community-led workshops, and residents are trained in monitoring energy and water systems. *Hibiscus* is a living system that blooms in response to need, weaving together the threads of tradition and technology.

Site plan

The exterior of a *Hibiscus* petal pod shows its elegant, biomimetic roof structure, providing shaded gathering space beneath its bamboo canopy.

Solar powered cold storage sits within the protected interior where fish are bought and sold.

Looking up from within the structure, the lightweight bamboo frame and woven roofing panels illustrate how traditional materials can be combined with contemporary design.

Herpolitha Weberi

DESIGNERS: Jose Carlos de Silva, Leonardo de Silva, Rodrigo Marquez

TECHNOLOGIES: solar photovoltaic, battery energy storage, rainwater harvesting and filtration

ANNUAL PRODUCTION: 140 MWh of electricity, 670,000 liters of filtered water

DESIGN TEAM LOCATION: Sweden

TOP: Aerial view of ***Herpolitha Weberi*** reveals the design's spiral pentagonal geometry nestled into the landscape—an organic form that shapes a solar canopy around a central elliptical garden, integrating renewable energy and ecological restoration.

Close-up of tilted solar panels mounted on galvanized steel spirals, designed to flex and adapt like coral—capturing sun and rain while defining walkable, shaded paths.

Inspired by the coral species *Herpolitha weberi*, this design unfolds as a living reef on land — a modular energy and water system that shapes both power and presence. Its spiraling pentagonal form, drawn from marine biology, adapts fluidly to the terrain, becoming both a shaded gathering path and a solar-generating canopy. It wraps around a central elliptical garden that may be cultivated, played in, or left wild.

Each "sail" — solar panels shaped like traditional Fijian drua—rests on galvanized steel pipes threaded into continuous pentagonal spirals. These tilted forms capture sunlight and direct rainfall into a network of passive filters, while casting protective shade across the ground. The result is a system that generates electricity, purifies water, and creates space for rest, play, and learning.

The structure is entirely modular. Assembled from threaded joints and anchored by the weight of local soil, rock, and integrated tanks, it requires no concrete. It can be deployed, removed, or reshaped with minimal disturbance. Batteries and inverters are suspended beneath the sails — secure, yet accessible.

Rainwater filters through gravel and sand beneath each module, then flows to a central UV and chlorination unit. With each new site, the form flexes — scaling, shifting, and orienting itself like coral responding to its surroundings.

Herpolitha Weberi proposes infrastructure that is humble, adaptive, and vital, emulating marine ecosystems while meeting the essential needs of island life.

LEFT: The modular design allows each sail structure to act independently for phasing and scalability.

Tree of Life

Towering canopy structures hover above a lush landscape, capturing sunlight and channeling rainwater to irrigate the gardens below—where renewable energy, food cultivation, and habitat restoration work in unison.

DESIGNERS: Alex Yakupov, Kirill Taravko

TECHNOLOGIES: solar photovoltaic, battery energy storage, rainwater harvesting and filtration, underground cisterns

ANNUAL PRODUCTION: 275 MWh of electricity, 360,000 liters of filtered water

DESIGN TEAM LOCATION: Russia

Aerial perspective reveals the modular layout of *Tree of Life*, where photovoltaic canopies and layered planting beds form a network of off-grid infrastructure.

Tree of Life is a modular energy and water farm designed to integrate seamlessly with the natural environment. Made from lightweight, semi-transparent materials, the structure offers a low-impact way to generate electricity, collect rainwater, and support local agriculture, while doubling as a space for gathering and rest.

The central canopy hosts photovoltaic panels that supply clean power to surrounding homes and systems. Rainwater is funneled into storage tanks, then filtered through an automated system that adjusts based on rainfall, water levels, and quality data from built-in sensors.

Beneath and around the canopy, food gardens flourish. Solar modules and planting beds are arranged to maximize both crop yield and environmental comfort. Some areas are partly shaded, while others are exposed to the sun. Together, they support food security and ecological resilience.

Built from durable, low-footprint materials, such as engineered polymers and polyvinyl-based glazing, the system is modular and easy to maintain. Local teams can handle daily operations, with minimal need for outside expertise.

Tree of Life is a concise and effortless way to bring comfort and well-being to communities—connecting energy, water, food, and nature in a single, regenerative system.

Beneath the canopies, dappled light filters through semi-transparent solar panels to create comfortable microclimates for farming, gathering, and community.

Solar Shelter

RIGHT: The design reinterprets the traditional Fijian bure as a resilient, solar-powered community hub. At ground level, shaded courtyards support daily life and recreation, while an aerial view reveals the modular hexagonal layout—optimized for solar capture, rainwater harvesting, and storm resilience through strategically placed storage and retention basins.

DESIGNERS: Dawid Andrzejczak, Mateuśz Kuczynski

TECHNOLOGIES: solar photovoltaic with retractable roller system, battery energy storage, modular thatched roof rainwater harvesting with filtration, above- and below-ground cisterns

ANNUAL PRODUCTION: 134 MWh of electricity, 900,000 liters of filtered water

DESIGN TEAM LOCATION: Poland

Solar Shelter reimagines the traditional Fijian bure for a climate-challenged future—fusing cultural heritage with durable, low-impact solar infrastructure. Designed for extreme weather, the system emphasizes resilience, simplicity, and community safety.

The village complex is arranged around a central path, with monocrystalline solar panels stretched horizontally between rooftops like woven shade mats. Thanks to Fiji's high solar insolation, the horizontal orientation yields strong energy returns while allowing design flexibility. During cyclones, the panels retract along rails into protective enclosures beneath the roofline, eliminating the need for overbuilt structural reinforcement.

Rainwater is harvested from thatched roof areas and filtered through a solar-powered reverse osmosis system. Storage tanks, placed above and below ground, double as ballast during storms and ensure year-round water access. A proposed retention basin manages seasonal overflow and reduces flood risk.

Construction draws on traditional building methods, adapted for strength and longevity. Materials include wood, bamboo, and coconut fiber, which minimizes carbon impact and reinforces cultural continuity.

A dedicated workshop enables local artisans to maintain and repair system components. Modular design simplifies rebuilding and expansion.

Solar Shelter is a canopy of protection and a foundation for independence—crafted by hand, grounded in tradition, and built to weather the future.

Classes on traditional weaving techniques take place rain or shine within the shelter.

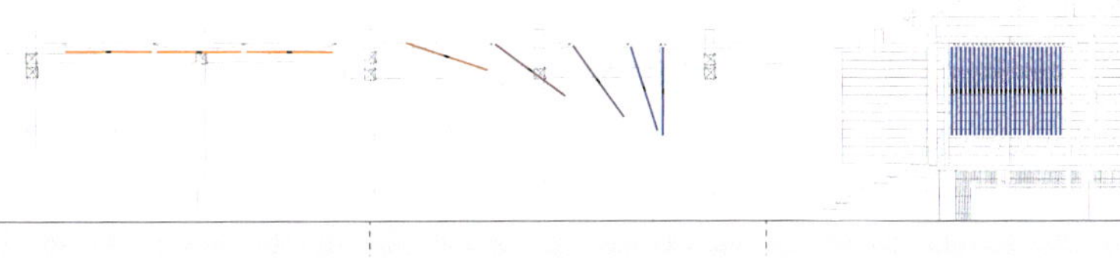

Fair weather setting
The horizontal orientation of the solar panels balances energy production with practical application.

Folding method
Pulling in the panels takes only a few minutes and stores them safely in the event of high speed winds.

Cyclone setting
PV panels are safely housed in a protected shed during storm events. When the skies clear they can be effortlessly hoisted back to provide energy for storm recovery.

Braided Nature
The Power of Welcoming

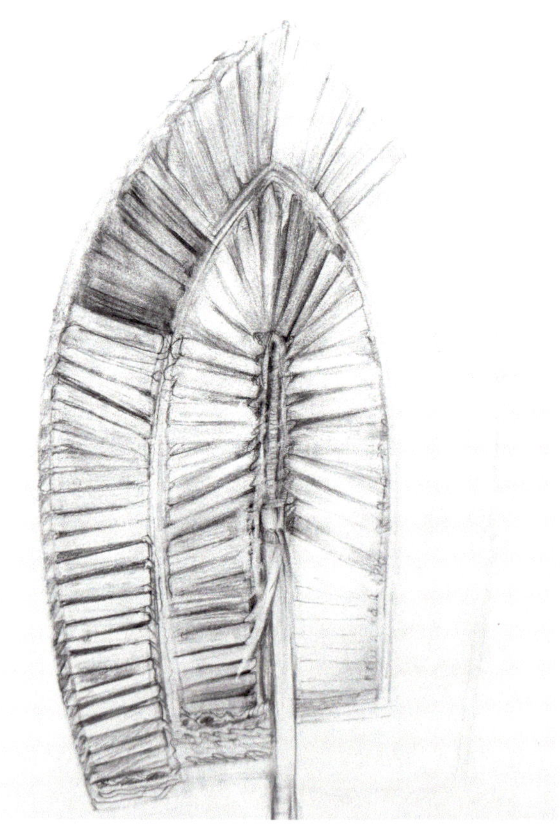

RIGHT: Concept sketch of the solar canopy structure, inspired by braided textures and vernacular forms such as fans and traditional mats.

DESIGNER: Kelly Lee Devrome

TECHNOLOGIES: solar photovoltaic, battery energy storage, photoelectric bricks, rainwater harvesting, graywater treatment

ANNUAL PRODUCTION: 33 MWh of electricity, 70,000 liters of filtered water

DESIGN TEAM LOCATION: United Arab Emirates

Braided Nature is a site-responsive installation shaped by the rhythms of Marou and the artist's own formative experiences in Fiji and Vanuatu. It brings together ecological design, ancestral knowledge, and traditional forms — ceremonial baskets, masks, and fans — to explore how people and place are braided together through time.

At its core is a modular solar canopy supported by marine-grade steel and volcanic rock, integrated with photoelectric modules and kinetic elements that move with the wind and tide. The system generates renewable electricity and collects rainwater, while treating graywater through natural reed beds. Paths are permeable and illuminated by soft solar lights to protect nocturnal wildlife.

Gardens planted with native and medicinal species surround the site. Together with shaded spaces beneath the canopy, they create a setting for community gathering, storytelling, and co-learning. Maintenance is shared among local stewards trained through collaborative workshops with artisans and educators.

This project is a personal gesture of gratitude. It offers a way to give back — to celebrate our relationship with the land, with one another, and with the enduring sense of welcome that defines these islands.

The sketch evokes the layered textures and sensory qualities that define the installation's relationship to the site.

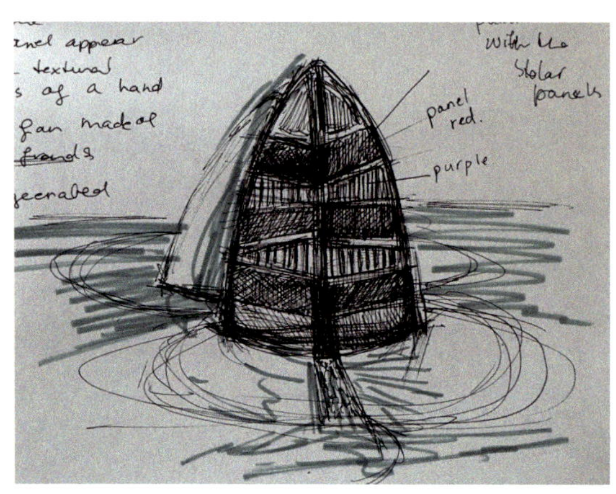

Early design notes showing the spatial layout and function of the canopy system, integrating solar energy, water harvesting, and gathering space.

Structural study exploring the vertical rhythm and movement of the braided photovoltaic modules in relation to prevailing winds.

Salusalu Marou Solar Park

RIGHT: Each petal-shaped pod harvests solar energy and rainwater, while providing shaded space for gathering, learning, and rest.

DESIGNER: Jason A. Balinbin

TECHNOLOGIES: solar photovoltaic rainwater pods, solar-powered water filtration, battery energy storage, above-ground cisterns

ANNUAL PRODUCTION: 125 MWh of electricity, 1 million liters of filtered water

DESIGN TEAM LOCATION: United States

Like a salusalu — the traditional garland woven to welcome and honor — *Salusalu Marou Solar Park* binds energy, water, and tradition into a living system. This reimagined utility blends clean power with educational space, gardens, and resilient public infrastructure.

At its core is a modular pod: a hexagonal photovoltaic canopy with integrated rainwater harvesting. Each 3.2 kW pod channels water into portable barrels, with overflow directed to a central pond for stormwater retention and aquifer recharge. Pods are linked along a landscaped path — like beads on a garland — woven through native plantings, edible gardens, and shaded rest areas. Underground conduits distribute water and power throughout the park.

The site includes a shaded amphitheater and outdoor classroom, co-designed with Yasawa School, alongside a solar tech demo zone and interpretive signage for hands-on learning. A community garden supports food resilience and stewardship.

Construction is comprised of local materials — bamboo, timber, masonry, and recycled components — and emphasizes low-tech, cyclone-resistant design. Tilted roofs and open canopies allow airflow and reduce wind pressure.

Salusalu Marou Solar Park is a scalable model for energy, water, and education — encircling the village in a garland of resilience and welcome.

Aerial view of the central hub, where educational gardens, energy infrastructure, and community spaces are interwoven.

The full park layout reveals the modular design of interconnected pods, linking energy, water, and education into a living garland.

The Breath of Marou

RIGHT: A corridor of elevated bamboo structures integrates reused solar panels and wind-activated flutes to create energy, shade, and gentle soundscapes for the village.

DESIGNERS: Wasif Ajwad, Zareen Mehzabin Tabassum

TECHNOLOGIES: solar photovoltaic, wind flutes, reused panel shading, and rainwater-cooled earthen pitchers

ANNUAL PRODUCTION: 547 MWh of electricity, 240,000 liters of filtered water

DESIGN TEAM LOCATION: Bangladesh

The Breath of Marou is a musical landscape that transforms sunlight, rain, and wind into sound, energy, and shade. Inspired by traditional basket weaving patterns, the artwork creates a space where climate infrastructure becomes an immersive, sensory experience—a breathing, musical organism.

Composed of six modular bamboo structures and 600 woven units, the canopy integrates functional and recycled solar panels to provide energy and shelter. Reused non-functioning solar panels shade visitors and harvest rainwater, while 1,000 functioning photovoltaic panels generate clean electricity. Rainwater flows into 2,400 earthen pitchers suspended beneath the canopy, where they cool the air through natural evaporation and provide a water reserve for village use.

Wind-activated bamboo flutes line the structure, creating gentle tonal shifts as breezes pass through. These sounds animate a quiet grove that doubles as a social space, cooling refuge, and educational site for community members and visitors alike.

The design emphasizes local craftsmanship, circular materials, and low-impact construction.

The Breath of Marou is a system that listens as much as it speaks. It channels the rhythms of wind, water, and sun into a shared ecological performance that resonates both spatially and culturally.

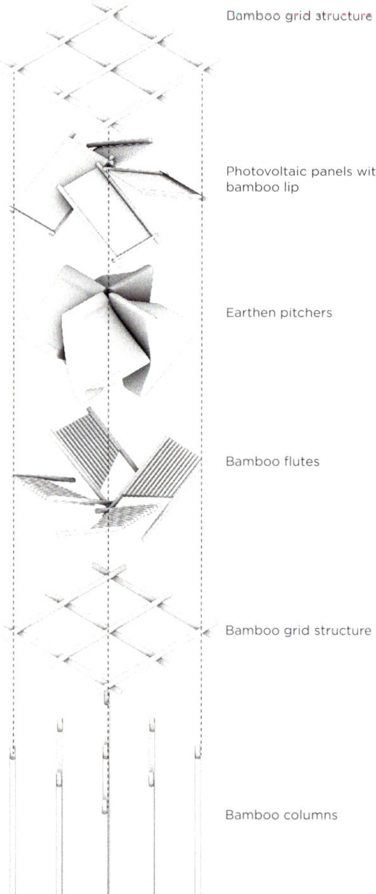

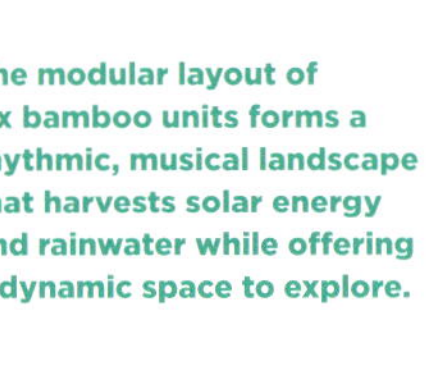

The modular layout of six bamboo units forms a rhythmic, musical landscape that harvests solar energy and rainwater while offering a dynamic space to explore.

Veilomani Energy Pavilion

TOP RIGHT: Interior view of the central pavilion, where angled wooden ribs form a soaring skylight—channeling sunlight and rainwater while anchoring the space for gathering and learning.

DESIGNERS: Henry Ronoh, Paul Maranga, John Paul Kata, Stephanie Ruto, Angela Nyambura Mbuthia

TECHNOLOGIES: solar photovoltaic, battery energy storage, rainwater harvesting and filtration

ANNUAL PRODUCTION: 120 MWh of electricity, 120,000 liters of filtered water

DESIGN TEAM LOCATION: Kenya

Exterior view of the *Veilomani Energy Pavilion's* iconic octagonal forms.

Veilomani Energy Pavilion is a community-centered installation inspired by the Fijian ethic of *veilomani*—encompassing love, kindness, and mutual support. Through three interlinked octagonal structures that signify prosperity and renewal, the design weaves together clean energy, water access, cultural education, and local food production.

Each pavilion serves a specific purpose. The Veilomani Learning Haven supports digital literacy and storytelling; the Matriarch's Circle centers women's wellness and craft economies; and the Drua Knowledge Hub offers climate resilience training and traditional skills development. Their architectural forms echo Fijian shipbuilding and vernacular architectures, constructed from timber, palm thatch, and bamboo using cyclone-resilient methods.

Solar panels integrated into the roof of each pavilion provide power for lighting, learning devices, and water pumps. Rain and condensation are harvested from the roofs and filtered using local materials for community use. The pavilions are surrounded by food gardens and illuminated paths, creating a welcoming and productive landscape.

Operated and maintained by local stewards, the *Veilomani Energy Pavilion* is a living, evolving system. It celebrates Fijian identity through a regenerative framework, creating a model of clean energy and shared knowledge for generations to come.

View from the edge of the pavilion showing shaded communal seating, educational spaces, and water-harvesting infrastructure integrated into the landscape.

Voivoi Future

RIGHT: Beneath a soaring woven canopy supported by clustered bamboo columns, community members gather to craft, share stories, and rest—showcasing a climate-responsive space that blends tradition, resilience, and beauty.

DESIGNERS: Michele Chen, Xingyu He, Tu Lan, Ruiqi Zhang

TECHNOLOGIES: solar photovoltaic canopy, fog harvesting net, rainwater catchment, biofiltration, underground cisterns

ANNUAL PRODUCTION: 372 MWh of electricity, 6.5 million liters of filtered water

DESIGN TEAM LOCATION: United States

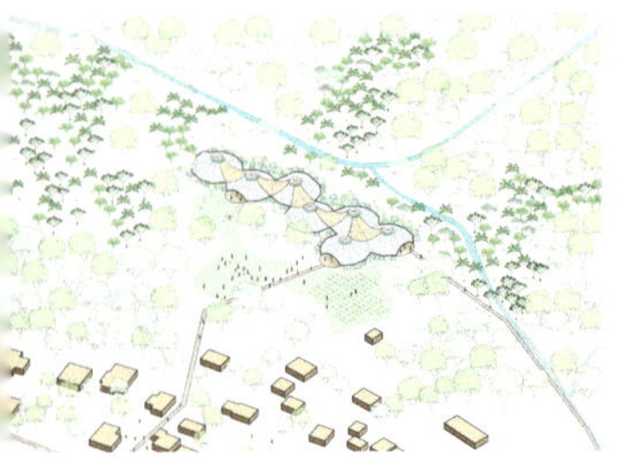

Site diagram

Voivoi Future honors the enduring tradition of Fijian women's weaving, reinterpreting their delicate craftsmanship of voivoi (Pandanus tectorius) leaves through a modular land art installation that generates energy, collects water, and supports ecological stewardship.

The design unfolds across three linked zones: a palm species nursery and conservation site, a network of deployable land art pavilions, and a multi-program landscape of co-weaving spaces, art markets, gardens, and playgrounds. The entire system is a living call to preserve palm tree biodiversity while offering infrastructure for community resilience.

Each pavilion consists of a foldable bamboo or voivoi-trunk structure supporting a lightweight, woven roof. Solar photovoltaic cells are embedded within the palm-leaf weave, forming a soft, curved canopy that adapts to light and wind conditions. The design generates sufficient electricity to meet immediate needs and accommodate future uses, such as expanded refrigeration or advanced water treatment.

Water is harvested in two ways: during the wet season, rain flows into bioswales and underground tanks for filtration and storage; during dry periods, fog-catching mesh condenses moisture from the air into central wells. Water is channeled to the pavilion's perimeter, where it is filtered through surrounding bioswales and stored in underground tanks, providing clean water for gardens and community use.

Construction is local and low-impact, using bamboo (bitu dina), recycled materials, and community-made elements. The installation adapts to a changing climate, designed to withstand wind, absorb flood water, and be disassembled if needed.

Maintenance is collective. Over time, the roof surface will evolve into a collective masterpiece: The roof becomes a canvas that is crafted by different community members across generations.

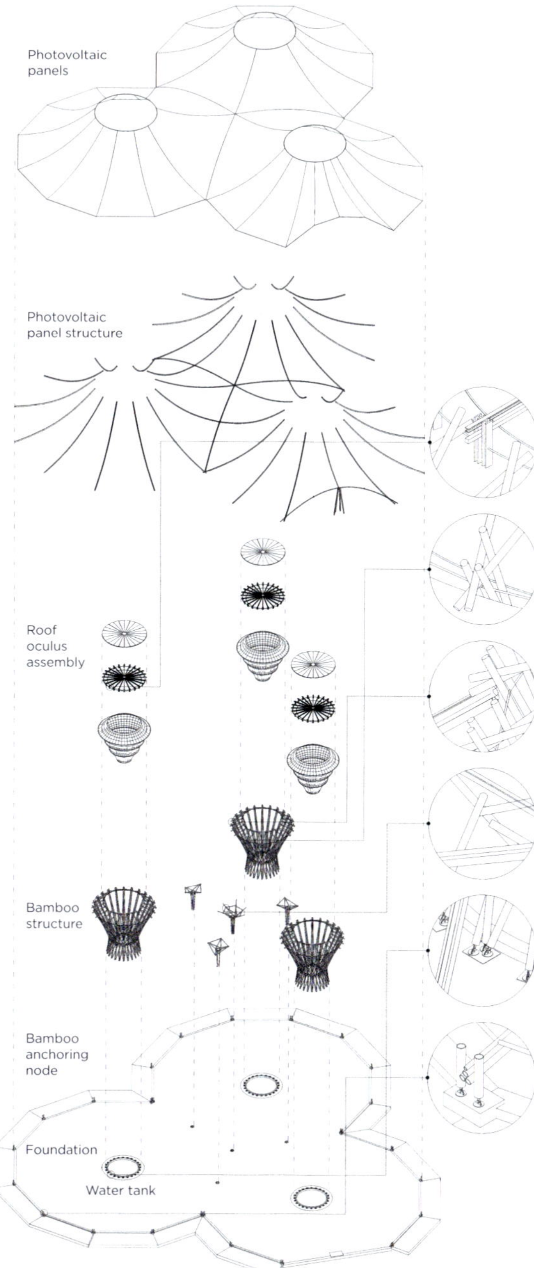

Section through the structure illustrating the primary system components

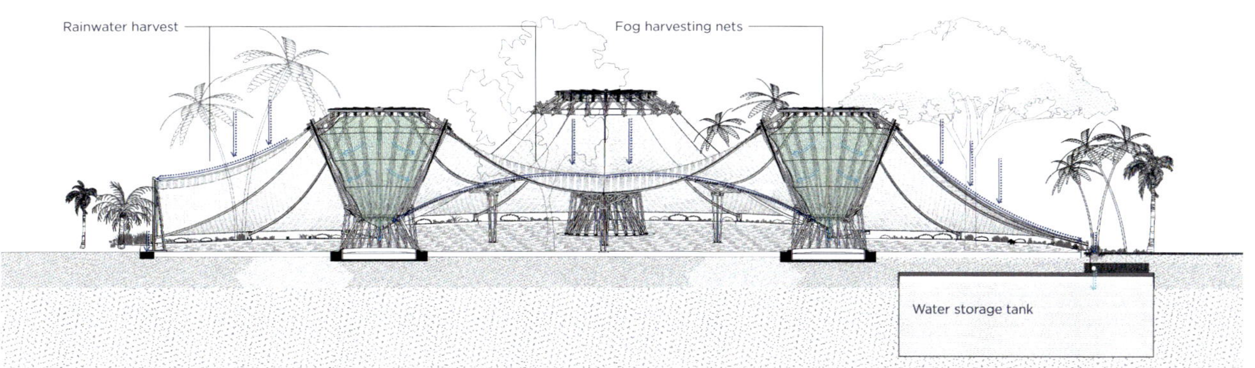

The Living Thread

The design centers around three key structures: a community hub for events, tool charging, and cold storage; a hilltop water tower surrounded by drought-resilient gardens; and a solar-powered water treatment plant co-located with aquaponics and agriculture. Supporting elements include satellite modules for homestays and health clinics, and smaller pavilions for play, rest, and reflection.

DESIGNERS: Emma Lubbers, Ellie Marigold, Irene Carlucci

TECHNOLOGIES: solar photovoltaic, battery energy storage, rainwater harvesting and water treatment via ultrafiltration and reverse osmosis, above-ground cisterns

ANNUAL PRODUCTION: 145 MWh of electricity, 105,000 liters of filtered water

DESIGN TEAM LOCATION: The Netherlands

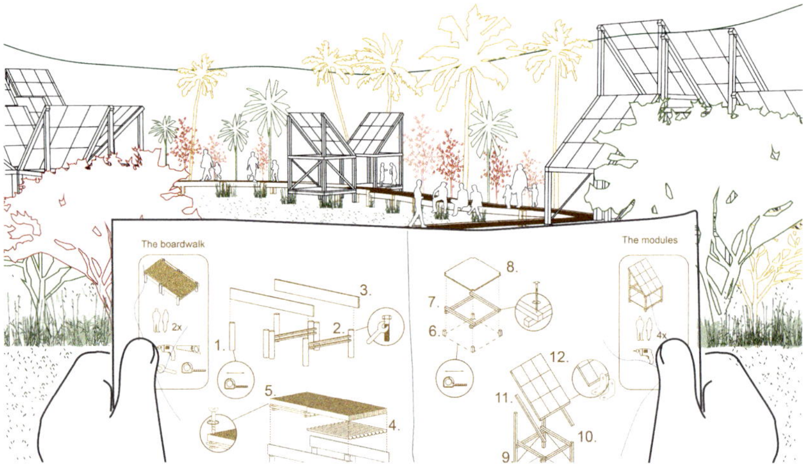

The Living Thread is a modular energy and water infrastructure woven through the landscape of Marou — a system of structures and spaces connected by a curving boardwalk that links sea, land, and village. Inspired by the logic of weaving and the flexibility of natural systems, the design emphasizes co-creation, adaptability, and ecological stewardship.

Built of palm timber and bamboo, the boardwalk twists across the site, rising to accommodate the terrain while preserving native vegetation below. Vertical slats and bamboo half-pipes direct rainfall to collection points, slowing runoff and reducing erosion. Along the path, simple modular units constructed of palm wood and upcycled plastic provide solar power, water harvesting, and shaded communal space. Just two base module types can be combined in different configurations to serve a variety of community needs.

Energy flows are monitored and shared across the system via a decentralized mini-grid. Water collected at the towers is gravity-fed downhill to treatment and distribution points, with overflow safely routed to the sea.

The Living Thread is a co-designed network for resilient living — grown from place, shaped by its people, and ready to evolve alongside the needs of Marou.

All systems are designed for long-term community stewardship. Components are locally sourced, structurally resilient, and easily replaceable.

Building the walkway

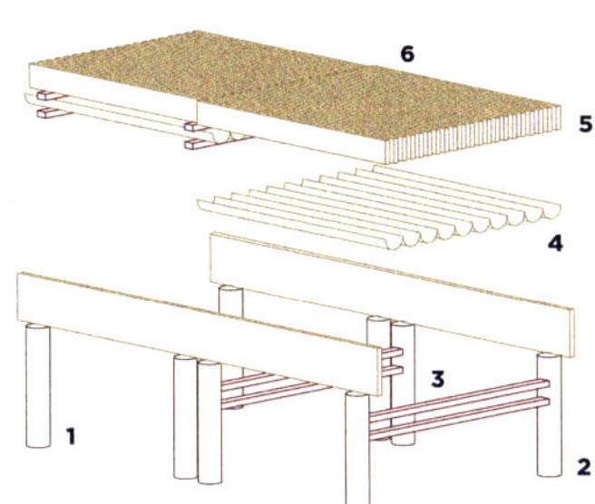

1. **Prepare the area**
Clear vegetation where the module will be installed. Mark the leg placements accurately according to the terrain.

2. **Install legs**
Cut legs from smaller palm trunks (height: 40–50 cm or as needed). Space them 2 m apart from each other in both length and width. Carve notches at the top of each leg to fit the outer wider planks.

3. **Build the base frame**
Cut two 10 cm × 10 cm timber beams. Each beam should be 2 m in length. Place the beams parallel to each other, allowing halved bamboo tubes to sit between them. Secure each beam into notches carved into the legs and reinforce using M10 bolts. Attach wider edge planks (40 cm height and 4 m length) on either side to lock decking into leg slits.

4. **Attach bamboo tubes**
Cut bamboo tubes in half lengthwise (~2 m). Place them lengthwise between the beams inside the frame.

5. **Lay walking surface**
Cut wooden decking planks (2 m long, 10 cm wide, up to 20 cm high). If necessary for curving modules, soften planks by soaking them in warm water. Lay planks side-by-side across the frame width. Alternate their pattern with adjacent modules for interlocking fit. Secure with galvanized screws into the beam below.

6. **Protect the wood**
Apply natural coconut oil on all wood components. Ensure bamboo and decking are fully treated for humidity resistance.

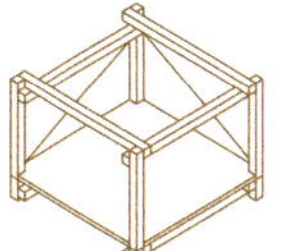

Module 1

Module 2

Example module configurations

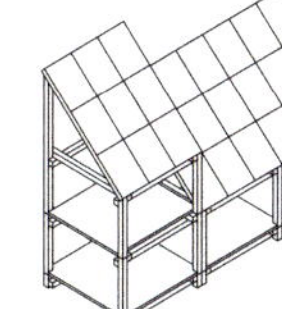

Community
Basic configuration of low and higher sections for community functions such as gathering, eating, and performance.

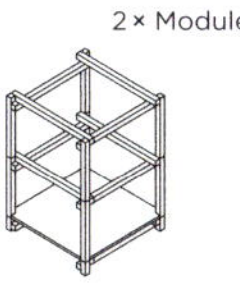

Play
In combination with natural features such as existing trees these structures can be used for play. Younger children can play on the platform. For older children, ropes and additional elements can be added.

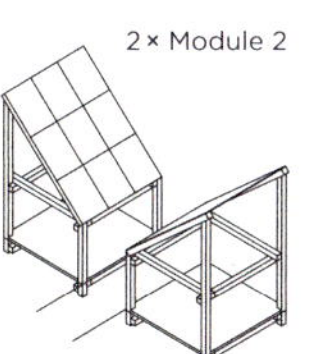
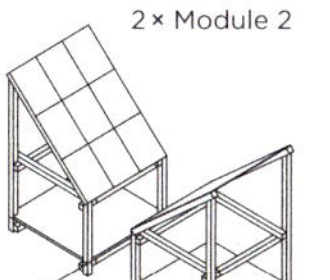

Shade and reflection
Along or over the boardwalk the modules can provide shade. Water from the roofs is collected in the bamboo gutters under the boardwalk.

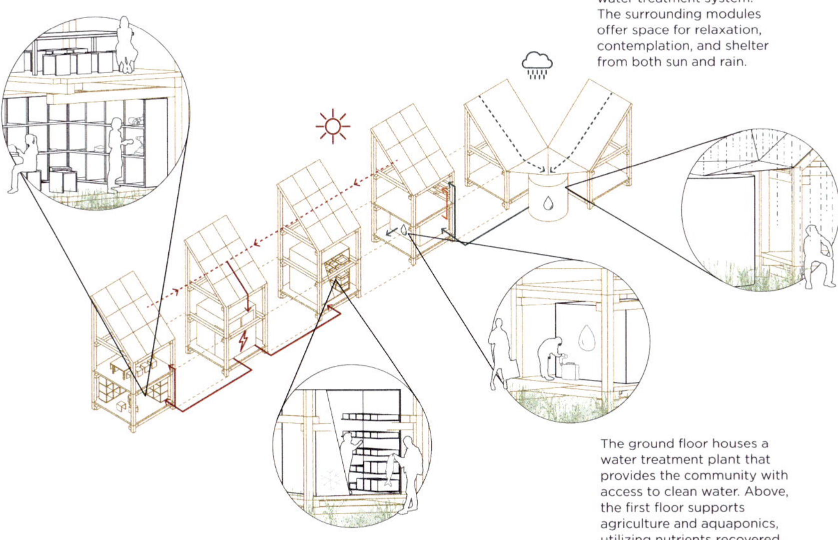

The ground floor includes charging lockers for local businesses to power tools and for community members to charge personal devices. The first floor provides a computer-equipped workspace, all powered by the on-site battery system.

At the center of four surrounding modules sits a water tank, which collects rainwater from the rooftops and channels it to the water treatment system. The surrounding modules offer space for relaxation, contemplation, and shelter from both sun and rain.

Cold storage modules offer secure spaces for food. They can also be connected to the medical center for the safe storage of temperature-sensitive medicines.

The ground floor houses a water treatment plant that provides the community with access to clean water. Above, the first floor supports agriculture and aquaponics, utilizing nutrients recovered from the treatment process to grow food sustainably.

Waqa ni Rarama
Canoe of Light

RIGHT: A concept illustration of the features of *Waqa ni Rarama* celebrates symbols of Fijian cultural heritage, adapted to double as regenerative infrastructure for Marou Village.

DESIGNER: Ethan Josiah Church

TECHNOLOGIES: flexible solar photovoltaic sail canopy, battery energy storage, rainwater harvesting, natural water filtration via engineered wetlands

ANNUAL PRODUCTION: 120 MWh of electricity, 100,000 liters of filtered water

DESIGN TEAM LOCATION: Fiji

Waqa ni Rarama, meaning "Canoe of Light," is a sculptural gathering place that honors Fiji's iconic double-hulled sailing canoe, the drua. The design integrates clean energy and water systems with traditional knowledge and materials, offering both shelter and storytelling.

The structure resembles a grounded canoe with a central spine and solar sail canopies that pivot to follow the sun. These sails generate electricity and collect rainwater, which is filtered through layers of gravel, biochar, and native aquatic plants before flowing into a shallow pond. The pond helps cool the surrounding space and supports local biodiversity.

Visitors are invited to walk through and around the structure, guided by lights, wind chimes, and the sound of flowing water. Interpretive signage shares information about the technologies alongside lessons from Fijian ecological traditions.

Constructed from bamboo, coral limestone, and salvaged timber, the installation is low-impact and resilient to weather.

Waqa ni Rarama is a vessel of light, knowledge, and community, bridging past and future with the grace of a canoe that always knows which way the wind is blowing.

Aerial view of the installation set against the backdrop of Naviti Island's double mountain peak, Vatu Rua.

Vakabula

RIGHT: Wind energy modules emerge from the constructed wetland as a sculptural feature in the landscape that complements the form of the surrounding coconut palm trees.

DESIGNERS: Patnicha Maneewan, Kritanai Pisutigomol, Pariyavat Promnamdum

TECHNOLOGIES: solar photovoltaic, battery energy storage, wind energy harvesting, rainwater harvesting, fog harvesting, graywater recycling, reservoir water storage, anaerobic digesters

ANNUAL PRODUCTION: 80 MWh of electricity, 1 million liters of filtered water

DESIGN TEAM LOCATION: Thailand

LEFT: Fog harvesting modules create a diaphanous texture against the tree line. TOP: Thatched domes create the perfect place to play.

Vakabula, meaning "to bring to life" in Fijian, is a modular infrastructure system designed to meet energy and water needs through locally grounded, culturally resonant design. Inspired by tropical flora, masi patterns, and vernacular architecture, the design uses a shared, foldable geometry to create multi-use structures: solar canopies, wind turbines, fog catchers, and shaded gathering spaces.

Each module is constructed from bamboo, tapa cloth, and magimagi rope made from coconut husk—materials rooted in traditional craft and ecological knowledge. Energy is generated through solar, wind, and biogas domes that are placed around the site to process agricultural and food waste. Water is captured via fog harvesting, rain collection, and graywater reuse, then stored in retention ponds.

The modularity of the design allows it to adapt to changing community needs. Structures can be deployed or folded away, replaced or reconfigured, using accessible tools and local labor. Assembly doubles as education: workshops teach rope-tying, sail-making, and bure construction, transforming the site into a living classroom.

Vakabula is a toolkit for climate resilience grown from within. It brings together Indigenous knowledge, simple tools, and shared labor to offer infrastructure that is flexible and enduring.

A visitor to Marou Village rests in the shade of photovoltaic modules.

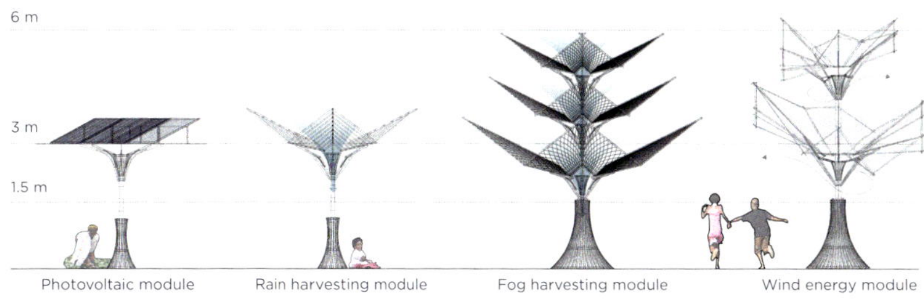

Grid of Light and Land A Living Framework for Village Resilience

RIGHT: Aerial view from the west shows how the grid responds to the site's topography, with photovoltaic modules aligned to solar exposure and agricultural fields running at an angle to the primary axis.

DESIGNERS: Chungyeon-Won, Yurim-Kim, Suah-Kim, Muzamil Naeem

TECHNOLOGIES: modular solar-rainwater collection integrated into tensile canopies and roof structures, battery energy storage, above-ground cisterns

ANNUAL PRODUCTION: 176 MWh of electricity, 330,000 liters of filtered water

DESIGN TEAM LOCATION: South Korea

This design begins by reading the contours of the land and tracing the path of the sun. Defining two intersecting axes—one of movement, one of light—these are not abstract inputs, but daily rhythms where people walk and shadows fall.

Stone markers along this grid invite the village to adapt and reshape the site over time. Three pavilions are arranged along looping footpaths, reflecting the informal geometry of traditional Fijian dwellings. A central shed anchors the site, while shaded spaces in between support daily life—resting, cooking, gathering, and playing.

Each module captures rainwater and solar energy. A tensile canopy offers shade and disengages in extreme winds, transforming weather into an opportunity for renewal. Modules can be added or reconfigured as the village grows without disrupting the whole.

The construction is comprised of metal and concrete frames, tensioned fabric, and photovoltaic panels. Low-tech and easy to maintain, the system is managed by locally trained stewards. With no permanent foundations and shallow anchoring, environmental impact is minimal.

Grid of Light and Land offers energy, water, and flexibility, growing with the community it serves.

The modular pavilion system with cisterns adjacent to fields being planted

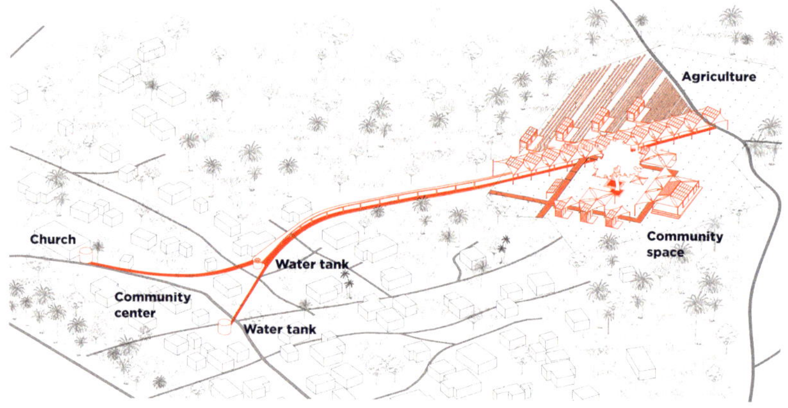

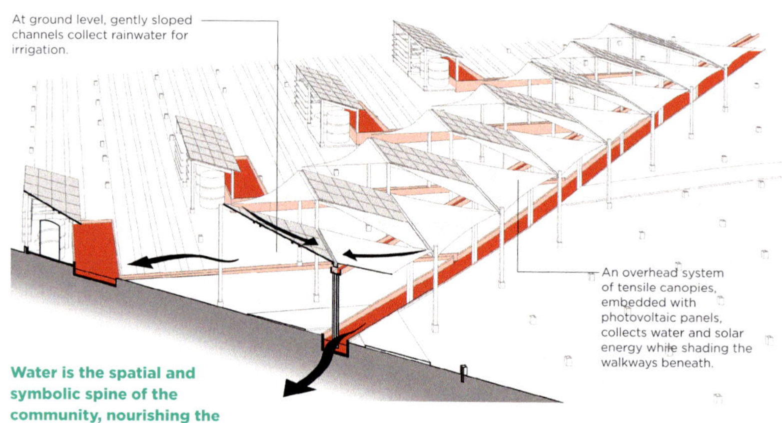

Water is the spatial and symbolic spine of the community, nourishing the land, activating public life, and serving as an expressive landscape element.

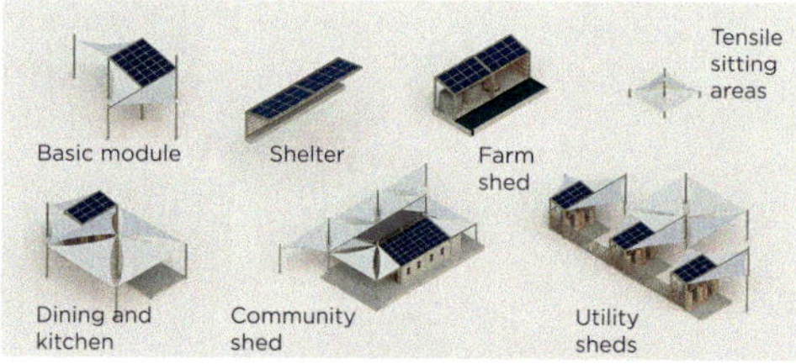

Central to the architectural language is the tensile canopy system designed with intentional impermanence. The lightweight membranes are engineered for controlled collapse under extreme weather, minimizing damage and maximizing safety.

Solar Village

RIGHT: View across the water garden toward sculptural solar towers, which rise from the landscape—integrating renewable energy generation with cultural symbolism and ecological planting.

DESIGNERS: Daipayan Sarkar, Shobana Sarkar

TECHNOLOGIES: solar photovoltaic, battery energy storage, rainwater harvesting, biofiltration, reservoir water storage

ANNUAL PRODUCTION: 320 MWh of electricity, 1.7 million liters of filtered water

DESIGN TEAM LOCATION: India

Rooted in the Fijian concept of *vanua*—land as kin, as culture, as responsibility—*Solar Village* reimagines renewable infrastructure as a celebratory act. Energy, water, and cultural expression are woven into a landscape that breathes with the rhythms of Marou life.

Sculptural solar towers rise like totems from the land, inspired by native trees, coral forms, and ancestral spirits. Each represents one of the five classical elements: air (cagi), fire (kama), water (wai), Earth (vanua), and sky (lagi). Their aerodynamic shapes reduce wind resistance while creating visual and spatial variety. Native plants are interwoven to support biodiversity and maintain ecological balance.

Paths inscribed with masi motifs guide visitors through symbolic zones: the Celestial Chorus Garden of light, the Mycelial Table for food and gathering, the Ancestral Piers of memory, and the Canopies of Culture, where storytelling, music, and dance unfold beneath the open sky. A restored stream supports rainwater harvesting and passive cooling.

Solar energy powers off-grid village needs, while rainwater reservoirs support households and gardens. Modular systems allow for easy expansion and community-led maintenance. Education, arts, and workshop pavilions foster intergenerational learning and cultural continuity.

Solar Village draws from ancestral wisdom and ecological design to offer a vision of renewable energy rooted in identity, place, and celebration.

Looking up from the Element of Fire at the aerodynamic forms of the solar towers, each one shaped to reduce wind resistance.

View of the Canopies of Culture solar power pavilion and the arrival zone.

Aqualillies

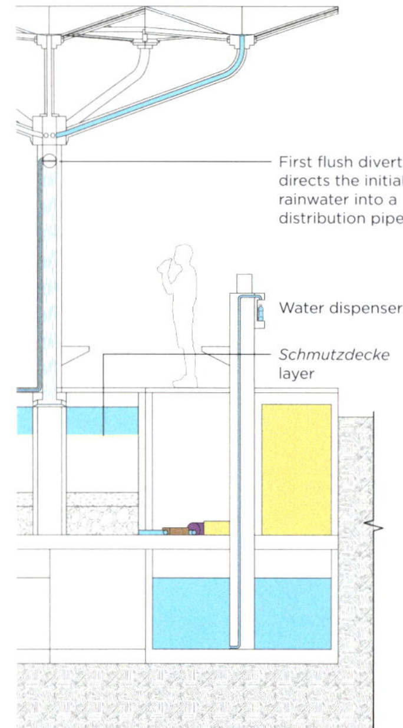

Rainwater is captured, filtered through slow sand and coconut-activated carbon, and stored in a reinforced concrete cistern beneath the modular canopy system.

DESIGNERS: Sheridan Stroop, Andrew Walker

TECHNOLOGIES: solar photovoltaic, battery energy storage, slow sand water filtration, coconut activated carbon filtration, UV treatment, underground cisterns

ANNUAL PRODUCTION: 120 MWh of electricity, 657,000 liters of filtered water

DESIGN TEAM LOCATION: United States

Site plan

Aqualillies is a place to gather. Rooted in community traditions and adaptable to future needs, this modular solar and water infrastructure system provides clean energy, potable water, and a space for play, ceremony, and learning. Designed with and for the people of Marou Village, *Aqualillies* honors Fijian hospitality, welcoming visitors who respect cultural practices, while strengthening self-reliance and well-being for residents.

The design forms a hexagonal canopy built above ferrocement capsules, where solar panels double as rainwater catchments. Beneath the walking surface, integrated systems store, filter, and treat rainwater with low-maintenance components: leaf screens, slow sand filters, coconut-activated carbon, and UV sterilization. The cool underground placement of the cisterns keeps water fresh and stable year-round.

Above ground, the gently elevated platform invites exploration. Trails approach from multiple directions, encouraging movement through the surrounding landscape and allowing each visitor to arrive on their own path. The modular pods are arranged to support multigenerational activity, from storytelling and craft to education, celebration, and rituals like the kava ceremony. Access panels integrated into the walking surface allow easy maintenance of the systems below, without disturbing daily life above.

Steel elements are used selectively for the catchment structure and piping, chosen for durability and recyclability in a humid, salt-rich environment. Excavated soil is repurposed for berms that reduce erosion and manage irrigation, while high-clay content may support future uses like pottery or brickmaking.

The modular design enables gradual expansion of the *Aqualillies* network across the village. Each unit can function independently or in connection with others, creating a decentralized infrastructure system that's easy to build, use, and sustain.

View beneath the *Aqualillies* canopy, where shaded gathering spaces provide room for ceremony, learning, and play—all while harvesting and purifying water within the platform below.

LAN'GI

RIGHT: Aerial view of the circular photovoltaic canopy, elevated above a clearing to collect solar energy and harvest rainwater while preserving open communal space beneath.

DESIGNERS: Agu Sienra Chaves, Cauane Lorrane Cunha

TECHNOLOGIES: solar photovoltaic, battery energy storage, rainwater harvesting and storage, passive cooling earthworks, distillation purification

ANNUAL PRODUCTION: 150 MWh of electricity, 500,000 liters of filtered water

DESIGN TEAM LOCATION: Brazil

Top-down plan highlighting the concentric structure of the installation—solar arrays oriented around a central courtyard that anchors cultural and environmental programming.

LAN'GI is a spatial threshold between sky (*lagi*) and Earth (*vanua*)—an immersive environment where energy and water systems are woven into atmosphere, structure, and land. Inspired by Fijian cosmologies, environmental traditions, and contemporary art, the design invites people to engage with the elements through sound, light, and movement.

A raised photovoltaic canopy floats above a volcanic soil clearing. Rainwater is guided by earthworks into a subterranean reservoir, where it is cooled, filtered, and pumped to nearby homes and gardens. Air currents are shaped by berms and canopy gaps, enhancing passive cooling.

Beneath the canopy, sculptural instruments harness solar and wind energy to generate subtle acoustic and kinetic effects. Pathways move visitors across three realms: The Telluric (semi-buried spaces linked to water and ancestry), The Communal Ground (gathering, workshops, daily life), and The Cosmic (the canopy, skyward gaze, universal resonance). Materials include bamboo, timber, limestone, and volcanic aggregate, assembled with dry connections for easy repair and reuse.

The experience unfolds through walking, listening, and feeling—a choreography of perception across elements and layers of being.

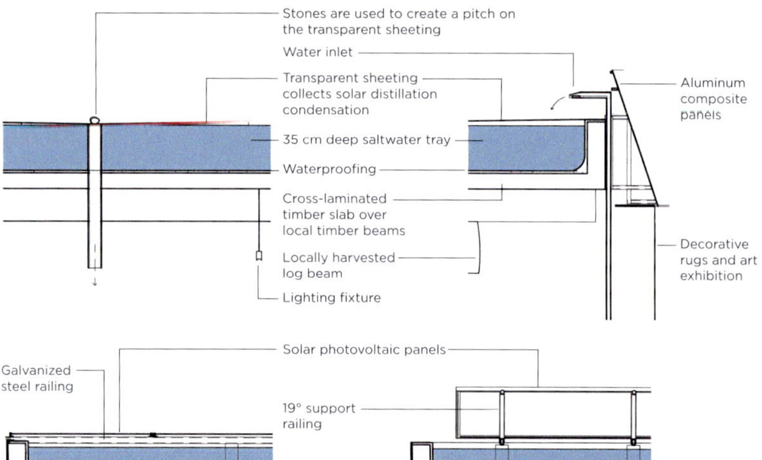

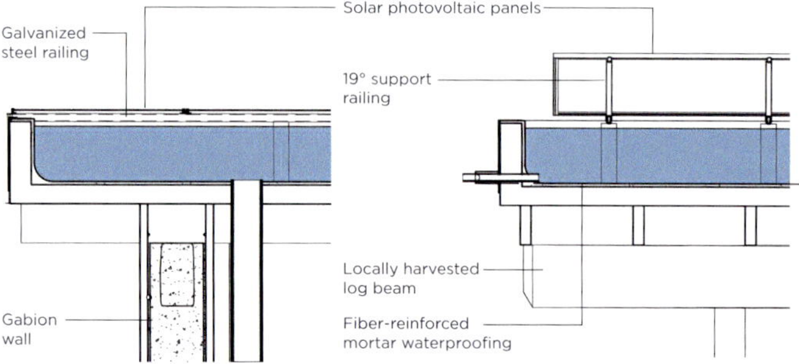

Construction details

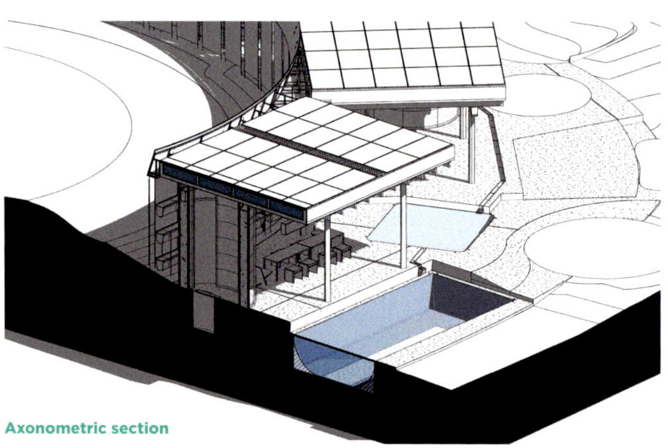

Axonometric section

de la terre

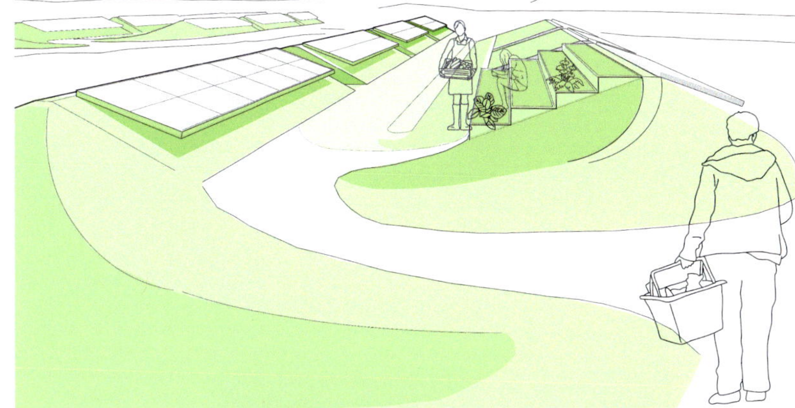

RIGHT: Photovoltaic panels are embedded within sculpted earthen berms, which also incorporate planting beds and shaded workspaces to support food security and everyday use.

DESIGNER: Susan Hickey

TECHNOLOGIES: solar photovoltaic on earth berms, battery energy storage, rainwater harvesting and filtration, decentralized stormwater management, underground cisterns

ANNUAL PRODUCTION: 113 MWh of electricity, 500,000 liters of filtered water

DESIGN TEAM LOCATION: United States

de la terre's berm network functions as public infrastructure—spaces for rest and learning.

de la terre, meaning "of the land," is a design shaped by topography, memory, and resilience. Inspired by the contours of the site and the strength of Fijian village life, it proposes a network of sculpted berms that blend energy, water, and culture into the landscape itself.

Low-lying berms anchor photovoltaic arrays on an east–west axis to optimize sun exposure. Electrical lines run through underground trenches to a central battery room, with storm-resistant mounting designed for tropical weather.

The berms are places to gather, garden, and learn. Shaded areas, seating, and planting zones are integrated into their form. Rainwater from nearby buildings is collected, filtered, and stored in tanks embedded within the berms, then distributed using gravity-fed systems.

Built from local earth, stone, bamboo, and timber, the system minimizes transport and supports traditional skills. Tensile shade structures and gabion walls offer durable, low-maintenance solutions.

Minimal excavation and balanced cut-and-fill preserve natural systems and tree cover. Community involvement is central, from data collection to construction and long-term care.

de la terre is a grounded vision for Marou Village, where infrastructure becomes landform, and resilience grows from the ground up.

Solar collection
Photovoltaic panels are mounted on the north-facing side of the architectural berm using a steel support structure. An underground conduit routes electricity from the solar array to the support building for storage.

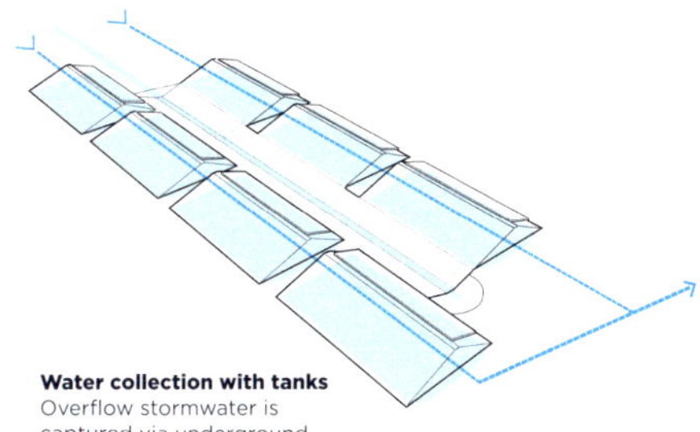

Water collection with tanks
Overflow stormwater is captured via underground piping from the main channel and directed to earthen mounds, where it collects in basins. From there, the water is transferred to a pumphouse equipped with a solar-powered pump, filtration system, and aerator, making it suitable for village use as potable water.

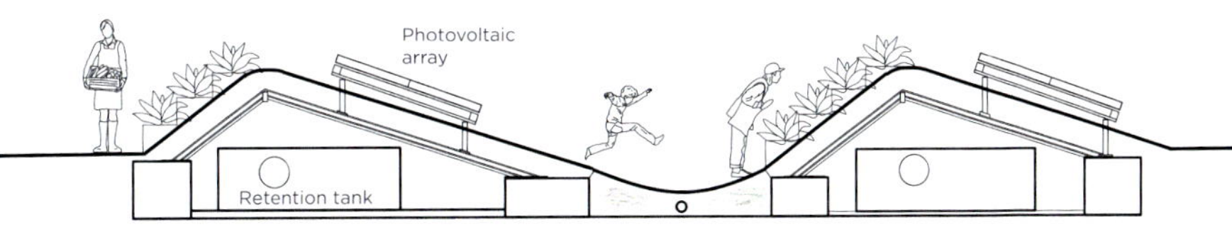

Section through architectural berms

RAY

DESIGNERS: Sam Chang, Peter Coombe, Charlotte Ho, Lee Kuhn, Michael Ray Navarosa Malonjao, Max St. Pierre Ostrander, Jennifer Sage, Kit Yan (Sage and Coombe Architects)

TECHNOLOGIES: thin-film solar photovoltaic, battery energy storage, tension-based bamboo structure, rainwater harvesting, flexible membrane water storage

ANNUAL PRODUCTION: 120 MWh of electricity, 500,000 liters of filtered water

DESIGN TEAM LOCATION: United States

RAY draws inspiration from the manta ray — graceful, resilient, and tuned to its environment. Suspended on a pliable bamboo frame and secured with coconut fiber lashings, the structure flexes under rainfall, channeling water through woven pandanus mats into a filtration system. The gentle deformation of the surface is intentional, allowing it to respond dynamically to changing weather.

A suspended array of lightweight, thin-film solar panels generates electricity, stored in lithium iron phosphate batteries. The minimal weight supports delivery by hand and traditional construction, reducing the need for heavy equipment. Materials are locally sourced — bamboo, coconut rope, and woven mats — ensuring that the structure can be assembled, maintained, and repaired by the community.

Elevated on shallow footings, *RAY* minimizes impact on the land. It can be relocated to allow the site to regenerate, extending its life cycle through stewardship. While solar cells will require periodic replacement, the structural components are long-lasting and culturally embedded.

RAY is a lightweight, adaptive infrastructure that merges local knowledge with responsive design — quietly delivering energy, water, and resilience to the residents of Marou.

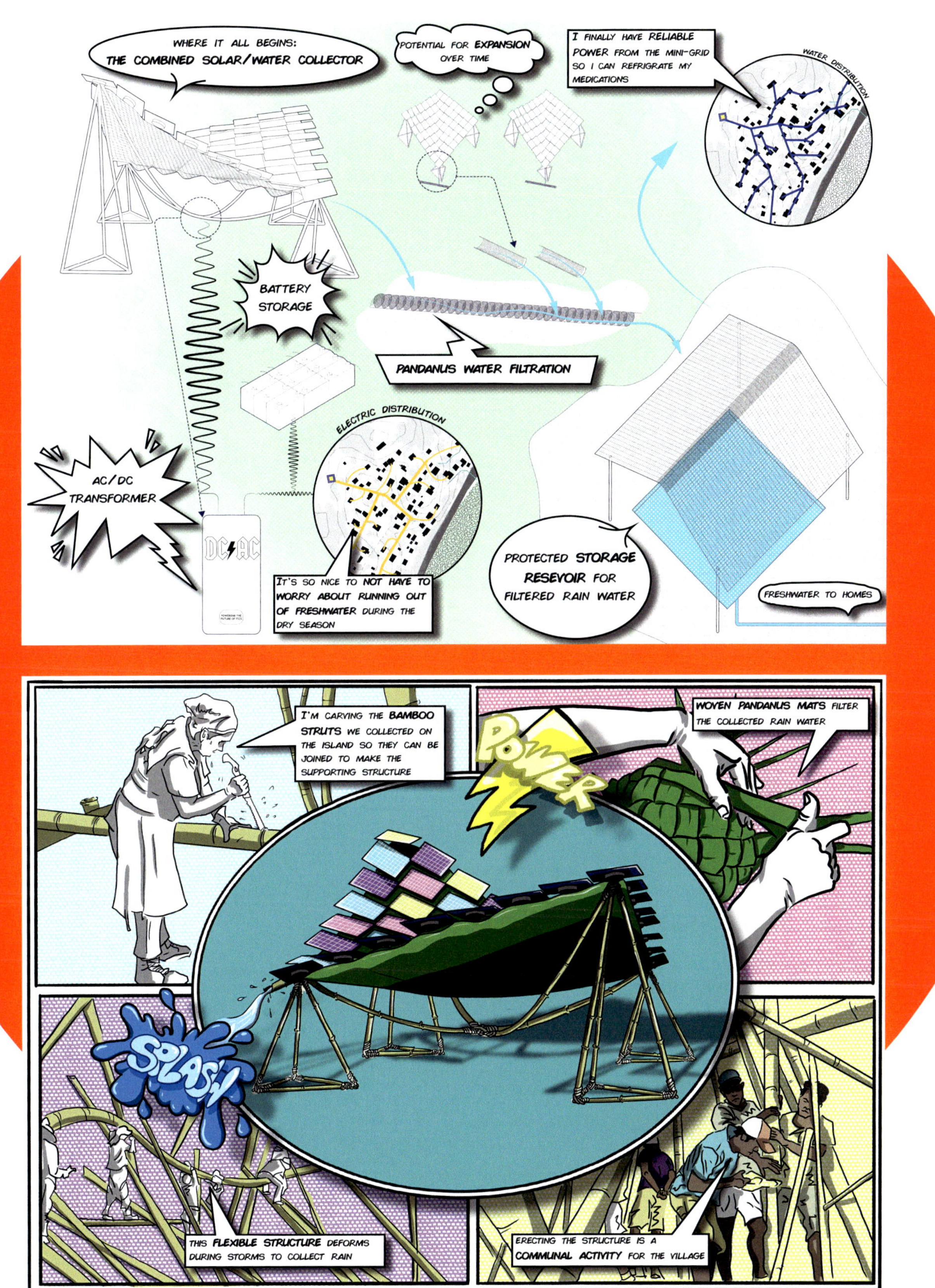
WHERE IT ALL BEGINS:
THE COMBINED SOLAR/WATER COLLECTOR
POTENTIAL FOR EXPANSION OVER TIME
I FINALLY HAVE RELIABLE POWER FROM THE MINI-GRID SO I CAN REFRIGRATE MY MEDICATIONS
WATER DISTRIBUTION
BATTERY STORAGE
PANDANUS WATER FILTRATION
ELECTRIC DISTRIBUTION
AC/DC TRANSFORMER
DC AC
IT'S SO NICE TO NOT HAVE TO WORRY ABOUT RUNNING OUT OF FRESHWATER DURING THE DRY SEASON
PROTECTED STORAGE RESEVOIR FOR FILTERED RAIN WATER
FRESHWATER TO HOMES
I'M CARVING THE BAMBOO STRUTS WE COLLECTED ON THE ISLAND SO THEY CAN BE JOINED TO MAKE THE SUPPORTING STRUCTURE
POWER
WOVEN PANDANUS MATS FILTER THE COLLECTED RAIN WATER
SPLASH
THIS FLEXIBLE STRUCTURE DEFORMS DURING STORMS TO COLLECT RAIN
ERECTING THE STRUCTURE IS A COMMUNAL ACTIVITY FOR THE VILLAGE

BIOGRAPHIES, GLOSSARY, INDEX, AND ACKNOWLEDGMENTS

BIOGRAPHIES

LISA M. FARMEN

Lisa M. Farmen formed Aquastry LLC to commercialize clean, green, and sustainable water treatment chemistries developed with funding from the National Science Foundation and the Oregon Nanoscience and Microtechnologies Institute. Prior to that, she founded Crystal Clear Technologies, Inc. (CCT), which was awarded four Small Business Innovation Research (SBIR) grants, won the California Clean Tech Open in 2006, and received the Clean Tech Open award in 2017 for Best Technology for Water. CCT raised $2.1 million in non-dilutive funding, secured four USPTO-issued patents in nanotechnology, and won the Global Symposium Business Plan competition in 2009. The company was also highlighted by the NSF to Congress in 2007 and by the Senate in 2008 as a showcase of SBIR program success.

Ms. Farmen earned her B.S. from Colorado State University in 1980 and her Executive M.B.A. in International Business from Golden Gate University (GGU) in San Francisco in 2000. She was honored with the Rising Star Alumni Award from GGU in 2007.

In 2025, Ms. Farmen served as a technical advisor to the Land Art Generator Initiative, providing expertise on water systems integration.

ROBERT FERRY

Robert Ferry is the founding co-director of the Land Art Generator Initiative and Studied Impact Design. Before co-founding the Land Art Generator Initiative in 2008, he collaborated with project management and design teams delivering sustainable and LEED-certified projects ranging from custom single-family residential to $500 million CAPEX mixed-use and corporate campuses. He spent four years as a consultant on large commercial projects in Abu Dhabi, where his focus shifted to ways in which buildings can move beyond net-zero and contribute to the regenerative infrastructure of the surrounding city. His concept designs pushing the envelope of building-integrated renewable energy technology have been published widely. Through the Land Art Generator Initiative, he supports the critical role of architecture and urban design as part of a comprehensive solution to climate change. Robert is a graduate of Carnegie Mellon University and a LEED-accredited licensed architect.

As co-director of LAGI he has received multiple National Endowment for the Arts grants and has been awarded the J.M.K. Innovation Prize, a program of the J.M. Kaplan Fund. His publications include *Land Art of the 21st Century*, *Regenerative Infrastructures*, *The Time Is Now: Public Art of the Sustainable City*, *New Energies*, *Powering Places*, *Energy Overlays*, *Return to the Source*, and *A Field Guide to Renewable Energy*.

ELIZABETH MONOIAN

Elizabeth Monoian is the founding co-director of the Land Art Generator Initiative (LAGI), an internationally recognized organization that brings together art, design, and renewable energy to shape sustainable public spaces. She has built global partnerships across public and private sectors—collaborating with cities, universities, corporations, cultural institutions, and community organizations to envision clean energy infrastructures within the cultural fabric of place.

Her work positions artists and designers as key contributors to climate solutions. Through public engagement she explores how the energy transition can be understood not only as a technical shift, but as a cultural and aesthetic transformation. Under her leadership, LAGI has received multiple National Endowment for the Arts grants and was awarded the J.M.K. Innovation Prize.

She holds an MFA from Carnegie Mellon University and is the co-author and editor of numerous publications, including *Land Art of the 21st Century*, *Regenerative Infrastructures*, *Energy Overlays*, *The Time Is Now: Public Art of the Sustainable City*, and *A Field Guide to Renewable Energy*.

ILISARI NAQAU NASAU

Ilisari Naqau Nasau is the Acting Chief (Sau Turaga) of Marou Village of the Mataqali Koro (Koro Clan), representing Marou Village. A respected leader, he brings deep knowledge and a generous perspective to the stewardship of Marou, whose cultural influence resonates across Naviti Island and beyond. As one of the earliest champions of LAGI 2025 Fiji, Ilisari Naqau extended the formal invitation on behalf of Marou Village in June 2024, offering to host the initiative and serve as site partner. His leadership has been, and will remain, instrumental to the development and realization of the LAGI 2025 Fiji results.

DR. RAMENDRA PRASAD

Dr. Ramendra Prasad is an Associate Professor, and Head of the Department of Science at The University of Fiji, where he is also affiliated with the Centre for Climate Change, Energy, Environment, and Sustainable Development. He holds a PhD in Modeling and Simulation from the University of Southern Queensland (Australia), as well as an MSc in Physics and a BSc from the University of the South Pacific (Fiji). His research spans modeling and simulation, advanced machine learning, data analytics, energy modeling and management, and environmental and atmospheric systems. Dr. Prasad has published widely in peer-reviewed journals and international conferences and is recognized among the top 2% of scientists worldwide by Stanford University.

ANN ROSENTHAL

As an artist, educator, and writer, Ann has interrogated the intersections of nature and culture through a range of environmental issues for more than four decades. Over the last few years, Ann has returned to her creative roots in painting and printmaking, celebrating her love of color, gesture, and form in nature and art. She is particularly drawn to places where water and land meet—fragile ecosystems that we endanger through ignorance, desire, and greed. Ann's recent creative and professional accomplishments include: Artist in Residence, HJ Andrews Experimental Forest, Oregon (2018); Co-Curator for "Crafting Conversations: A Call and Response to Our Changing Climate," Contemporary Craft BNY Mellon Gallery (2019); awarded "Woman of Environmental Art" from PennFuture (2020); one of four editors for *Ecoart in Action: Activities, Case Studies, and Provocations for Classrooms and Communities* (New Village Press, 2022); selected to design and execute two asphalt art murals with collaborator JoAnn Moran for Friendship Park in Pittsburgh, PA (2022–2023). Ann received her MFA from Carnegie Mellon University in 1999.

PAUL SCHIFINO

Paul received his degree in graphic design from the Art Institute of Pittsburgh in 1979. His work has been included in the design publications *Communication Arts (CA)*, *Graphis*, *Print*, *How*, and *ReadyMade* magazine. His art has been included in shows at The Andy Warhol Museum (*AMP*), the Mattress Factory (*Gestures #4* and *#14*), TRAF Gallery (*By Design*), TRAF Gallery (*Best of Pittsburgh Show*), and most recently *The John Show*. His work is also included in the permanent archive of the Mattress Factory.

He has served as president of the Pittsburgh chapter of the American Institute of Graphic Arts (AIGA), and is a former Advisory Board member of the American Shorts Reading Series and the Art Institute of Pittsburgh. Paul currently serves on the Board of the Land Art Generator Initiative.

ELENA VAN HOVE

Elena van Hove is the Director of Global Energy Access, Laboratory for Energy and Power Solutions (LEAPS), within the Julie Ann Wrigley Global Futures Laboratory at Arizona State University where she manages a number of diverse energy access and electrification projects. LEAPS is a unique academic group that focuses on technical assistance and scaling of impact projects, developing appropriate solutions that directly benefit communities.

Elena has had a variety of experiences working on energy projects around the globe, including in Europe, Africa, South America, and North America. She received a Bachelor of Science in Electrical Engineering from Purdue University and a Master of Science in Sustainability from ASU. Both degrees focused on power and energy.

The Flow of Life: Currents of Continuum

Austin Lim, Phang Lim

See page 164

GLOSSARY

ABSORPTION

A process by which ions, molecules, or atoms are taken up into the volume of a material.

ABSORPTION CHILLER

A refrigeration system that uses heat energy (such as that from the sun) to drive the cooling process. The system is a closed loop containing a solution of a low-boiling point refrigerant (e.g., ammonia or lithium bromide) and an absorbent (e.g., a salt solution). At various stages, the refrigerant is either evaporated from or absorbed into the water. The process was invented by the French scientist Ferdinand Carré in 1858 using sulfuric acid. One variation is referred to as the Einstein refrigerator, patented by Albert Einstein and his former student Leó Szilárd. Adsorption (with a "d") refrigeration systems are similar, except that the refrigerant is not absorbed into a liquid, but rather adsorbs onto the surface of a solid, such as a silicone gel.

ACRE-FEET

A measure of the volume of water equal to one flat acre of area filled evenly with one foot of water. One acre-foot of water is the same as 325,851 gallons. For metric scale equivalents, one acre-foot equals 1,233.5 cubic meters or 1,233,481 liters.

ADSORPTION

A process by which ions, molecules, or atoms adhere to the outer surface of a material.

AGRIVOLTAIC

Sharing land use for simultaneous solar energy production and food production. In sunny and arid climates, the use of solar panels to partially shade crops can increase yields.

ANAEROBIC DIGESTER (BIODIGESTER)

A system that enables the decomposition of organic matter (biomass) in an oxygen-poor (anaerobic) environment through microbial activity, producing biogas as a byproduct. This gas, primarily composed of methane (CH_4) and carbon dioxide (CO_2), is similar in composition to conventional natural gas and can be used for cooking, heating, lighting, electricity generation, and transportation. On farms, anaerobic digesters convert manure and other organic waste into biogas, significantly reducing emissions of methane and nitrous oxide — two greenhouse gases with global warming potentials far greater than carbon dioxide (methane ≈ 83×, nitrous oxide ≈ 273× over a 20-year timeframe). The remaining solid material, called digestate, can be used as a nutrient-rich fertilizer. Biomass used in biodigesters is considered a renewable resource, as it is derived from biological processes that regenerate quickly, unlike fossil fuels which take millions of years to form.

ANTHROPOCENE

A proposed geological epoch that marks the period during which human activity began to exert significant global impacts on Earth's systems, leaving measurable geochemical signatures in ice and sediment cores. It is theorized to follow the Holocene, our current epoch. While widely used in scientific and public discourse, the formal recognition of the Anthropocene was rejected by a panel of two dozen geologists in March 2024, following a proposal led by the Anthropocene Working Group (AWG). In the humanities and arts, the term is often used to underscore the destructive environmental consequences of industrialization, resource extraction, and anthropogenic climate change.

AQUACULTURE

The cultivation of aquatic organisms — such as fish, shellfish, and aquatic plants — for food, habitat restoration, or commercial products. Practiced in both freshwater and marine environments, aquaculture can range from small-scale ponds to large, managed ocean farms. When integrated into sustainable systems, it can contribute to food security, ecosystem services, and water reuse.

AQUAPONICS

Combining aquaculture (the raising of fish or other aquatic animals) with hydroponics (growing plants with little or no soil), aquaponics is an efficient and environmentally friendly system for food production that recycles water and requires few regular inputs. Those include: oxygen, sunlight, fish feed, water (to replace losses to evaporation and plant root uptake), and electricity (to pump, filter, and oxygenate the water). The ammonia-rich water of the aquaculture tank is cycled through biofilters where nitrifying bacteria provide nutrients to the plants downstream. After passing through the plant roots, purified water returns to the fish tank to repeat the cycle.

AQUIFER

An underground body of water or water-saturated soil occurring below the water table (unconfined aquifer) or within a naturally occurring rock cavity (confined aquifer). The study of water flow in aquifers is called hydrogeology.

ATMOSPHERIC WATER GENERATION (ATMOSPHERIC CONDENSATION)

A technology that produces clean water by extracting moisture from the air through condensation. Warm, humid air is drawn into the system and cooled below its dew point using an electrically powered condenser—often run on grid energy, solar panels, or other renewable sources. As the air cools, water vapor condenses into liquid, which is then collected and filtered for safe use. Atmospheric water generators are particularly valuable in regions with limited access to surface or groundwater but consistent ambient humidity. These systems range from compact, solar-powered units to large-scale installations designed for off-grid or emergency water supply.

BIFACIAL SILICON SOLAR PANEL

A type of photovoltaic panel that has solar cells on both the front and back sides, allowing it to generate electricity from direct sunlight as well as reflected or diffused light from the surrounding environment. Bifacial panels are typically made with monocrystalline silicon and mounted on reflective surfaces or elevated structures to maximize rear-side exposure. Under optimal conditions, they can produce more energy than traditional monofacial panels, improving overall system efficiency.

BIOFILTRATION OR BIOREMEDIATION

Living material can be used to take pollution from water, soil, or air. Through chemical processes inside plants or microorganisms, pollutants become biologically degraded or less harmful.

BIO-RETENTION POND

A landscaped basin designed to manage stormwater by slowing, filtering, and absorbing runoff through layers of soil, gravel, and vegetation. Unlike wet ponds, which retain standing water, bio-retention ponds — also called rain gardens or bio-cells — temporarily hold water before allowing it to infiltrate into the ground. Native plants and engineered soils help remove nutrients, sediments, and pollutants, making these systems effective for water quality treatment, urban cooling, and habitat enhancement.

BIOSAND FILTRATION

A household-scale water purification method that uses layers of sand and gravel to remove pathogens and suspended solids from contaminated water. As water passes slowly through the sand, a biological layer (*schmutzdecke*) forms near the surface, where microorganisms consume harmful bacteria and organic matter. The combination of physical filtration, biological activity, and sedimentation makes biosand filters a low-tech, effective solution for providing safe drinking water in remote or low-resource settings.

BITU DINA

A fast-growing, hardy species of bamboo native to parts of the Pacific Islands, commonly used in traditional construction, weaving, and water harvesting. Known for its straight, durable culms and ability to thrive in tropical climates, bitu dina plays an important role in sustainable building practices and local ecological systems. Its versatility makes it valuable for both structural and craft applications.

BLADDER STORAGE

A flexible, collapsible container used to store harvested rainwater or graywater, typically made from durable, UV-resistant materials. Bladder tanks expand as they fill and can be installed above or below ground, making them ideal for tight or irregular spaces where rigid tanks are impractical. Common in remote, emergency, or off-grid applications, bladder storage offers a lightweight, transportable solution for temporary or long-term water containment.

BURE

A traditional Fijian structure typically built with locally sourced materials, such as timber, bamboo, and thatch. Bures are designed with deep cultural significance and adapted to the tropical climate, featuring elevated floors, steeply pitched roofs, and open-air ventilation. Historically used as homes, meeting houses, or spiritual spaces, the bure embodies principles of communal living, environmental harmony, and vernacular resilience in Pacific Island architecture.

CAMAKAU

A traditional Fijian sailing vessel with a single outrigger and triangular sail, used for inter-island travel, fishing, and trade. Crafted from hollowed logs and lashed timber without nails, the camakau is designed for speed, balance, and efficient navigation across open ocean. Deeply rooted in

Fijian maritime heritage, it reflects generations of Indigenous knowledge in boatbuilding, wind patterns, and ocean stewardship — skills now being revitalized as part of cultural and environmental resilience efforts.

CARBON DIOXIDE (CO_2)

A naturally occurring chemical compound essential to life on Earth, carbon dioxide also acts as a greenhouse gas (GHG), trapping heat in the atmosphere and contributing to anthropogenic climate change. Human activities — primarily the combustion of fossil fuels — have increased atmospheric CO_2 concentrations by approximately 50% since the onset of industrialization. Pre-industrial levels were at or below 280 parts per million (ppm), according to ice core records. Since 1960, concentrations have risen from around 320 ppm to approximately 430 ppm (as of 2025). Continued increases risk accelerating global temperature rise and sea level change. To limit warming to below 2 °C, scientific consensus holds that between two-thirds and four-fifths of known fossil fuel reserves must remain unburned. Elevated CO_2 levels also affect ocean chemistry; as carbon dioxide dissolves into surface waters, it forms carbonic acid and related compounds, leading to ocean acidification and disruptions to marine ecosystems.

CARBON FILTER

A water purification device that uses activated carbon— a porous form of charcoal—to remove contaminants through adsorption. As water passes through the filter, impurities such as chlorine, pesticides, volatile organic compounds (VOCs), and unpleasant tastes and odors are trapped on the surface of the carbon particles. Common in household and portable filtration systems, carbon filters effectively improve water quality without the use of chemicals or electricity.

CIGS (COPPER INDIUM GALLIUM SELENIDE)

A thin-film solar cell technology made from a semiconductor compound of copper, indium, gallium, and selenium. CIGS panels are lightweight, flexible, and can be applied to a wide range of surfaces, making them ideal for building-integrated photovoltaics and portable solar applications. While generally less efficient than conventional silicon-based panels, CIGS cells maintain strong performance in low light and high-temperature conditions, offering a promising alternative for specialized or design-driven solar installations.

CISTERN

A waterproof container used to collect and store rainwater or other non-potable water, typically for later use in irrigation, flushing, or filtration. Cisterns can be installed above or below ground and range in size from small domestic tanks to large communal reservoirs. In water harvesting systems, they play a crucial role in managing supply during dry periods.

COCOPEAT

A natural, fibrous growing medium made from coconut husks, commonly used as a soil substitute or conditioner. Lightweight, highly absorbent, and rich in organic matter, cocopeat retains moisture while providing good aeration for plant roots. Common in hydroponics, container gardening, and seed starting, it is valued for being renewable, biodegradable, and free from pathogens and weed seeds.

COIR

A coarse natural fiber extracted from the outer husk of coconuts, used in water filtration systems for its durability, porosity, and biodegradability. In filtration, coir mats or bundles act as both a physical and biological medium, trapping sediments and supporting microbial activity that breaks down pollutants. Common in constructed wetlands, bioswales, and erosion control applications, coir offers a sustainable alternative to synthetic materials in eco-friendly water treatment designs.

CONCENTRATED SOLAR POWER (CSP)

Concentrated solar power (CSP) describes a variety of systems that use mirrors or lenses (see *heliostatic*) to concentrate the power of the sun to create heat energy that can then be converted into electricity.

CONDENSER

A heat exchanger that converts a gas or vapor into a liquid by cooling it, thereby releasing latent heat into the surrounding environment.

CROSS-LAMINATED TIMBER (CLT)

A composite wood panel produced by laminating multiple layers of wood in alternating grain orientation for increased strength. CLT can be fabricated from smaller and younger trees compared to dimensional lumber, which requires larger trees for conventional milling. CLT is therefore compatible with more sustainable forest management practices.

DESALINATION

The process of removing dissolved salts and other impurities from seawater or brackish water to produce freshwater suitable for human use. Common methods include thermal processes, such as distillation, and membrane-based technologies, such as reverse osmosis.

DISTILLATION

A thermal separation process that purifies water by converting it into vapor and then condensing it back into liquid, leaving behind salts, contaminants, and other impurities. Common in water harvesting systems, distillation harnesses heat—either from the sun or other sources—to replicate the natural water cycle in a controlled environment. Especially effective for producing potable water from saline or polluted sources, it relies on phase change rather than chemical treatment.

EARTH BERM

A mound or bank of soil used to block wind, control water flow, reduce noise, or insulate buildings. Earth berms are often integrated into landscape design and passive solar architecture to enhance environmental protection and energy efficiency.

ECOTONE

The transition zone between two biological communities.

ELECTROLYSIS

A process that uses an electric current to drive a chemical reaction, typically used to split water into hydrogen and oxygen gases.

ENGINEERED WETLAND (ALSO "CONSTRUCTED WETLAND")

A designed landscape system that mimics the ecological functions of natural wetlands to treat wastewater, manage stormwater, or support biodiversity. Engineered wetlands are built with hydrological precision and planted with native or adaptive vegetation, offering a low-energy, site-responsive solution for water purification and habitat creation in both urban and rural contexts.

ETHYLENE TETRAFLUOROETHYLENE (ETFE)

A fluorine-based plastic known for its high strength, light weight, and excellent resistance to corrosion and UV radiation. ETFE is widely used as a building façade and roofing material where high light transmission and flexible, curved forms are desired. Notable architectural applications include the Eden Project in Cornwall, United Kingdom, and the Beijing National Aquatics Centre. In photovoltaics, Flexic ETFE refers to a type of solar panel that uses ETFE as the outer (face) layer instead of glass, allowing the entire panel to remain flexible and suitable for curved or irregular surfaces.

EVAPORATOR

A heat exchanger that reduces the pressure on a liquid helping it to vaporize, which has the effect of pulling heat from the surrounding environment.

FLOATOVOLTAICS

Solar photovoltaic (PV) modules installed on floating platforms over bodies of water, such as reservoirs, lakes, or canals. This approach conserves land, reduces water evaporation, and can improve panel efficiency through passive cooling from the water surface. Floatovoltaics are increasingly used in regions with limited land availability for ground-mounted solar arrays.

FOG HARVESTING NETS

Fine-mesh structures designed to capture water droplets from fog as it passes through. As moisture-laden air condenses on the mesh, the droplets coalesce and drip into collection channels, producing clean water without the need for electricity. Used in regions where fog is frequent, fog harvesting nets offer a low-tech, sustainable method of water collection that can support communities during periods of low rainfall.

FOOD FOREST

Forest gardening is an ancient practice in which a variety of species of trees and plants are grown in close proximity, mimicking the biodiversity of a healthy natural forest. When practiced at large scale, the technique can also be referred to as agroforestry. Each species of plant has a unique set of roles to play in the system—some healing soils, others producing food, and others attracting a diverse population of healthy insects that reduce the risk of blight.

GEOFABRIC OR GEOTEXTILE

Any permeable fabric used in landscaping, construction, geotechnical engineering, or agriculture to separate, reinforce, or protect soil, or to filter or drain water within or around soils.

GRAVITY ENERGY STORAGE

A method of storing energy by using electricity to lift a mass to a higher elevation and converting it back into electricity as the mass descends. This process relies on changes in gravitational potential energy to enable energy retrieval. Common examples include pumped hydro (raising water into an elevated reservoir), hydraulic mass systems (lifting a heavy piston within a shaft), gravity rail (using an electric locomotive on a sloped track), tower crane systems (stacking heavy blocks), and earth bucket conveyors. Gravity energy storage offers a mechanically simple, long-duration storage solution that supports grid flexibility and renewable energy integration.

GRAVITY FED CONVEYANCE

A passive system that transports water or other fluids from one location to another using the natural force of gravity, without requiring pumps or external energy. Common in irrigation, water supply, and drainage systems, gravity-fed conveyance relies on elevation differences and carefully designed channels, pipes, or aqueducts to maintain steady flow. It provides a simple, energy-efficient solution well-suited for remote or off-grid applications.

GRAYWATER

Water that has been used once for a light-duty purpose, such as hand washing or dishwashing. Graywater can be collected and used for other secondary purposes, such as toilet flushing or irrigation, thus reducing the demand for potable water.

GREEN INFRASTRUCTURE

A network of natural and engineered systems that use vegetation, soils, and natural water processes to manage stormwater, improve air and water quality, and enhance urban resilience. Examples include green roofs, rain gardens, bioswales, and urban forests. Unlike traditional “gray” infrastructure, which relies on pipes and concrete, green infrastructure works with nature to provide ecological, social, and climate benefits in both urban and rural settings.

HDPE (HIGH-DENSITY POLYETHYLENE)

A strong, weather-resistant plastic valued for its durability and versatility. HDPE is commonly used in infrastructure and design applications — from water pipes to modular structures — because it resists cracking, UV degradation, and corrosion. Made from petroleum, it is also one of the most widely recycled plastics, making it a frequent material choice in sustainable construction.

HELIOSTATIC (HELIOTROPIC)

The ability to follow the location of the sun in the sky and maintain an object’s consistent relationship to it throughout the diurnal and seasonal shift. In solar energy technology, heliostatic mechanisms can maintain a solar cell perpendicular to the sunlight for ideal absorption and conversion, or mirrors can maintain an angle-of-incidence relationship to the sun to consistently reflect sunlight to a central collector.

HELOPHYTE FILTRATION

A natural water purification method that uses wetland plants — known as helophytes, such as reeds, cattails, and bulrushes — to filter and break down contaminants. These plants grow with their roots submerged in water and soil, where microbial activity in the root zone helps remove nutrients, pathogens, and suspended solids. Often used in constructed wetlands, helophyte filtration offers an effective, low-maintenance approach to treating wastewater and stormwater while enhancing biodiversity and landscape aesthetics.

HIGH-TRANSMITTANCE NANO-FILM

An ultra-thin, engineered surface coating that allows most sunlight to pass through while selectively manipulating specific wavelengths to produce visible colors — such as white, blue, or gold — on solar panels. Applied to the front glass of photovoltaic modules, these nano-films maintain energy efficiency while modifying visual appearance, enabling solar technologies to blend with architectural surfaces or align with cultural design preferences without compromising performance.

HYBRID PHOTOVOLTAIC THERMAL (PVT)

Any system that converts solar energy into both electrical and heat energy simultaneously. Because photovoltaic panels operate at approximately 20% conversion efficiency, much of the potential solar energy is lost to heat. This heat build-up has a detrimental impact on the performance of the solar cell due to increased electrical resistance within the circuitry. PVT systems can operate at 75% total conversion efficiency (electricity + heat).

HYDROGEN FUEL CELL

A device that generates electricity by recombining hydrogen (from a canister) and oxygen (from the atmosphere). The reaction generates water and an electrical current (the opposite of electrolysis).

HYDROPHILIC

A material that has an affinity for water — it readily adsorbs moisture to its surface, absorbs it into its volume, or dissolves in it. This behavior is thermodynamically favorable. All hydrophilic materials are hygroscopic, though not all hygroscopic materials are hydrophilic.

HYDROPHOBIC

A material that repels water, resisting wetting or dissolution. This surface behavior is thermodynamically unfavorable, causing water to bead and roll off rather than spread or absorb.

HYDROPONICS

A method of growing plants without soil, using a nutrient-rich water solution to deliver essential minerals directly to the roots. Plants are typically supported by inert growing media, such as gravel, sand, or clay pellets. Hydroponic systems can be highly efficient, enabling faster growth, reduced water use, and controlled cultivation in indoor or greenhouse environments. Commonly used in urban agriculture and space-constrained growing systems.

HYGROSCOPIC

Tending to absorb moisture from the air. Examples of hygroscopic materials include cotton, wood, and sugar.

ICE BATTERY

A thermal energy storage system that uses excess solar power — typically generated during peak sunlight hours — to freeze water and store cooling capacity as ice. In off-grid settings, ice batteries provide reliable, low-tech refrigeration by preserving cold rather than storing electricity, enabling essential cooling during nighttime or cloudy periods when power is limited. By converting surplus solar energy into thermal storage, ice batteries offer an efficient, long-duration solution for preserving food, medicine, and other temperature-sensitive goods without relying on continuous electrical supply.

KILOWATT (kW)

Equal to 1,000 watts. See *watt*.

KILOWATT-HOUR (kWh)

Equal to 1,000 watt-hours. See *watt-hour*.

LED (LIGHT-EMITTING DIODE)

A solid-state semiconductor device that emits light when an electric current passes through it. LEDs are highly energy-efficient, long-lasting, and more durable than traditional light sources, such as incandescent or fluorescent bulbs. An OLED (organic light-emitting diode) is a related technology that uses organic compounds to emit light and is commonly used in display screens and lighting applications.

LITHIUM IRON PHOSPHATE (LFP)

A lithium-ion battery chemistry known for its high thermal stability, long cycle life, and enhanced safety profile. Unlike other lithium-based batteries, $LiFePO_4$ uses iron and phosphate in its cathode, making it significantly less prone to overheating or combustion. While it has a lower energy density than alternatives, like lithium cobalt oxide, $LiFePO_4$ is favored for stationary energy storage, electric vehicles, and off-grid renewable systems due to its durability, consistent performance, and comparatively lower environmental impact.

MEGAWATT (MW)

Equal to 1,000,000 watts. See *watt*.

MEGAWATT-HOUR (MWh)

Equal to 1,000,000 watt-hours. See *watt-hour*.

MICRO-HYDRO

A small-scale system that generates electricity from flowing water, typically without requiring large dams or reservoirs. Micro-hydro systems harness the kinetic energy of streams or rivers using technologies, such as run-of-the-river setups, which divert a portion of the flow through a turbine, or vortex systems, which create a spinning current in a basin to drive a low-speed generator. Ideal for off-grid or rural areas, micro-hydro offers a reliable and renewable energy source with minimal environmental impact.

MULTI-EFFECT DISTILLATION (MED)

An active desalination method that produces potable water by passing seawater through a series of chambers, each operating at a lower pressure than the last. Heat introduced in the first chamber causes evaporation, and the resulting vapor is used to heat the next stage. This cascading process reuses thermal energy to efficiently separate water from salts and impurities, yielding distilled water at each step. MED is commonly used in large-scale systems where waste heat or low-grade thermal energy is available. See *distillation*.

MWhe

Megawatt-hour equivalent. This unit of measurement for energy is often used when quantifying liquid fuel in comparison to electricity.

MYCELIUM

The vegetative part of a fungus, the branching threads of which are called hyphae. Mycelium can break down complex organic compounds and remediate polluted soil. When cultivated in molds, mycelium can be used to rapidly make packing materials, leather substitutes, furniture, building materials, and insulation that outperforms fiberglass, mineral wool, or polystyrene.

MYCOREMEDIATION

A form of bioremediation that uses fungi — particularly their root-like networks called mycelium — to break down, absorb, or immobilize environmental pollutants. Fungi can metabolize a wide range of harmful substances, including hydrocarbons, pesticides, and some heavy metals, transforming them into less toxic or inert forms. Mycoremediation is valued for its low-impact, ecologically adaptive approach to cleaning contaminated soil, water, and industrial waste sites.

PANDANUS

A tropical plant with long, tough, blade-like leaves traditionally harvested and prepared for weaving in many Pacific cultures, including Fiji. Once stripped, softened in hot water, and dried, the leaves are used to create mats, baskets, roofing, and ceremonial textiles. Valued for their durability and flexibility, pandanus fibers carry deep cultural significance and continue to play a central role in both daily life and artistic expression across the region.

PARAMETRIC DESIGN

Any design process that incorporates mathematical algorithms to derive form. An early analog version of parametric design can be found in the structural design process of Antonio Gaudí, who used inverted force models that resulted in catenary arches, vaults, and domes. Adjusting one parameter of the model results in downstream changes to other components. Parametric techniques allow designers to mirror complex organic and natural forms and to rapidly iterate variations.

PERMACULTURE

Adapting the cycles observed within healthy natural ecosystems to agricultural practices, thereby maintaining healthy soil, enhancing ecosystem services, improving resilience, and diversifying crop yields, while eliminating the use of pesticides and herbicides. Permaculture often incorporates Indigenous knowledge and traditions, as well as regenerative agricultural practices that draw atmospheric carbon into soil (biosequestration).

PHOTOVOLTAIC (PV)

The photovoltaic effect, first recognized by A. E. Becquerel in 1839, is the ability of a material to produce direct current electricity when exposed to solar radiation. Silicon (Si) is a semiconductor material that displays the photovoltaic effect. It was the first material to be employed in solar cells and is still the most prevalent. It can be applied for use in either a crystalline (wafer) form, or in a noncrystalline (amorphous) form. There are two types of crystalline silicon: monocrystalline and polycrystalline (aka multicrystalline). Monocrystalline is expensive to manufacture (because it requires cutting slices from cylindrical ingots of silicon crystals that are grown with the Czochralski process), but it displays a high conversion efficiency (around 23%). Polycrystalline is easier to manufacture than monocrystalline silicon and is more versatile, but has lower conversion (around 18%).

PHOTOVOLTAIC THERMAL (PVT)

A hybrid solar technology that captures both electrical and thermal energy from the same surface area. While standard photovoltaic panels convert only about 20% of incoming sunlight into electricity, the remainder is lost as heat, often raising cell temperatures and reducing electrical efficiency. PVT systems incorporate a circulating fluid that absorbs this excess heat, improving overall energy yield and helping photovoltaic cells operate closer to their optimal temperature. By harvesting both power and heat, PVT systems can achieve total conversion efficiencies of up to 75%.

PHYTOREMEDIATION

Using plants to clean up polluted soil, water, and air.

POLYCULTURE

A type of agricultural practice where multiple species are grown together, imitating the diversity of natural ecosystems. Common industrial farming tends to grow crops as monocultures, depleting soils and limiting biodiversity, which can lead to increased pest infestation.

POTABLE

A liquid (usually water) that is considered safe to drink and that meets established health and safety standards. Potable water is free from harmful contaminants, pathogens, and pollutants, making it suitable for human consumption and everyday use. For uses such as irrigation, it is not necessary to expend the energy required to purify water to potable standards. See *graywater*.

PUMPED HYDRO

See *gravity energy storage*.

REGENERATE

To defy entropy through the maintenance of systems that cycle and recycle energy. Employ systems that produce resources to support human thriving and biodiversity. To leverage the power of the sun, human energy, and rapidly renewable resources to give back more than is input or invested into the system—generating resources such as energy, biomass, or clean water, or generating new investments into social systems.

REVERSE OSMOSIS

A method of water desalination that uses high pressure to counteract natural osmotic pressure, forcing water through a semi-permeable membrane that blocks dissolved salts and other impurities while allowing freshwater to pass through.

SODIS (SOLAR WATER DISINFECTION)

A simple, low-cost method for purifying drinking water using sunlight. Contaminated water is poured into clear plastic or glass bottles and placed in direct sun for at least six hours, allowing ultraviolet (UV) rays and heat to destroy harmful pathogens. To ensure effectiveness, bottles must be clean, transparent, and free of scratches that block UV light. Users should avoid touching the bottle's mouth or interior after disinfection to prevent recontamination, and water should be consumed directly or transferred with sanitized containers. Ideal for sunny, low-resource settings, SODIS is widely used in off-grid and emergency contexts.

SOLAR STILL

A passive, single-stage device that replicates the natural water cycle to produce distilled water using only sunlight. A transparent cover — typically glass or clear plastic — is placed over a basin containing saline, polluted, or moisture-rich material. Solar heat causes evaporation, and the resulting vapor condenses on the cooler inner surface of the cover. The purified droplets then run down into a collection trough. Simple and low-maintenance, solar stills are ideal for off-grid or emergency use in sunny climates. The humidification-dehumidification (HDH) method enhances this process by using solar-heated air to accelerate evaporation and condensation. See *distillation*.

SOLAR THERMAL

Solar radiation used to heat a medium, such as water or air.

SWALE

A shallow channel with gently sloping sides designed to manage water runoff, filter pollutants, and increase rainwater infiltration. Bioswales are planted with hearty local species that provide additional water filtration and stormwater attenuation.

TENSEGRITY

A structural design principle in which isolated rigid components, such as rods or struts, are held in place by a continuous network of tensioned elements like cables or tendons. The result is a stable, lightweight form that distributes forces efficiently through a balance of tension and compression. Found in both engineered systems and biological structures, tensegrity enables flexibility, resilience, and elegant spatial configurations with minimal material use.

THERMAL BATTERY STORAGE

A system that stores energy in the form of heat, which can later be converted into electricity, used directly for heating, or applied in cooling systems via absorption chillers. Thermal batteries typically use materials such as molten salts, sand, or ceramics to retain heat over extended periods. Salt-based systems store high-temperature heat for industrial or grid-scale applications, while sand batteries offer a cost-effective and scalable solution for district heating. These systems are gaining attention as durable, low-maintenance options for integrating renewable energy into energy grids and off-grid systems.

THIN-FILM

As applied to photovoltaics, any of a variety of non-crystalline solar cell technologies that can be applied in very thin layers, thus reducing material costs. Sometimes referred to as *second-generation photovoltaic cells*.

ULTRAFILTRATION

A membrane filtration process that removes suspended solids, bacteria, and some viruses from water using a physical barrier with microscopic pores. Ultrafiltration membranes allow water and small dissolved molecules to pass through while blocking larger contaminants. Often used as a pre-treatment step before reverse osmosis or as a standalone purification method, ultrafiltration provides high-quality water without the need for chemical additives. It is common in both municipal and decentralized water systems.

UTILITY-SCALE

Significant enough power generation to warrant the distribution of the energy to the utility grid (as opposed to on-site power generation for local use).

VERTICAL AXIS WIND TURBINE

A type of wind turbine with a vertically oriented rotor shaft, enabling it to capture wind from any direction without needing to reorient. Unlike horizontal axis wind turbines (HAWTs), which operate most efficiently at higher elevations with steady, unobstructed wind, VAWTs are well-suited for environments with turbulent or variable airflow, such as rooftops, lower elevations, or areas obstructed by buildings or trees. They typically have lower cut-in wind speeds, making them ideal for decentralized, small-scale energy generation in locations with inconsistent wind conditions.

VERTICAL FARMING

An agricultural method that grows crops in stacked layers or on vertically inclined surfaces, often within controlled indoor environments. Using hydroponic, aeroponic, or aquaponic systems, vertical farms optimize space, minimize water use, and eliminate the need for soil. Integrated technologies, such as LED lighting, climate control, and nutrient management, enable year-round production with a minimal land footprint. Especially suited for urban areas, vertical farming supports local food systems and helps reduce transportation-related emissions.

WATER-ENERGY NEXUS

This term refers to the important intersections that exist between energy and water infrastructures. To a great extent, water systems support energy systems and energy systems support water systems. For example, roughly half of all freshwater consumption goes to the cooling needs of thermal power plants, and a significant percentage of the electricity we generate goes to pumping water. The Colorado River Aqueduct, which supplies water to Los Angeles, consumes 2,000,000,000 kWh of electricity every year to pump water over 1,600 feet in elevation. Sometimes the food system is included in the water-energy-food nexus, since there are many overlaps between energy, water, and agricultural systems as well. When we design improvements to all of these systems through an integrated approach (rather than considering each in its own discrete silo), we can often discover system efficiencies and reduce our overall consumption of natural resources.

WATT (W)

Unit of measure of electrical power equivalent to 1/746 horsepower. W = Volts × Amperes

WATT-HOUR

A measure of electrical energy equivalent to one watt of power used or produced for a one-hour duration.

WET POND

A man-made basin designed to retain a permanent pool of water, used to manage stormwater runoff and improve water quality. As runoff flows into the pond, sediments settle and pollutants are removed through natural processes, such as sedimentation, microbial activity, filtration, and plant uptake. Wet ponds help reduce flooding, recharge groundwater, and support aquatic habitats, making them a key component of sustainable urban drainage and green infrastructure systems.

WIND TURBINE

A rotary engine driven by the force of passing wind that can convert rotational force into electrical power.

INDEX OF SOLUTIONS

ACKNOWLEDGMENTS

It has been an extraordinary privilege to work in collaboration with the Village of Marou to host the 2025 Land Art Generator Initiative design competition. From our very first visit, we were welcomed with warmth, generosity, and a spirit of true partnership. The beauty of the land is matched only by the deep care and cultural stewardship of those who call it home.

We are deeply grateful to Ilisari Naqau Nasau, Sau Turaga (Chief Maker) of Marou Village of the Mataqali Koro (Koro Clan), for inviting LAGI to work alongside the community of Marou. This invitation made possible a collaboration that will surely continue for many years to come.

We extend our heartfelt thanks to the residents of Marou: Ilisari Naqau Nasau (Acting Chief), Paula Nakarawa, Vesivesi Bose, Seru Lasa, Naibuka Kamayavu, Onisimo Yabakidrau, Solomoni Naqoli, Apasai Kaitoga, Samuela Nabolaniwaqa, Meciu Vuli, Viliame Tuwawa, Siliveno Tuitavua, Inia Lesu, Meli Tauvoli, Joseva Nasau, Vika Seru, Siteri Sawea, Melita Buna, Malelita Nainiata, Miriama Tuwawa Bainivalu, Rota Salio, Lanieta Mavama, Vika Tuirotuma, Timaima Cagilau Ralulu, Akanise Tipo, Lewatu Rejieli, Sera Tamudere, Aralai Vuranovo, Asilika Momoyalewa, Vasiti Talatoka, Ruci Drau, Remivani Toga, Watisoni Daku, Ilisari Vuda, and others whose presence and insights shaped this project.

We extend our sincere appreciation to the distinguished local leaders who generously offered their time and insights during our visits. Their contributions were invaluable to our work and vision—including the Hon. Deputy Prime Minister and Minister for Tourism and Civil Aviation, Mr. Viliame Gavoka; Hon. Semi Koroilavesau, Member of Parliament; Hon. Lenora Qereqeretabua, Assistant Minister for Foreign Affairs; Mr. Mikaele Belena, Director of the Department of Energy; and Mr. Isoa Tuwai, General Manager of Estate Services, iTaukei Land Trust Board.

We are grateful for the academic support and expertise that contributed to the depth and impact of this initiative. Thank you to: Elena van Hove, Director of Global Energy Access, Laboratory for Energy and Power Solutions, Arizona State University; Nathan Johnson, Associate Professor, The Polytechnic School and Director, Laboratory for Energy and Power Solutions, Arizona State University; Dr. Ramendra Prasad, Associate Professor, Department of Science, The University of Fiji; and Ayu Abdullah, Executive Director at Energy Action Partners whose COMET (Community Energy Toolkit) workshop results for Marou Village established the future mini-grid energy demand information that was used by participating design teams.

The involvement of Jale Samuwai and Aminisitai Delaisainiai was essential. As representatives of Rocky Mountain Institute (RMI) in Fiji, their depth of knowledge and thoughtful guidance helped steer us in the right direction at every turn.

Special thanks to the logistical support team at Crystal Island for helping to ensure the program ran smoothly in the Yasawas: Ilisari Naqau Nasau, Captain Paul McCulloch, David Paka, Rani Ranjini, Sevina Namale, Tabua Batiniu, and Manasa Bogiwale.

Thank you to Dr. Katrina Igglesden for introducing us to Maciusela Raitaukala, Director of the Fiji Arts Council, who warmly welcomed the project. The Fiji Arts Council in Suva provided an invaluable platform for sharing the ideas and outcomes of LAGI 2025, hosting the exhibition in November of 2025, and displaying the prototypes for the public in 2026.

We are grateful to the LAGI 2025 Fiji jurors, who brought their insights to the evaluation process. Their names are listed at the front of this book, and we thank them for lending their time and expertise to help shape the outcome of this important initiative.

Thank you to Lisa Farmen for her generous technical guidance on water systems and to the team at Global Support and Development (GSD) for offering guidance on the feasibility of water treatment systems as the project moves into the next stages of design and implementation.

As always, we are indebted to Paul Schifino for his impeccable design of this book and to Ann Rosenthal, who has once again provided her incomparable copy editing skills to ensure the clarity and quality of every paragraph.

Our sincere appreciation goes to the LAGI Board of Directors — Todd Bartholf, Christopher Choa, Deborah Hosking, Tim Mollette-Parks, Martin Pasqualetti, Victor Pérez-Rul, Paul Schifino, and George Riley Thomas II — for their ongoing guidance and support.

We extend our deepest thanks to the brilliant designers, artists, and thinkers whose visionary ideas form the heart of this book. Their imagination illuminates new pathways for regenerative design and inspires hope for our shared future. It is their work that transforms the abstract into the tangible — offering solutions, stories, landscapes, and living systems in which we might all thrive.

And finally, thank you to Bruce Rauhe and Abby Paiva, whose commitment to a regenerative future shaped by creative possibility anchors this work. It has been a joy to share this path with you both.

This book is dedicated to those who are most vulnerable to the uncertainties of our global energy and climate systems. May the ideas within these pages serve as a beacon, lighting the way toward a future of human abundance and resilience in mutual symbiosis with nature.

© Hirmer Verlag, Munich, and Land Art Generator Initiative, 2025

All text © the authors or their estates unless otherwise noted. All works © the artists, artist teams, or their estates unless otherwise noted. All project descriptions © the artists, artist teams, or their estates unless otherwise noted.

Front cover: *Solar Leaf*, Iman SheikhAnsari
Back cover: *Unleashing the Vanua: Living Systems for Community Resilience*, Jisoo Kim, Seung Hyo Chang, Jisoo Kim

Published by:
Hirmer Verlag
Bayerstraße 57-59
80335 München Germany
www.hirmerverlag.de

Editorial direction: Robert Ferry, Elizabeth Monoian
Project management Hirmer Publishers: Rainer Arnold
Senior editor Hirmer Publishers: Elisabeth Rochau-Shalem
Copy editing and proof reading: Ann Rosenthal
Design: Paul Schifino
Paper: Gardamatt Eleven, 150 g/m_2
Pre-press: Reproline Mediateam, Unterföhring, Germany
Printing and binding: Optimal media GmbH, Röbel/Müritz
Printed in Germany

Bibliographic information published by the Deutsche Nationalbibliothek
The Deutsche Nationalbibliothek lists this publication in the Deutsche Nationalbibliografie; detailed bibliographic data is available on the Internet at http://www.dnb.de.

All rights reserved. The automated analysis of individual or multiple digital or digitized works for the purpose of obtaining information, in particular about patterns, trends, and correlations, is prohibited (German Copyright Act § 44b: Text and Data Mining).

ISBN 978-3-7774-4518-2

Land Art Generator Initiative is a US-based non-profit organization.
https://landartgenerator.org
https://lagi2025fiji.org